THE WEIGHT
OF GLORY

Peter Baelz

THE WEIGHT OF GLORY

*A Vision and Practice for Christian Faith:
The Future of Liberal Theology*

Essays for Peter Baelz

edited by
D. W. Hardy and P. H. Sedgwick

T&T CLARK
EDINBURGH

T&T CLARK
59 GEORGE STREET
EDINBURGH EH2 2LQ
SCOTLAND

First Published 1991

British Library Cataloguing in Publication Data
Weight of Glory : essays for Peter Baelz.
1. Church of England. Christian doctrine
I. Hardy, Dan   II. Sedgwick, Peter   III. Baelz, Peter
1923–
230.3

ISBN 0 567 09579 7

Typeset by Buccleuch Printers Ltd, Hawick
Printed and bound in Great Britain by Billing & Sons Ltd, Worcester

CONTENTS

CONTRIBUTORS

Peter Baelz was Dean of Durham and formerly Professor of Moral and Pastoral Theology and Canon of Christ Church, Oxford, and Fellow and Dean of Jesus College, Cambridge.

Simon Barrington-Ward is Bishop of Coventry and formerly Dean of Chapel, Magdalene College, Cambridge.

Don Cupitt is Dean of Emmanuel College and Lecturer in the Philosophy of Religion at Cambridge University.

Peter Donovan is Senior Lecturer in Religious Studies at Massey University, New Zealand.

Monica Furlong is a religious journalist and writer.

John Habgood is Archbishop of York and formerly Bishop of Durham.

Daniel W. Hardy is Director of the Center of Theological Inquiry, Princeton, New Jersey and formerly Van Mildert Professor of Divinity, University of Durham, and Residentiary Canon, Durham Cathedral.

Brian Hebblethwaite is Fellow, Dean of Chapel and Director of Studies in Theology and Religious Studies, Queens' College, Cambridge.

Jean Holm was Head of Religious Studies, Homerton College, Cambridge.

William Jacob is Warden of Lincoln Theological College.

Michael Langford is Professor of Philosophy and Professor of Medical Ethics at the Memorial University of Newfoundland.

Ann Loades is Reader in Theology, University of Durham.

James W. McClendon, Jr, is Distinguished Scholar in Residence, Fuller Theological Seminary, Pasadena, and formerly Professor in the Church Divinity School, Berkeley, California.

Donald M. MacKinnon was Norris-Hulse Professor of Divinity and Fellow of Corpus Christi College, Cambridge.

Jack Mahoney is F. D. Maurice Professor of Moral and Social Theology and Mercer School Memorial Professor of Commerce at Gresham College, and Director of the Business Ethics Research Centre, King's College, London.

Hugh Melinsky was Principal of the Northern Ordination Course, Manchester, and formerly Chief Secretary of the Advisory Council for the Church's Ministry.

Basil Mitchell was Nolloth Professor of the Philosophy of the Christian Religion, Oxford University.

Helen Oppenheimer writes on Christian ethics and philosophical theology.

David Paton was a Missionary to China.

Arthur Peacocke is Director of the Ian Ramsay Centre, Oxford, and formerly Dean of Clare College, Cambridge.

Peter Sedgwick is Lecturer in Theology at the University of Hull and Adviser in Industrial Issues to the Archbishop of York.

John Sweet is Fellow of Selwyn College, Cambridge, and University Lecturer in New Testament.

Peter Walker was Bishop of Ely and formerly Canon of Christ Church and Bishop of Dorchester.

Alan Webster was Dean of St. Paul's and formerly Vicar of Barnard Castle.

Maurice Wiles is Regius Professor of Divinity in the University of Oxford.

INTRODUCTORY SECTION

INTRODUCTION

Peter Sedgwick

This collection of essays sets out to honour a person, explore a position and analyse some of the underlying issues in the often heated debates within contemporary British Christianity. In his life and through his writings Peter Baelz has been one of the foremost exponents of 'liberal Christianity' in the Church of England. There is a consistency stretching back over five decades about the vision which has inspired him: a vision of Christ active in His world through the Spirit, so that men and women may come to know God their Creator and have their lives transformed.

The liberal position is not easy to define. Nevertheless in Peter Baelz's work there are some clear directions. It is necessary to understand the experience of the knowledge of God: how is this possible at all in the modern world? What are the conditions which allow this disclosure to take place? Throughout his writings there is a concern with a sense of the transcendent and an awareness of the numinous in an apparently secular world. As he wrote in a report to the Friends of Durham Cathedral in 1983:

> True art discloses the 'many-splendoured thing' which we with our 'estranged faces' all too easily miss. Thus art can assist that conversion of the imagination which precedes the response of faith. It can open our eyes to see 'the many-splendoured thing' which is the refraction of the glory of God in creation and redemption. To this glory the Cathedral, I hope and pray, bears a constant and continuing witness.

There must therefore be a coherence and intellectual rigour about a theological restatement of the experience of revelation. Aesthetics and epistemology both form part of the philosophical justification of claims about the nature of transcendent reality. Beyond such claims there are the implications of a belief in the presence of God in the world. The centrality of personal existence to theological ethics is one of the clearest implications of the liberal position. Throughout the last two decades Peter Baelz, with several other theologians some of whom have contributed articles in this volume, has rethought the nature of personal

1

relationships in such varied spheres of modern life as marriage, homosexual relationships, and the care of the dying.

There is no one final restatement of liberalism, and certainly not all the contributors to this volume would accept the 'liberal' classification. Nevertheless many of the reports which the Church of England has received on ethical issues in recent years do contain a concern to balance the Anglican tradition with a restatement of personal existence. The Church of England has often served to mediate this restatement of Christian vocation. It has sometimes seemed as if the Church of England has been subject to dangerous polarization, yet there is little in these reports which sought such division and opposition. Indeed, precisely the opposite is the case. It is easy to caricature a dogmatic liberalism, but the constant wrestling with contemporary issues in Peter's writings is marked far more by a concern for freedom of thought, and a desire to set the conditions for the right kind of liberality. It is, as John Habgood indicates in his article, prepared to live with 'loose ends, partial insights, and a measure of agnosticism, without losing its grip on the essentials of faith.' (p. 9)

Therefore this volume does not reflect the same theological viewpoint in each of its contributors. Some of the articles may well oppose each other on fundamental issues. Yet there is, I hope, a coherence and a strategy to the volume. It begins, after a reflection on the liberal position by John Habgood and a personal reflection by Peter Baelz, with what must surely be one of the most central issues in theology today: our knowledge of God, and its relationships to other forms of knowledge. How too does Christian worship relate to the tentative explorations of modern theology? In his ministry in Durham Cathedral Peter Baelz continually sought, through many different forms of worship, to evoke the presence of God in contemporary life.

The succeeding sections take up the implications of our knowledge of God. First, the nature of theological ethics is explored. How is the balance between creativity and tradition worked out? Is Christian morality a particular morality, or is it applicable to all human beings? Secondly, there are particular concerns which have been problematic for the Churches in the last few years, such as medicine and wealth creation. In these articles there is an awareness of past tradition and pressing modern debates.

Liberalism has always sought to place itself in a world: it is not simply individualist, but exists in a Church. Therefore much of Peter Baelz's time in the last decade was taken up with the twin areas of the ministry of a Cathedral, and the theological education of the clergy. Yet it would be wrong to see these interests as simply inward-looking. Some of the articles in these sections are concerned with the nature of spirituality in a pluralist, environmentally threatened world. Others take up the evolving tradition of Anglican ministry and worship.

In the final section, the volume broadens out again. Two articles reflect on the experience of Africa and China. Others point to the multi-faith world in which we now live in Britain. The context for Christian theology is no longer simply the Western heritage. So we return to the opening section of the volume, on how knowledge of God is possible.

If this volume has a coherence, it seeks to point to a story of accomplishment in theology over the last few decades. Considerable work has been achieved on reformulating theological ethics, and revising the nature of ministry and worship. There is much more agreement that the apparent picture of division and threats of schism would seem to allow. Peter Baelz has played a major part in this work, covering an astonishing range of activities in his life and writings: philosophical theology; medical, sexual and social ethics; education and ministry; worship and spirituality. The contributors to this volume wish to honour someone who has always placed his life at the service of that tradition, which is the central theme of this collection of essays.

> Lord, shall we not bring these gifts to Your service?
> Shall we not bring to Your service all our powers
> For life, for dignity, grace and order,
> And intellectual pleasures of the senses?
> The Lord who created must wish us to create
> And employ our creation again in His service
> Which is already His service in creating.
>
> (T. S. Eliot, The Rock, Chorus IX)

REFLECTIONS ON THE LIBERAL POSITION

John Habgood

Liberalism is a slippery concept. I doubt whether 'the liberal position', about which I have been asked to reflect, exists as such, or whether there is any one set of ideas or attitudes on which those who value the word 'liberal' would agree. It is best described in the lives of individuals. The wide range of topics discussed in this book conveys something of the breadth of interest, and the questioning, and the interplay between theology and secular concerns, which are characteristic of liberal spirits, and notably of Peter Baelz himself. But the notion, frequently canvassed these days, that there is a cohort of liberals within the Church of England who share certain definite aims and assumptions, and who consciously foster what has been called 'the liberal ascendancy' seems to me to reveal a deep misunderstanding of the liberal phenomenon.

I intend therefore to start by describing two individuals, both of whom I had the good fortune to know in Cambridge at a formative period in my own life, and who were liberal in strikingly different ways.

To hear Charles Raven lecturing or preaching at the height of his powers was unforgettable. The sustained eloquence, the breadth of vision and knowledge, the sense of intellectual adventure, swept his audiences along, and Cambridge undergraduates in the immediate post-war years packed the lecture halls and churches to hear him, myself among them. In later years when he felt Cambridge had rejected him, as a lonely ex-Regius Professor of Divinity and ex-Vice-Chancellor demoted to being Warden of Madingley Hall, I came to know him personally, and found he could work the same magic in a room with half-a-dozen students. The last time I met him he came bounding up the stairs to my room, apologising for being late because he had had a heart attack that morning.

This larger-than-life quality infused all his teaching. He was at his most impressive in talking about science and religion, and in particular in his exposition of the seventeenth century Cambridge Platonists. The first volume of his now largely forgotten Gifford lectures, *Natural Religion and Christian Theology* (1953), is a valuable historical summary telling the story of science and religion, unusually, from the perspective of Natural History rather than Physics. But the second volume which attempts a synthesis between religious experience and a scientific world view reveals serious weaknesses, both scientific and theological.

Despite his strong advocacy of science and scientific ways of thinking there were occasions, particularly in his account of evolution, when he abandoned them. Ill-defined claims about the work of God's spirit substituted for scientific explanations, and left him vulnerable to advances in knowledge. I remember feeling uneasy when listening to him expatiate in his lectures on the inexplicability of the evolution of the cuckoo,[1] and in this respect, as in others, time has passed him by. Theologically, too, despite current enthusiasm in some quarters about the work of the Spirit, it is easy to see the weakness of a theology of nature in which the Spirit is identified with more or less everything that is going on. In Daniel Jenkins's words, Dr Raven's 'diffused world-spirit manifesting itself everywhere with large-hearted comprehensiveness' is 'like a sign-post pointing in all directions and therefore giving no guidance at all'.[2] In the 1990s some eyebrows would also doubtless be raised about a Christology based on Christ's power 'to awaken and quicken our sensitiveness . . . All else, the works of power, the fulfilment of prophecies, the Virgin birth, the physical resurrection, are no doubt appropriate but surely secondary; and if the evidence for them does not convince us, we need not therefore feel that we are outcast from Christendom'.[3]

This was a liberalism rooted in a major attempt at synthesis. The vision was there, a vision of a religio-scientific world brought together in at least a provisional harmony. Teilhard de Chardin's numerous books expressed a similar, and more widely acknowledged, vision when they began to be published a few years later. But in both Raven and Teilhard the synthesis involved some cutting of the corners; their theologies avoided the awkward questions being raised by neo-orthodoxy about the particularity of Christ, and sin, and human limitations, and their science tended to lapse into vagueness at crucial moments. Teilhard was unfortunately never criticised in his lifetime. Raven, as I knew him, was better at talking than listening. It was said of him, perhaps unkindly, that 'he did not become the leader he might have been because of his utter inability to absorb or relate himself to a contrary idea'.[4]

Alec Vidler is a liberal in a totally different tradition. He prefers the word 'liberality' with its suggestion that what is at stake is an attitude of mind, rather than some grand synthesis, or party, or identifiable tradition. It is significant that the title of the book for which he is most likely to be remembered is *Soundings*, and his theological hero is F. D. Maurice who described himself as 'only a digger'.

I was fortunate in being able to watch Alec Vidler at work over a number of years as a member of an informal group which advised him in his work as Editor of *Theology*. There was the same breadth of interest as in Raven, the same impatience with what he saw as narrow-minded ecclesiasticism, but a historian's suspicion of extravagant claims and over-simple answers. He has described his work in this context as 'theological midwifery'. The fact that *Theology* under his editorship hardly ever carried editorials is further evidence of his desire not to pursue a particular line, but to encourage exploration. He wrote of himself, 'I remember that in the early years of my editorship some readers used to complain that they could not make out what *Theology* now stood for : and I took this as a compliment rather than the reverse!'.[5]

In a different context, writing about the N. T. character possessed by a 'legion' of devils, he spelt out the dividedness of the digging, as opposed to the synthesizing, liberal.

> I allow that in the end a man needs to be one, unified, just as mankind does. But *in the end*. Is this what the theologians with their inelegant jargon, call an eschatological possibility or promise?
>
> But on the way to the end it may be better to be more than one man, pulled this way and that, with plenty of discords and jagged edges, trailing uncertainties, with clashing loyalties, ever and again amazed and perplexed and tongue-tied. Perhaps again this is why theologians have had so much to say about being justified by *faith*, for faith, unlike sight, stammers and is dumb.[6]

Soundings tried to convey something of this attitude in a time of theological complacency. Biblical theology ruled the roost. Theological questions were to be answered by careful study of the language of the Bible. Questions which fell outside this narrow circle of interest could safely be ignored. Vidler wrote in his introduction: 'We believe that there are very important questions which theologians are now being called upon to face, and which are not yet being faced with the necessary seriousness and determination'.[7]

The impetus came from a group of Cambridge theologians, and once again Vidler acted as midwife. I was invited to join the group in 1960 for a crucial meeting at Launde Abbey where the decision was made to produce a volume of essays. These became the first public stirrings of the theological revolution which was to overtake the churches in the decade which followed. In terms of publicity *Soundings* was soon swamped by John Robinson's *Honest to God*, and members of the group reflected wryly that John Robinson had not been invited to join it on the grounds that he was too firmly wedded to Biblical Theology – as many of his subsequent writings demonstrated.

Predictably the main public interest in *Soundings* centred on the essay by Harry Williams which was a plea to take seriously the insights of Freud, and which interestingly began with a dismissal of Raven's attack on Freud in his Gifford lectures. What set the correspondents buzzing, though, was a hint that in certain psychological circumstances fornication might be appropriate and right, and that what prevented it was not morality but fear. The suggestion was made in very modest terms, but with hindsight it can be seen as a prelude to the sexual revolution of the sixties. Most of the other authors of *Soundings*, including Vidler himself, had grave doubts about whether the essay should be published. In the end Harry Williams's argument prevailed on the ground that he was being honest to his own experience and that of the authors he was quoting. What claim could the book make to be an honest exploration of contemporary issues if it were censored at this vital point? But here we run straight into a typical liberal dilemma. How far can honesty be taken before it becomes destructive of confidence in those who pursue it?

Vidler's own concern was to bring theology out of its intellectual ghetto. 'When theologians are on speaking terms only with themselves they are doomed to frustration and indeed to damnation',[8] was his way of putting it. But taking theology out of the divinity schools also entails risks, risks to which Raven exposed himself only too obviously by trying to Christianise a broad sweep of secular knowledge. Vidler's strategy was to use secular methods of criticism, but to hide his own faith under a veil of theological inscrutability, which during his time as Dean of King's teased and fascinated his fellow dons. 'If we must have preachers,' he said in his final Cambridge sermon, 'I like them to be oblique and reserved and even enigmatic'.[9]

He tells the story of how on his arrival at King's as its Dean, and finding himself responsible for college discipline, he went round the walls of the college directing that the spikes and broken glass on top of them should be removed. In a sense he has been doing that all his life: not underestimating the importance of limits, but making it easier to move in and out by unorthodox routes. His ministry as a 'theological midwife' rested on his historian's sense of the survivability of Christianity even through tumultuous change, and his conviction as a critic that the only way to knowledge is through open enquiry. As David Edwards said of him on his retirement in 1964, he saved the Church of England from stagnation.

I have chosen to concentrate on these two men from an age now vanished, partly because Peter Baelz was himself in Cambridge not long after their heyday, and more particularly because a little historical distance can help us to take a cooler look at contemporary controversies. I am not an historian, and feel safer in writing of things I know at first hand.

Ian Ramsey was yet another kind of liberal, driven by his need to come to terms with the Oxford philosophy of his day. His elaborate recastings of Christian theology, his insistence that all theological language can do is to provide models pointing towards a disclosure of God, and his rather elusive thoughts about the extent to which these models are rooted in empirical reality, would surely have made him an object of much suspicion in the nineteen eighties. Yet he went to Durham, revered as its bishop, and hailed as the brightest intellectual light in the Church of England. How, I wonder, would he have reacted to today's controversies? And, more to the point, was there a fundamental difference in degree between his liberalism and that of David Jenkins who followed him to Durham eleven years after his death?

A constant feature of liberalism is the wish to take seriously the intellectual climate in which faith has to be lived. This is not the same as following intellectual fashion. At the frontiers of academic conversation there obviously has to be an engagement with ideas which are currently in vogue. Much theological writing at this level, like any other writing, tends to be ephemeral and is only dangerously misleading if it is assumed at that instant to express the faith of the church. But underneath such temporary eddies there are much more enduring ground swells, perhaps even permanent alterations in human consciousness and perceptions. These are not mere matters for fashionable intellectual debate. In the long term they affect everybody. And the hard question which has to be answered by theologians is how far these ought to shape theological development.

Serious liberalism does not start reconstructing its theology at the first hint of secular change. Nor is it wise, in my view, to be too busy with reconstruction à la Raven even when so-called modern knowledge seems well established. But it needs to take seriously the questions posed by fundamental sea-changes, and be ready to live with loose ends, partial insights, and a measure of agnosticism, without losing its grip on the essentials of faith.

What are these long term changes? The development of science and the broad understanding of the nature of the universe it has given us is one of them. A sense of historical perspective often manifesting itself in terms of historial relativism is another. The discovery of hitherto unknown depths in the human psyche is a third. It would not be hard to list others.

All of these can be, and have been, attacked. There are fashionable attacks on science, for instance, on the grounds of its reductionism and in the name of various kinds of holism. There is a general critique of the Enlightenment which has exposed the shaky philosophical foundations of many of the more extreme claims made on behalf of science. Theological liberalism has no vested interest in ignoring these attacks. But it has to ask whether they place serious question marks over prevailing secular orthodoxies, or whether they simply represent marginal adjustments to a major intellectual construction which will easily survive them.

My own view is that the changes scientific discoveries, for instance, have made to our perception of the world are so firmly based, so deeply rooted in modern western consciousness, and so bound up with our way of life, that Christians ignore them at their peril. I can give a rather extreme example of this by quoting a letter I received recently after speaking in Parliament on embryo research. I had been making the point that the development of individual lives is as gradual, and as obscure, as the transition from hominid to human in the course of evolution. The letter was signed in his official capacity by the Secretary of a reputable organisation sponsored by 27 MPs, and the first part of it read as follows:

> Thank you for so clearly stating in the House of Lords what many of us had suspected, namely, that you are not a Christian. This is particularly helpful for those of us who are concerned about who should become the next Primate within the Anglican Church.
>
> If the report is correct, during the discussion on the Embryology Bill you said that 'Christians are not required to believe in the historical existence of Adam and Eve.' Furthermore, you evidently went on to subscribe to the completely unproven and indeed even scientifically unsound theory of evolution.
>
> One wonders what other parts of the Bible you do not believe.

There are several points of interest here. The first is the definition of 'Christian' by reference to a particular moral judgment which historically has never before carried this weight or even been generally agreed. The second is the linking of that judgment to particular historical claims about the Bible which were in principle set aside by most theologians more than a century ago. The third, and most revealing, is the claim to have scientific evidence to support a face-value interpretation of the Biblical story. Science, in other words, is not set on one side. It is used selectively to bolster a theological position which seems weak if held on purely theological grounds.

This kind of argument, based on naive fundamentalism and suitably doctored science, is only beginning to make inroads into Britain, but is already a serious threat to orthodox science and scientifically informed theology in the USA. Liberals of whatever kind may find themselves fighting in such circumstances, not only for the intellectual integrity of theology, but also for the integrity of science. The whole exercise is richly paradoxical. A travesty of science is used in argument against mainline scientific theories, thereby unconsciously revealing the extent to which the power and prestige of science are now accepted even by those who for theological reasons want to reject some of its findings. This has nothing to do with the normal process whereby scientific theories are constantly criticised and sometimes overthrown. It has everything to do with the desire to use science for one's own purposes. Theologians need to be alert to the difference, and this is a yet further reason for taking science seriously.

In gentler academic climates the difficulties may be greater, because the frontiers are more blurred and the influence of new knowledge on theological understanding more subtle. Away from the battle lines drawn between various kinds of dogmatic conservatism, whether religious or secular, it is hard to know how much new knowledge can be absorbed by a traditional faith without turning it into something else. What are the essentials of faith on which believers have to maintain their grip while accepting criticism and allowing a measure of agnosticism? If Adam and Eve belong to the margins of theology, and if nothing essential is lost by treating their story as non-historical myth, can the same be said of the various stories of the Resurrection?

As recent events have proved, such questions can appear highly threatening, even when every allowance is made for the different historical, scientific and literary provenances of the two kinds of stories. But it is worth noting how the most perceptive liberal theologians, Ian Ramsey for instance, have treated the oddities in the Resurrection stories, not as a basis for making negative historical judgments, but as pointers to their transcendent meaning. We don't understand anything about the Resurrection at all unless we see them, not just as narrative, but as stories which make an overwhelming claim on us and which disclose God by their very oddness.[10]

Perhaps the safest guideline in this difficult territory is the belief that the readiness to receive new truth itself belongs to the essence of faith. F. J. A. Hort, the least well-known of the famous 19th century trio Lightfoot, Westcott and Hort, made this point memorably in his lecture, 'Christ – The Truth'.

> It is not too much to say that the Gospel itself can never be fully known till nature as well as man is fully known; and that the manifestation of nature as well as man in Christ is part of his manifestation of God. As the Gospel is the perfect introduction to all truth, so on the other hand it is itself known only in proportion as it is used for the enlightenment of departments of truth which seem at first sight to be beyond its boundaries . . . 'I am the Truth' . . .

marks every truth which seems alien to Christ as a sign that the time is come for better knowledge of Christ, since no truth can be alien to him who is the Truth.[11]

The search for truth, in other words, through rational critical understanding (which needs of course to be self-critical as well) has theological roots no less significant than the theological basis of revelation. Both are from God : in different modes and degrees, maybe, but both originating and finding their fulfilment in him. It is this kind of faith, I believe, which undergirds the best liberal approaches to theology. I want to emphasize that this is a theological undergirding, not an absence of faith in God, but a conviction that he is to be found wherever the human mind can reach.

This is why the equation of liberalism with lack of faith is frequently so wide of the mark. I cannot speak for all liberals because, as I have tried to show, liberalism is a complex phenomenon and I approach it from its conservative rather than from its radical side. But from my perspective an intoxication with the greatness and the mystery of God lies at the heart of it.

I end with a brief mention of so-called 'liberal causes'. Raven pursued some, notably pacifism and feminism. Vidler didn't, unless it was the constant defence of academic freedom. Theological liberals in our own day are accused of knee-jerk reactions on a variety of fashionable issues. But I am not sure matters are as simple as this. Pacifism, for instance, does not seem to me to be characteristically liberal. On the contrary it is frequently grounded in moral absolutism and a refusal to learn the lessons of history. Other forms of adherence to causes, whether liberal or conservative, owe more to political than to theological orientation. Other causes, and these are perhaps the only ones which belong truly within a liberal tradition of theology as I have described it, emerge from new facts, or new interpretations of old facts, or a new willingness to face facts which have hitherto been ignored. Agonizing over such issues as homosexuality belongs here. But the idea that, because somebody adopts a liberal attitude in some matters he or she must be liberal in everything, seems to me to be plainly untrue.

There is, in short, no identikit for being a liberal. It is possible to recognise, however, some whose lives have clearly been shaped by the gracious liberality of God, and who display its marks in their own liberality towards all that God has made. These are lives for which both Church and world can rightly give thanks.

References

[1] See, for example, *Natural Religion and Christian Theology*, Vol. II, C.U.P. 1953, p. 137 ff.

[2] Quoted in *Charles Raven* by F. W. Dillistone, Hodder and Stoughton, 1975, p. 287 f.

[3] *Natural Religion and Christian Theology*, Vol. II, p. 80.

[4] Dillistone, p. 415.

[5] Quoted by D. L. Edwards in *Theology*, January 1965, p. 7.

[6] *Scenes from Clerical Life* by Alec Vidler, Collins 1977, p. 172.

[7] *Soundings*, edited by A. R. Vidler, C.U.P. 1962, p. xi.

[8] Vidler 1977, p. 177.

[9] ibid., p. 169.

[10] See, for example, *Religious Language* by I. T. Ramsey, S.C.M. 1957, p. 127 ff.

[11] *The Way The Truth The Life* by F. J. A. Hort, Macmillan (2nd edn.), 1894, pp. 83 and 85.

PENITENT CATHOLIC, IMPENITENT LIBERAL

Peter Baelz

When in June 1967 Alec Vidler preached a farewell sermon to Cambridge,[1] he remarked that if ever he were 'to utter a last word for public consumption, it would be something like what Père Lacordaire said: "I hope to live and die a penitent Catholic, and an impenitent liberal."'

'Penitent Catholic, impenitent liberal'. These words have lodged in my memory ever since I first read them. I felt then – and still feel now – that here was a banner under which I too should be happy to serve. I do not know precisely what the words signified to Père Lacordaire, or even to Dr Vidler. Indeed, on the few occasions when I have quoted them in public, I have met with bewilderment rather than understanding. Nevertheless, they still seem to me to convey in a nutshell the essentially two-sided character of a living Christian faith.

First, catholicism. Catholicism is not to be interpreted narrowly in opposition to something equally narrowly termed protestantism. Rather, it emphasises the fact that Christian identity is first and foremost one of belonging. To be a Christian is to belong to a universal human community which itself belongs to God. In the name of Jesus Christ and in the power of the Holy Spirit, this community bears witness in worship, thought and action to the one God and Father of all, who is over all and through all and in all, ever creating, ever redeeming and ever bringing to fulfilment. Furthermore, the faith in which this community lives is a *given* faith. Historically, it flows from the life, death and resurrection of Jesus of Nazareth: ultimately, it is grounded in the eternal givingness and grace of God.

Second, penitence. Acceptance of the gift of God's grace calls for a fundamental reconstruction of outlook and endeavour. Penitence is more than godly contrition for past sins. It is, first and foremost, a conversion of the imagination, a transformation of heart and mind, an ex-centering of perception and response, a self-forgetfulness in saying 'Yes' to God, a process in which men and women are drawn out of themselves and into the life of that ultimate Other whom we name God. It is not only the mystic but also the philosopher, such as H. H. Price or Bernard Lonergan, and the man of affairs, such as Dag Hammarskjöld, who find themselves persuaded, maybe much to their surprise, that (in Price's words) 'love comes first in the epistemology of faith'.[2] It is a paradoxical fact of experience that one can begin to love God before intellectually believing in him.

Third, liberalism. Liberalism means different things in different contexts. Within the context of catholicism it can, I suggest, be given a distinctive if open-ended meaning. Here it expresses the manner in which God's grace, freely given, is freely received. If God's being and action are truly characterised by the power of love rather than the love of power, then in his self-giving God will have full regard for the personhood of those to whom his gift is being offered. Grace may in some sense constrain, but by reason of its very graciousness its constraints are those of love and not of compulsion. Grace respects as it transforms and fulfils nature, it does not reject or over-ride it. Therefore the experience of faith has to be appropriated and interpreted, personally and communally, in the same way as any other experience has to be appropriated and interpreted. It has to be sensitively but critically sifted, sorted and assessed.

Even though the heart has its own reasons of which the intellect knows nothing, it is also true that the heart is prone to deception and idolatry. It needs the support of the critical intellect, not to establish its insights on some purely rational and impersonal basis, but to give them reasonable backing and coherence. Granted that it is the heart that makes the initial advance into the Other's territory, it is the intellect that consolidates and integrates the positions that the heart has taken up. A fundamentally contemplative theology needs also to be a radically critical theology. The catholic liberal is such, not because of some unacknowledged commitment to secular humanism, but because of a prior commitment to a comprehensive catholicism. His impenitent liberalism is grounded in his understanding of the character of God himself and of his self-giving in creation and redemption.

To sum up. The dialectical relation between a contemplative catholicism and a critical liberalism combines an emphasis on the givenness of Christian faith with a corresponding emphasis on its questing and questioning. What is given is the life of Jesus Christ and life in Jesus Christ. What is sought is an appropriate understanding and response to that life. In his essay in moral philosophy *After Virtue* Alastair MacIntyre describes a living tradition as one that is 'always partially constituted by an argument about the goods the pursuit of which gives to that tradition its particular point and purpose'.[3] Similarly, I suggest, we might describe the living Christian tradition as a tradition in which the Christian community continues to search, singly and together, for the One by whom, in Christ, it has already been found.

Back now to the beginnings. My initiation into the life of the Christian community was neither catholic or liberal. My parents had both been born and brought up among the expatriate German families living in south-east London. Their church connections, such as they were, had been with the Lutheran congregation in Forest Hill; but after their marriage in 1914, shortly before the outbreak of the First World War, these had largely lapsed. When, then, I was born in 1923, there was no obvious church and congregation into which I should be baptised, and I was privately christened by a Unitarian minister whose congregation had become the spiritual home of my serious-minded and high-principled grandmother. This caused me no problems at the time. Indeed, it did not seem to cause any problems later when, still at school, I followed the lead of my devout elder brother and was received into the Methodist Church; nor again when, an undergraduate at Cambridge and continuing my ecclesiastical pilgrimage, I decided that my real spiritual home was the Church of England. Although I was already a communicant both in the Methodist Church and in the College Chapel, I somewhat grudgingly consented to be confirmed by the Bishop of Ely, on the understanding that this was a matter of church order rather than sacramental necessity. For some reason or other the matter of my baptism was not raised. However, when it came to my ordination three years later, a stricter regime prevailed. To dispel all conceivable doubt – on the parts of others rather than of myself – I was conditionally baptized and confirmed by Stephen Neill, formerly Bishop of Tinnevelly and then living and working in Cambridge. This chapter of my story may possibly explain why I have never felt as clear about the sacrament of initiation as I feel about the sacrament of holy communion. Nowadays, if ever I am asked about my so-called churchmanship, I tend to reply that at heart I am a 'eucharistic Quaker'!

As my parents did not attend church, so neither did I. My parental education in the Christian faith consisted of Bible stories read by my father after Sunday breakfast, and I remember finding those from the Old Testament much more exciting than those from the New. However, I was soon taken in hand by my elder brother. Left to my own devices I should have spent Sunday afternoons playing tennis with my father, but under fraternal guidance I went along, somewhat reluctantly, to the Crusaders, a non-denominational Sunday School of biblical-evangelical persuasion. Here I was first informed and convicted of my sins and then given the good news that I had been saved from them by Jesus Christ, with whom I could now enjoy a personal relationship. This was strong stuff for a youngster already introverted, diffident and by nature or nurture a perfectionist. Perversely it fostered in him a religion of works rather than grace. Among other things he became, at least in theory, a fervent sabbatarian, convinced it was a grave sin to play games on a Sunday or even to listen to the popular dance music broadcast by Radio Luxemburg. He also got hold of the strange idea that, if he personally could not establish beyond reasonable doubt the existence of God, God himself was liable to go out of existence. (This latter idea may have stemmed from a visit with his grandmother to the theatre to see J. M. Barrie's improving play *Peter Pan*. In this play, as I remember it, the audience is asked if it believes in fairies. If anyone is presumptuous enough to confess that he does not, he is told that his expression of disbelief deals a death-blow to yet another of these fanciful creatures!)

Although I have since rejected much of what I was taught by the Crusaders, I should wish to acknowledge my debt to them for giving me a grounding in the Scriptures and awakening in me some sense of the all-pervasive reality of God.

The move from school to university proved something of a liberation. Although it was wartime, a severe illness resulted in my being allowed to continue and complete my studies, first in classics and then in theology. Before illness struck, I had registered as a conscientious objector and been before a tribunal, which had approved my proposal to join the Friends Ambulance Unit. My pacifism had taken root while I was still at school, when I declined to join the Officers Training Corps; but it was greatly strengthened at university by the teaching of Charles Raven, Master of Christ's College, Cambridge, where I was an undergraduate. Raven's influence with Christian youth at that time was by no means insignificant, and it is not surprising that the intellectual support of Rheinhold Niebuhr, a distinguished American theologian who stoutly defended the Just War tradition, was enlisted to counteract it. I have to confess that I am now less certain about the pacifist witness than I was then. The opposing positions taken up by Raven and Niebuhr both seem to me to be tenable from a Christian point of view. Their fundamental divergence stems from a difference of judgment concerning the kind of responsibility which the Christian community is called to accept for the way things go in a world where sometimes, it seems, violence can be contained and counteracted only by opposing violence.

At university horizons were enlarged, not least the horizon of faith. Here again I owe a great debt to Charles Raven. It was he who taught me that the God of redemption is also the God of creation, that the Creator Spirit is at work not only in the church, nor in the privacy of the soul, but also in the world. He combined devotion to Jesus Christ as the focal expression of the creative and redemptive activity of God with a recognition of the traces of the same activity throughout the whole of creation. The Word made flesh was the Word enlightening everyone, and the whole of the created order was groaning in travail until it should find its fruition in the glorious liberty of the children of God. When in later years the works of the Jesuit scientist and theologian Teilhard de Chardin were published, Raven was among those who greeted them with acclaim. The basic approach to science and religion that I now found in Teilhard I had already learned from Raven.

The other teacher to whom I am equally indebted was my supervisor in the philosophy of religion, Ian Ramsey, Fellow and Chaplain of Christ's. He taught me, among other things, that all experience, including religious experience, combines intuitive and interpretive elements. Religious faith provides no exception. It combines the flash of insight with the effort to understand and communicate. Whereas the former might be accompanied by a practical sureness of conviction,[4] the latter has always to be contextual and tentative. Faith itself is gift rather than accomplishment, but a gift which, if authentic, may be expected to illuminate as it transforms the whole of experience. Hence a reasonable faith will transcend any religion that is restricted within the bounds of 'pure reason'.

It was at university too that I discovered the reality of grace and community. I was fortunate enough to find my way into the college branch of the Student Christian Movement. Here was a group of diverse individuals, with different backgrounds and prejudices, held together by a common concern to explore the Christian faith and by a shared worship in the college chapel, broadly Anglican but also ecumenical. Here we all accepted and supported one another, even when we passionately disagreed with one another. Here we learned at first hand the truth of what Paul Tillich later expressed in a celebrated sermon, *You are accepted:* 'It would be better to refuse God and the Christ and the Bible than to accept Them without grace. For if we accept without grace, we do so in the state of separation, and can only succeed in deepening the separation. We cannot transform our lives, unless we allow them to be transformed by that stroke of grace. It happens or it does not happen.'[5] It was my good fortune that it happened.

It was at university too that I was introduced to the liturgical riches of the Book of Common Prayer and to the tradition of English church music. It was, I suspect, the worship of the college chapel which, more than anything else, prompted me to become an Anglican, a decision which in my schooldays I should have viewed with dismay. Since then I have maintained a kind of love-hate relationship with the Church of England, but I doubt whether I should now be happy in any other tradition than the Anglican. It is here that I feel most 'at home'. In the words of the Psalmist: 'Thou hast not shut me up into the hand of the enemy, but hast set my feet in a large room.'[6]

Ordination came as something of a surprise, both to myself and to my family. It was not what had been envisaged. My elder brother was the 'religious' member of the family, not I. I experienced no strong interior calling to orders. Rather, the idea was put into my mind by one or other of my S.C.M. friends, and having without success done my best to dislodge or forget it, I finally gave in to it. It has been my experience all along that God works in and through natural and human processes rather than despite them. Although it may have the merit of emphasising that God really is active in the world, in the end the language of divine 'intervention' seems to me to cause more problems than it solves: one intervenes only in a situation in which one has so far played no part.

One of the last candidates for ordination in the Church of England before selection conferences were instituted, I was accepted, more or less on trust, by Bishop Barnes of Birmingham and ordained in 1947 to serve a curacy in the parish of Bournville, the home of chocolate and Quakerism, for both of which I acquired a predilection. My memories of this curacy are few – for example, churching newly delivered mothers in the linen cupboard of Selly Oak Hospital maternity ward; or lecturing at Fircroft College on the history of philosophy to men who had ceased their formal education at the age of fourteen and were for the most part ardent socialists. I lasted in the parish for only a few months before succumbing to a persistent bone infection which took me to hospital for two years and which was to dog me off and on for the next twenty years. A long stay in hospital can teach you patience but it can also encourage passivity. Patience and passivity may look the same but they are not the same. Patience is akin to receptivity, responsiveness and life; passivity is akin to torpor, disdain and death.

My parochial ministry lasted from 1947 to 1960. Beginning in Birmingham, and then beginning again, after two years in hospital, in Sherborne in Dorset, I returned to the diocese of Birmingham in 1953 to become rector of the small country parish of Wishaw, situated between Four Oaks and Coleshill. This parish, made up of two hundred or so souls, cabbages and farmland, with half a public house – the parish boundary divided the public bar from the saloon bar – and a post-office in a cottage parlour, was used by the Bishop for clergy with special needs, either of health or of occupation. My two predecessors, G. D. Kilpatrick and A. R. C. Leaney, were both biblical scholars, the former moving on to a chair at Oxford, the latter to a chair at Nottingham. While at Wishaw I resumed lecturing at Fircroft College and was also invited to give some lectures at the Queen's Theological College. Perhaps most rewarding of all were lectures I gave under the auspices of the Workers

Educational Association to a mixed but highly motivated group of students in Coventry. Their direct, intelligent if unsophisticated questions were often the most pertinent and incisive, and I found it an exciting challenge to try to answer in a similarly direct, intelligent and intelligible manner. Here, I suspect, were laid the foundations of a continuing desire to provide stepping-stones between the experience of the many and the learning of the few. In 1956 I was invited to return to Bournville as vicar, where I stayed through intermittent bouts of bad health until 1960. I kept my links with Fircroft College, and through Fircroft with the Selly Oak Colleges, which presented a strongly ecumenical approach to mission and ministry and so provided my own day-to-day work with a wider and deeper context. Loyalty to the same Lord went hand in hand with a rich variety of understanding and response.

In 1960 I was invited to become Dean of Jesus College, Cambridge, and for the next twenty years my work was in an academic environment. The sixties were notorious for student unrest and for a general rejection of authority in the name of the 'permissive society'. In retrospect it is possible to see that one underlying cause of the unrest was a failure, in an increasingly fragmented and individualistic culture, to move beyond the false antithesis of personal freedom and shared values. Freedom and belonging both constitute the good life for human beings. Freedom without belonging tends to a *laissez faire* liberalism, belonging without freedom to an authoritarian collectivism. A distinction needs to be drawn between 'wilful' freedom, which increases only as external values and influences are rejected, and 'responsive' freedom, which recognises goods beyond itself to which it is receptive. Michael Polanyi had already made this distinction in his book *Personal Knowledge: The freedom of the subjective person to do as he pleases is overruled by the freedom of the responsible person to act as he must.*[6] The practical implications of this distinction have still to be worked out in individual, social and political life.

The office of Dean at Jesus College carried with it responsibility for the life and worship of the chapel rather than for the discipline of the college. The tradition of the College, founded by Bishop Alcock of Ely in 1496 on the site of a Benedictine nunnery, was religious; the pursuit of learning and education was largely secular. If the chapel were to continue to play a significant role in the life of the college, rather than cater simply for the religious predilections of a diminishing number of its members, it was important that it should both deepen its life of worship at the centre and at the same time be open to the questions of all and sundry at the circumference. Beliefs and attitudes might diverge; but in an institution of higher education there was the opportunity and need to probe and explore, with academic rigour, the reasons and grounds for these varying beliefs. It helped, at least symbolically, the work of bridge-building if the Dean had an academic as well as an ecclesiastical role, and I was fortunate, after a few years in Cambridge, to be appointed to a university lectureship in the divinity faculty.

In 1972 I left Cambridge for Oxford. Appointed by the Crown to a canonry of Christ Church and the chair of moral and pastoral theology, for which I was signally unprepared, I divided my research and teaching between underlying questions of method and specific problems thrown up by advances in scientific knowledge, for example, in medicine, and developments in social outlook and practice, for example, in the field of sexual ethics. It is the practice of the Church of England from time to time to set up small working groups of men and women, lay and ordained, with varying experience and expertise, to study and report on some specific moral issue. I had the privilege of belonging to a number of such groups. With time I began to perceive that a distinctive pattern was emerging, in which the moral and pastoral concerns for norms and justifiable exceptions interweave. While the basic values characteristic of Christian faith and life remain the same, the structures and practices which embody these values may with the changes of history themselves change. This pattern of argument has been aptly described by Basil Mitchell, himself a member of many of these working groups: 'Whether the issue is suicide, euthanasia, abortion, or divorce and remarriage, the same basic pattern emerges. The Christian tradition yields a strong moral imperative – against taking one's own life, against killing the innocent, against the dissolution of marriage; and the question then arises whether there can be any justifiable exceptions.... To insist upon an absolute prohibition, no matter how painful or abnormal the circumstances, would, it was felt in all these cases, threaten the values underlying the principle itself or other principles to which the Christian is equally committed. To abandon the principle altogether and range all cases on a single scale of lovingness would be to ignore moral distinctions which are required by the nature of human life as God created it.'[7]

While in Oxford I became involved in another area of church life. At that time the Church of England had an Advisory Council for the Church's Ministry. The Council itself had a number of committees, one of which was the Committee for Theological Education, which was concerned with the education and training of the Church's ministers. I succeeded Sydney Evans, Dean of King's College, London, as its chairman, and retained the post for some ten years. One of my concerns was to seek to bring together theological and ministerial training and to ensure that the Church provided a firm and coherent base for them both. To this end I urged the need to offer *an integrating theology*, based on a sense of *the living whole informing its various parts*. 'An integrating theology', I wrote, 'is intended, not only to hold together the different disciplines into which the study of theology is divided, but also to draw together into a creative unity understanding and response.'[8] The practice and understanding of Christian faith go hand in hand.

In the summer of 1979 I received a letter asking me if I would consent to my name being proposed for the Deanery of Durham. My immediate reaction was that I would not. It was true that, largely because of my own fault, I had never felt as settled in Oxford as I had in Cambridge – Oxford I respect, Cambridge I love – and had been entertaining for some time the idea of returning to parochial life. However, I had at last worked through this period of indecision and my mind was made up to stay in my present situation until retirement. I therefore put the letter in the waste paper basket. However, a good friend and counsellor told me that I must not react so hastily and cavalierly, and that I ought at the very least to go to Durham and find out what the job involved. That, it could be said, was my undoing!

I had visited Durham only once before, at the invitation of the Bishop, to give a couple of lectures to his clergy, and on that occasion I had little time to give to the cathedral. In any case, cathedrals, I knew, were only buildings, while Church was people; and it was necessary, I thought, for the Church to travel light into an uncertain future. But something happened on that occasion which made me change my mind, and for the next eight years I began to discover what it might mean to be caretaker of one of the most beautiful buildings in the world. There is something about Durham Cathedral which only those who have lived and worshipped and worked in and around it can fully appreciate. In my more imaginative moments I associate this 'something' with Cuthbert and Bede, the one, saint and bishop, buried behind the high altar at the east end of the cathedral, the other, saint and scholar, buried in the Galilee Chapel at the west.

The cathedral was a meeting-place of church and world, of civic religion and Christian commitment, of tourist and pilgrim. Overwhelming in its grandeur, it could also be as welcoming as home. Its peculiar ministry was to the senses rather than the intellect, and it was one of my desires to foster a closer relationship between the cathedral and the arts, not only in word and music, but also in the visual arts, including drama, sculpture, stained glass, painting, metalwork and embroidery. In conjunction with Northern Arts, Hatfield and Trevelyan Colleges, Sunderland Polytechnic and the Chaplaincy to the Arts and Recreation in the North-East for Leisure and the Arts, the Cathedral initiated and supported a yearly artist in residence. The scheme proved a success. It fostered the powers of the imagination and encouraged the renewal of vision. And 'where there is no vision, the people perish.'[9]

Surrounding and impinging on all that was going on in the Cathedral was the day-to-day life of the people of Durham, caught up in the social and political unrest caused by such factors as the decline and demise of traditional industries, the miners' strike, or the financial stringencies imposed on the University. Nor was it to be expected that the cathedral which contained the chair (*cathedra*) of David Jenkins, Bishop of Durham in succession to John Habgood, would be allowed to pass its days in rest and peace!

Bridges. Stepping-stones. At its best a cathedral exercises an indirect ministry of its own, in addition to the more direct ministry of its servants. It touches the springs of feeling and imagination. It frees heart and mind to respond with courage, determination and hope. In a talk to the Cathedrals Finance Conference of 1988, to which I gave the title *Fabricating the Gospel*, I said:

> The essence of the cathedral's existence, and the justification for all the time and money we spend on it, is not simply that it is a wonderful building, but that it is a symbol and sign of God's presence. Indirect evangelism begins where people are and with the concerns they have. If they want the loos, then tell them where the loos are to be found. If they have lost their kids, then help them to find them. If they want architecture or social history, talk to them about the tracery of the windows or the miners' memorial.
>
> Underlying all our encounters and conversations is the conviction that these immediate and surface interests and concerns are part of our common humanity, and that it is in this humanity that God deigns to become enfleshed. These ordinary concerns may become stepping-stones to deeper concerns. We ourselves may call these deeper concerns worship, or prayer, or exploration, or what-have-you; but I believe that deep down these are the concerns of our visitors too, whether they recognise them as such or not. They too need to celebrate, to get things off their chests, to have a fresh look at themselves and at the world they live in. They too need to discover new sources of forgiveness, hope and love. It is not for us to dictate the direction or force the pace of their journey.
>
> In our desire to share with them something of the glory that has, God knows how, grasped us, and to receive from them something of another glory that has grasped them, we may enter into a conversation with them which will lead God knows where. And if he knows where, and our times are in his hand, then perhaps we may leave to him the outcome of this peculiar but far-reaching ministry.[10]

Retiring in 1988, shortly after my sixty-fifth birthday, some two years earlier than I had intended, but increasingly harassed by the arthritic legacy of my earlier illness, I now live with Anne, my wife, among the hills and sheep of mid-Wales. This is for both of us a new and engaging chapter in our shared story, and we now have the space and time to get to know one another better. When we married in 1950, neither of us realised what lay in front of us. What with my recurrent illness and frequent disappearances to hospital, life for both of us was something of a struggle for survival. I was not the world's most helpful husband or father, and Anne shouldered the responsibilities of family life more or less on her own. Only when our three sons had grown up and left the nest – one of them had to be asked, most respectfully, whether it was not time for him to leave! – did she have the chance to develop and use her own special gifts. There is no formal position of wife of the Dean of Durham, but by warmth of character and consistency of concern Anne made it a focus of friendly and caring relationships – so much so that, on the occasions when I have been back to Durham, the first question I have been asked by all and sundry has been 'And how is Mrs Dean?'

In retiring to the Victorian watering-spa of Llandrindod Wells we have broken all the rules which pre-retirement advisers are anxious to inculcate. We have struck camp and gone into a far country, where life and friendships have had to be begun anew. We have one worry, namely that after two years and more we are still undeniably happy! We live on the edge of a small but remarkably cosmopolitan country town, and we have around us the hills, the railway, a swimming pool, a cottage hospital, a community arts centre and, most important of all, a lively parish church. Here too, then, in the heart of Wales we are discovering still more of what it means to be 'at home' and to know that one belongs.

References

[1] Alec Vidler, *Cambridge, Farewell!*, in Theology, July 1967, p. 299 f.

[2] H. H. Price, *Faith and Belief*, in 'Faith and the Philosophers', ed. John Hick (Macmillan 1964), p. 25.

[3] Alastair MacIntyre, *After Virtue* (Duckworth 1981), p. 206.

[4] Ian T. Ramsey, *On Being Sure in Religion* (Athlone Press 1963).

[5] Paul Tillich, *The Shaking of the Foundations* (S.C.M. 1949), p. 161.

[6] Michael Polanyi, *Personal Knowledge* (R.K.P. 1957), p. 309.

[7] Basil Mitchell, *The Homosexuality Report*, in Theology, May 1980, p. 188 f.

[8] Peter Baelz, *An Integrating Theology*, A.C.C.M. Occasional Paper No. 15, December 1983.

[9] Proverbs 29.18.

[10] Published in the Thirty-first Annual Report of the Friends of Cathedral Music, April 1988.

APPROACHES TO
THEOLOGY

INTELLECT AND IMAGINATION

Donald M. MacKinnon

The range and limit of human imagination in advancing knowledge of the world around us was a topic of general importance to David Hume and Immanuel Kant. Thus in Pt. IV Section 4 of his *Treatise* Hume urged his readers distinguish habits of imagination that were 'permanent, irresistible and universal' from those which were 'changeable, weak and irregular.' The former he illustrated by reference to inference from effects to causes, and from causes to effects, the latter by the transition from a noise heard to the presence of a spectre. Both inferential procedures were natural, the latter, however, natural in the way a disease may be said to be so. One quickly realises that in fact the perverted assumption of the presence of a ghostly visitant takes for granted and builds on the more general procedure of inferring from effects to causes. A creaking sound on the stair outside a closed door *must* have a cause. But how is that cause to be identified? The superstitious will immediately entertain the possibility or likelihood of a spectre, following the basic habit of imagination, without which (in Hume's own words) 'human nature would inevitably perish and go to ruin.'

So in naturalistic terms Hume anticipates Kant's method of transcendental argument, establishing the conditions of human survival in such procedures as the imaginative movement to an identifiable and relatively stable cause of a bewildering effect. For Kant of course the imagination was the 'understanding working blind', its activity associated particularly with the second synthesis in the subjective 'deduction of the categories', (named 'synthesis of reproduction through imagination'). Later in the structure of the *Critique of Pure Reason* imagination is treated as the effective agent of the schematism of the categories, whereby in fact the forms of understanding are transmagnified into the conditions of objective awareness, the pure category of ground and consequent, for instance, into that of cause and effect. The latter is vindicated in the 'second analogy' as the assumption that we must bring to the manifold of our experience if we are able to consider an objective time-order, wherein before and after are not matters of our caprice or situation, but following one another with the inevitability of night or day. It was Kant's conviction that only if we assumed the reality of sequences in which one event *must* follow another with the necessity of a man's death following his consumption of potassium cyanide, could it conceive any sort of sequence in which the before and after, even if there were no casual linkage between them (as in the case of my writing this essay and the departure five hours before of a train from Aberdeen to Edinburgh), were objectively as they were. Causality is as it were, ingredients in the very notion of objectivity.

So two great philosophers in different, but related ways, acknowledged a crucial part played by imagination in human knowledge; but both alike insisted on the need of a sharp discipline, supplied in the case of Immanuel Kant, by understanding, distinguished alike from sense-awareness and from that Reason he sought to criticise. Yet for Kant understanding was in his own word spontaneous, and this spontaneity required the *Critique of Pure Reason* itself to secure it against the indulgence of sheerly undisciplined extrapolation of its resources to achieve no longer the conditions of objective experience, but to delineate in ways that would outrun any procedure of confirmation or falsification, the ultimate secrets of the universe.

Are there lessons here to be learnt that can be formulated in terms of less rigorously scholastic precision than those to which his enterprise constrained Kant? In particular are there lessons to be learnt by the Christian theologian for whom faith has a perceptual basis? I say: perceptual rather than historical, recalling that the author of the first Johannine epistle (whether or not he is to be identified with the author of the fourth Gospel) speaks in his first sentence of that which 'we have heard, we have seen with our eyes, and our hands have handled of the word of life' (1 Jn. 11). If Paul found it necessary to remind the Corinthians that they no longer see Christ 'after the flesh', this reminder is warranted by the fact that once he was so seen. It is, of course, the fourth Evangelist who with dazzling intricacy, emphasises and then seems to depreciate, the perceptual basis of the disciples' faith. He is less dismissive certainly than Paul; yet at the end of his twentieth chapter, rich as it is, in subtle presentation of the risen Lord's visual self-manifestation to his own, he records that same Lord's blessing of those who unlike Thomas, have not seen, yet like him have believed.

One may seem a long way from Kant's rigorous mapping of the complementary roles of sense, imagination, understanding, reason in the concluding chapters of John's Gospel. Yet if one includes the supper discourses in one's review, there is an analogous refusal to speak of faith as if it were all a matter either of sense or imagination, let alone of intellectual insight akin to that of the mathematician. The very unnoticed richness of perceptual experience with the inter-penetrating resources that make it what it is are wonderfully uncovered by Kant in his quest for the conditions of objectivity. We are not in bondage to sense-awareness in the manner suggested by the uncritical empiricist, who disdains skills enabling us transcend the immediate, and for whose conceptual activity is reduced to a mere *Vorstellungs-ablauf.* So in the fourth Gospel faith demands a reference-point; it does not disdain ostentation whether by sight, hearing or touch. Yet that reference-point by itself is insignificant, even as Kant judged sense without conceptual activity to be blind. But the analogue of that activity, the exercise of imagination that will enable perception yield its secrets, must be disciplined. It must be the gift of the Spirit, not the prompting of an unchecked aspiration that will bend the deliverance of sense to confirmation of its own ill-disciplined fantasy. So Mary Magdalene, called out of near despair by the address of the one she had taken for the gardener, had immediately to be delivered from the further error of supposing herself confronted with the one she had known, and watched in his agony, come again to her as Lazarus from his charnel-house to his sisters. By correction of her fantasising her perception itself was enlarged, and deepened further by the mission entrusted to her.

To some readers such analogizing may seem little more than anachronistic self-indulgence. To impart a quasi-Kantian architectonic into treatment of John's exploration of the relations of perception and faith may be dismissed as little more than a tired academic's frivolity. Yet in a very interesting lecture delivered at Keble College, Oxford, in 1987, and published in the Epworth Review for September 1989,[1] Professor Dennis Nineham, who is deeply, almost obsessively preoccupied, with questions concerning the relations of faith and history, raises a very similar question in discussing contemporary response to an event which might (in his view) very well have been treated by the Evangelists, as a case of demoniac possession (pp. 43/4). Diagnostic identification of the case as one of diabetic coma, although supervening on first perception of the patient's seizure, and distinguishable from it, is also continuous with that perception as enjoyed by contemporary experients. We do not *see* the victim's collapse as the effective action of alien forces; we anticipate clinical identification of the symptoms by the medically trained. Again we do not anticipate any sort of miraculous intervention proving an effective alternative to clinically tested therapeutic response. Yet we have to allow that on occasion, medical practitioners have to reckon, for instance, with the spontaneous regression of a carcinoma. It would be a mistake to characterize such an event as miraculous; but it does reveal the importance of reckoning with perceived discontinuities, occurring within the framework of the clinically identified, familiar advance of a disease. And this suggests that while experience is deeply saturated with assumptions derived from prevalent culture, there is also a hard perceptual base, not easily disentangled from the overlay of contemporary belief, but providing a context within which common reference is possible, and a starting-point provided for argument and evaluation.

So I would plead that those who argue most strongly the significant claims of historical and cultural relativity do not forget the world of perception: a far richer world moreover (as the testimony of artists and poets makes plain) than what has been conveyed in these somewhat cursory and elliptical comments. In the presentation of the miraculous by the four evangelists we have to reckon with a half-conscious engagement with the question of divine intrusion at the level of the perceptually familiar. Apart from the crudities of the Acts of the Apostles (allegedly Luke's second volume), there is an implicit rejection of the sheerly thaumaturgical. It is rather very often the significance of a sudden recognizable breach with familiar routine that is at issue, the raising rather than the answering of questions. Yet this always takes place at the level of the perceptually familiar where radical discontinuity advertises the presence of the transcendent unknown. But how is that presence to be grasped? We are surely coming to see that presence, *parousia, praesentia,* is a fundamental theological category. But we are tempted to indulge our imagination in ways that imprison or at least delimit its operation; we confirm the reach of imagination (as the great poet understands it) with the capacity to fantasise, to form mental images. So without realizing it, we show ourselves in bondage to Bentham's dogma: 'Poetry is misrepresentation.'

Yet the very introduction of the topic of miracle must serve as a reminder that the treatment of perception in this essay may rightly be judged excessively abstract. There has been a failure sufficiently to emphasise that perceptual experience is experience of a common world to which human response is a great deal more complex than is suggested by a model arguably in too close bondage to the highly specialized, concentrated and sophisticated observation characteristic of the laboratory. The situation of the individual observational scientist is of course abstract in the sense of only partly recognized dependence on a wealth of subsidiary activity on the part of other agents, not forgetting, of course, highly elaborate technical apparatus. And this dependence is one that cannot be treated as if it were a dependence on *zōa organa,* the living tools to which Aristotle in his *Politics* reduced the slave population on which the common life of the *polis* depended. The laboratory assistant is not such a servant, and it is a serious mistake to avert attention from his active participation in the enterprise of the investigator whom he assists.

Yet of course the world of the laboratory is a specialised world; whereas the world in which miracle is still sometimes half-believed, is the human world in which men and women cry out to their God that he should rent the heavens and come down. The entreaty of men and women, condemned to the death camps of Nazi Europe, provides the context in which the alleged experience of miracle must be discussed, when the prayer of millions went unanswered, and the death-trains continued to roll. If ontologically miracle must in part be identified with radical discontinuity, it is the setting of human anguish, of prayer seemingly unanswered and judged impatient of any answer save a total silence, that helps to define the event as miraculous. But the manner in which that definition is carried out must be judged in part an act of creative interpretation, whereby the seal of a religious experience is set upon a hardly expected deliverance from ill of body and/or mind, and it is regarded as an answer to prayer. So the understanding of prayer, of the life of faith itself is in peril of perversion. All this is clear enough from the Gospels even if their authors must be judged totally ignorant of the most commonplace material assumptions of modern science of nature. The ambiguity of the faith of those who kept company with Jesus, believing because of signs and wonders, is plain. It demands the transformation that comes (to recall the vivid and shocking language of John 6) from 'eating the flesh of the Son of Man and drinking his blood', from recognizing that the Messianic road is one that leads through Crucifixion to Resurrection. Yet such recognition is more a disciplining of the imagination than obviously a flight from perception.

This elementary reference to the theme of miracle may serve as a reminder that perceptual experience is anchored in human life, which is never something in which practical and theoretical, emotional and intellectual concerns can fly apart. If we abstract, as abstract we must for concentration of argument, we must never forget that from which we abstract: the flow of human life, in which our words receive and give meaning, shaping our experience, even as they receive their sense from its rich variety. There is no problem in the philosophy of logic more difficult, and yet more fundamental, than that of the status of logical necessity: whether it is something found, or something that in the last resort is conventional in foundation, however disturbing the paradox of attributing truth to what is determined as true by a common refusal to abandon it. The reference to the community of that refusal is crucial, and distinguishes such obstinacy from intransigent commitment to individual inventiveness. If the frontiers of acceptable discourse are matters of decision, this decision is not arbitrary, but the achievement of a common mind, assigning limits to the remotely acceptable.

Although these issues are of the greatest technicality, it is important to recall their significance as indication of the extent to which it is with the limits of human creativity and the conditions of its exercise that we are ultimately concerned in these reflections on the interplay of intellect and imagination in the life of faith. If the faith that concerns the Christian theologian is an activity or a disposition that demands continual reference to a perceptually definite occasion, if not the intentional object, its oscillation between fashioning and finding resonates a familiar epistemic tension. Its exploration demands continued recourse to the insights gleaned from classical epistemology. If it is manifestly the case that in the world of Christian faith, we are in a world that is uniquely *sui generis*, it is also true that its birth and growth attest the presence of the conditions that beset every enterprise of human discovery, whether concerned with the world around us, to which we belong, or with the more intimate areas of personal self-knowledge.

It is unfortunate that a certain clotted obscurity especially in the earlier pages, has earned Professor George Steiner's book *Real Presences*[2] a hostile reception, and obscured the importance of the issues he is raising by fastening on the significance of presence as a metaphysical category. The brief discussion of miracle in this essay has advertised its significance for theology. For faith is seen to be born in part at least by the purifying imagination of every taint of fantasy, of retracting from the fantastic embroidering of the familiar to glimpsing in that familiar itself, the presence of the transcendent. So the fourth Evangelist purges his Passion-narrative almost entirely of any suggestion of the fantastically miraculous, relying on a near-poetic irony to indicate that in the events recorded the transcendent is uniquely discernible. Apart from the prostration of the posse come to arrest Jesus at his self-avowal (the pregnant *egō eimi*) the narrative eschews every hint of portent, yet is all the time compelling the reader to reckon with layer below layer in its sense, and by his reckoning, come to acknowledge the action of the eternal.

Yet always this presentation takes for granted, may even be judged parasitic upon, the familiar perceptible reality of our common world. If we allow a perfectly proper sensitivity to the historical remoteness of first century Judea to check any rashness in our imaginative reconstruction of the judicial process whereby Jesus was brought to his death, we must also insist that the writer constrains us to find the presence of the transcendent there in that which is familiar in principle.

So in this essay, offered in great respect to my former colleague Peter Baelz, I suggest that if we learn to set side by side what initially must seem to belong to different universes of discourse, namely Kant's epistemology and the theology of the fourth Evangelist, we learn lessons that will enlarge our understanding of the nature of faith. It will not be the whole story; we must never ignore by facile abstraction, the richness and the cruelty of the common world. But as Kant also argued, distinctions of good and evil in themselves transcend the changes of the centuries, and enter into the definition of that world which is both starting-point and setting of our common life.

References

[1] *The Last Half-Century of Theology:* a personal impression. (Epworth Review: Sept. 1989, pp. 47–57.)
[2] Faber (1989).

THE CHALLENGE OF SCIENCE TO THEOLOGY AND THE CHURCH [1]

Arthur Peacocke

Any contribution to a volume celebrating the lifework of Peter Baelz cannot but take account of the dominance of pastoral concerns in both his academic and ecclesiastical activities. Notable amongst these concerns is his continuous effort to bridge the gap between the study and men and women in the pew and in the street. For he has recognised more than most that one of the most urgent pastoral needs of men and women in Western societies is to be given grounds for seeing the Christian perceptions on nature, humanity and God as, at least, plausible and believable. This plausibility and believability has long been in jeopardy under the onslaught of the Enlightenment and, even more in this century, from the continual pressure exerted by the growth in scientific knowledge and influence.

To contribute to the task of facing this general challenge, a gauntlet that Peter Baelz has always been willing to take up, I shall, in this essay, be seeking to reflect again, in the light of the understanding of the natural world which we have from the sciences, on certain ideas, images and models that have traditionally prevailed in Christian theology. If the truths, as I believe, these traditional modes of thinking have conveyed in the past are to be handed on to the future they have to be re-thought, new images have to be re-born, in the light of the best contemporary knowledge we have of what is in the world and what is going on in it. And that means the perspectives of the sciences have to be taken into account in any viable 20th-century theology. This hazardous task has to be undertaken with no sense of repudiation of the past. For, in fact, one is constantly encouraged by what rich treasures there are in the past of the Christian church waiting to be revived and brought into the light of a new day. Like the householder of St. Matthew's Gospel, we need to bring out of our store 'things new and old' (Matt.13v.52, REV).

For the most vital theology in the history of the Church has always been that which has been hammered out in response to new intellectual challenges and to new social and political pressures. One could instance the great contribution of the Cappadocian Fathers, who met the challenge of Greek philosophy; or the conflicts that led to the formulation of the Nicene Creed and the affirmations of the early church councils; or St. Thomas Aquinas who, despite much opposition, after the rediscovery of the writings of Aristotle in the West refashioned the philosophical basis of Christian theology so well that it lasted until quite recently – when it, too, became a straitjacket like the theology of his own contemporaries had become.

The presuppositions of what I say will be 'critically-realist' with respect to both science and theology. That is to say, I think both science and theology aim to depict reality; that they both do so in metaphorical language with the use of models; and that their language and models are revisable within the context of the continuous communities which have generated them.

We cannot but take seriously the features of the history of the natural order that the sciences have broadly established, but not, however, some recent speculations too seriously. For a theology that marries the science of today may well be a widow tomorrow. Even so, there are broad features of the world which have become so well established that Christian believers, indeed members of all theistic religions, would be foolish not to take account of them. It is true that human beings make mistakes, but there is no virtue in believing that they make nothing but mistakes. There are some features of the world that have emerged from the scientific endeavours of the last three centuries with which theology simply has to reckon.

The resources for our theology continue, of course, to be scripture and tradition, ways God has spoken in the past through the frameworks of thought of the past. Today we still wish to affirm the activity of God in Christ through the Holy Spirit, yet we must do so with the means provided by our own frameworks of thought if we wish to be understood by our contemporaries. God is still actively revealing himself, and the new wine of today needs new wineskins.

We have to apply our reason to our resources – the scriptures and tradition – and to our experience, and that experience includes a new awareness of the world through the natural sciences. We seek intelligibility and meaning for ourselves as individuals for our brief sojourn in this world of God's creating. We need to hear the Word that is eternally uttered by the Creator to his creation in a language that we can understand and respond to and communicate to others – and today we have to recognise that the one universal language that knows no cultural boundaries is that of science. As a well-known astronomer, R. Hanbury Brown, put it informally at the 1979 World Council of Churches gathering at Boston on *Faith, Science and the Future*, 'Quantum theory does not change when you cross the Equator'.

So let us look at some of the 'heads' of Christian doctrine and see what images and metaphors might be the best way of thinking about them in the light of the broad, best-established features of the scientific picture of the world.

GOD

The primary attribute of God in the monotheistic religions is that of *transcendence* over the world, over all-that-is. For we have to recognise that the existence of all-that-is is not self-explanatory. Even the original quantum fluctuation, from which our observable universe is currently thought to have expanded, had to have a mode of being of a kind to which quantum mechanics could specifically apply, so that it had to be a fluctuation in a 'field' of a kind describable by the laws of that science. It was not just 'nothing at all' even if it was 'no thing'! The affirmation of the existence and transcendence of God is, then, a response to the question 'Why is there anything at all?', a response to the sheer givenness of it all – and the need for such a response is, if anything, enhanced by the scientifically perceived subtlety and rationality of the observed universe. This response involves the recognition of God as Creator, of God as giving being to all-that-is, of God as the ground of all being, Being itself; and of the world as having a derived and dependent being. This constitutes one of the fundamental pillars of Christian theology, indeed of all the monotheistic religions and I shall be taking this as a premise and presupposition in what follows.

The givenness of the parameters of the universe has been sharply brought into focus recently in that cluster of physical considerations which is referred to as the 'anthropic principle' – the fact that this universe is characterized by a particular set of laws and fundamental constants which prove to be just those that could allow to the development of living matter, of life, and so of ourselves. The anthropic principle re-emphasizes what, in the theological tradition, is perceived as the contingency of all-that-is. Everything could have been otherwise; it need not have been at all in the forms it now has. The anthropic principle contributes new grounds for us to recognise the contingency of our own existence and God's transcendence.

In 20th-century physics there has been a development, initiated by Einstein, in which the categories of space and time, which seemed so given and *a priori* to Kant, are themselves interlocked with each other in a new kind of relation. For space, time, matter and energy have become mutually defined concepts which modern physicists link closely together. We now have to talk about four-dimensional space-time, the curvature of which is related to the gravitational field and this is related to the concept of mass, itself now seen as interchangeable with energy.

Any doctrine of creation, any notion that God gives being to all-that-is must include time, as St. Augustine and the Fathers knew, for God is, in some sense the creator *of* physical time. The doctrine of creation is not, in the first instance, a statement about what happened 'in' space-time, for space-time, matter and energy are all aspects of the created order. God has to be regarded as other than, and transcending, the space-time, matter and energy of the physicists. The doctrine of creation is fundamentally about the relation of God to all-that-is, and this includes space-time-matter-energy. So modern physics has emphasized a fundamental insight of theology which goes back to Augustine and even earlier.

But, with biblical authors, modern Christians also believe that God is not entirely 'timeless'. For we regard God as, in some sense, personal and so experiencing, as we do subjectively, a sense of succession in relation to the history of the world, humanity in general, and ourselves in particular. We cannot put God, as it were, on a mountain top from which he views all time – past, present and future – and thus foresees all future events (including those involving ourselves) laid out before him, for that limits, indeed destroys, our freedom. For us to be free, God cannot know certainly what we will decide. There is no simple fact of the matter ('At 10.30 a.m., I will do X . . .') for God or for us *to* know. It seems we can best think of God bringing into existence, i.e. creating, each moment of our physical time (in our particular relativistic framework) – which is what the traditional notion of God sustaining and preserving matter-energy in space-time must now be taken to signify.

There is in modern physics, it must be accepted, a great mystery in our understanding of matter, energy, space and time – and the further we go down into the fundamental entities of the universe, the harder it is to say what they are in themselves. But the universe is also mysterious in its later developments, in the most complex of existing entities. For the natural sciences have not dispelled the ultimate mystery about the nature of human personhood, both as we perceive ourselves and other persons, and our relation to them. The traditional sense of the transcendence of God is enhanced by such recognition of the existence of boundaries that limit even our most sophisticated scientific endeavours.

The scientific perspective also enriches our notion of another classical attribute of the God of Christian faith, namely the *immanence* of God in the world. We observe, through the sciences, the operation of natural processes that are continuously and inherently creative, for matter has the ability to be self-organising into new forms. The process is open-ended and the details of the processes are often unpredictable in principle – either because of 'Heisenberg' uncertainty at the sub-atomic level or because of the unpredictability of certain, far from uncommon, non-linear macroscopic systems. Though not strictly always predictable, they are often intelligible *post hoc*. There seems to be an in-built tendency in matter, and the processes it undergoes, towards complexity, awareness, information transfer, and ultimately, consciousness, cognition and self-consciousness. Potentialities appear to be being actualized. The original 'hot big bang', with its cloud of neutrinos, quarks or whatever, has becomes *us*. Nature not only has, but *is* a history of events. There seems to be no inert stuff in the universe, for all entities and structures are in dynamic process in which the universe manifests emergence of the genuinely new. These emergents have to be described and explicated by means of concepts that are not reducible entirely to those appropriate to the structures and entities from which the new have emerged. *New realities go on appearing.*

If we are to think of God as creator of such a universe, then we are bound to re-emphasize that God is still creat*ing* in, with and under the processes of the natural processes of the natural world all the time. God is *semper Creator*. The world is a *creatio continua*. God as Creator not only, in this perspective, sustains and preserves the world (the traditional understanding) but must now be regarded as continuously creating in, with and under these creative processes – and I deliberately use sacramental language here. God is now understood to be exploring and actualizing the potentialities of creation, achieving ends flexibly without laying down determinate lines in advance. God is improvising rather as did J. S. Bach before the King of Prussia or perhaps like an extemporizing New Orleans jazz player in Preservation Hall. Creation is the action of God-the-Composer at work.

The processes of creation, as unravelled by the sciences, appear to be open-ended. There is increasing individuality of organisms as one goes up the biological scale, culminating in the freedom of *homo sapiens*. It seems that God as Creator self-limits his omniscience and omnipotence by allowing to emerge, through the processes to which he himself gives existence, openness and flexibility and freedom, most notably in *homo sapiens*.

We also see, through our scientific spectacles, that death is the pre-condition of new-life. Consciousness, and so awareness, cannot evolve without the development of nervous systems and sensitive recording organs which inevitably have to be able to react negatively to their environment with what we call pain. It appears that pain and suffering are the pre-conditions of sensitivity and consciousness, and that death of the individual organism is the pre-condition for new life to appear. What theologians used to call 'natural evil' now appears in a new light as a necessary part of a universe capable of generating new forms of life and consciousness. This has the corollary that, for our notion of God to be at all acceptable morally, we have to regard God as himself suffering in, with and under the creative processes of the world. God is, then, to be conceived as enduring what we call natural evil for achieving the ultimate good and fruition of what is being created.

The world also shows an enormous fecundity and variety in its organic life. Yet science can demonstrate the extraordinary unity that underlies this diversity, how the operation of relatively simple principles has led to this amazing variety. We dare not, in all humility, assume that all this marvellously rich life is there simply in order that some chance flick of the genes will produce us! God must be taken to have joy in the created order in its own right, in its own vitalities, at its own levels, and for its own sake. (Here, incidentally, is the basis of a theo-centric ecological ethic.) God must be seen as delighting in the existence of all forms of the created order – inorganic and living, and not only in *homo sapiens* (as Psalm 104 expresses so well).

In the light of the scientific picture of a creative universe, God's immanence in the creating process needs to be strongly re-affirmed and re-emphasized after having gone underground for three or four centuries, especially in our theologies of salvation (soteriology), as we shall later discuss. It needs to be brought to the surface again. For, in some sense, the world is 'in' God, yet God is 'more than' the world. God, in this respect, is more Creator-Mother than Creator-Father, for God gives new forms and life to what is *in* God, in 'God herself', we find ourselves having to say. The ultimate being of God is, of course, other than space, time, matter and energy. So when we say the world is 'in' God, the preposition 'in' here is a spatial metaphor and we do not mean to imply that the created world is of the same nature, possessing the same kind of being, as God him/herself – only that God is present to all-that-is, the circumambient Reality that flows in and around all.

There is still in all this, and it has been perennial in Christian theology, a tension between transcendence and immanence as attributes of God. Both are necessary, yet it is hard to hold them together coherently as referring to God's relation to the world. We very much need a model that brings these two ideas, distinct though they are, into some kind of overlapping focus of transcendence-in-immanence. I think we can begin to see such a model in our human experience. (In the next section we shall also discuss how further reflection on human nature in the light of the sciences helps us to conceive of how God might interact with the world.) For we are self-transcendent in our consciousness over our bodies, yet there is a sense that we are ourselves immanent in and through those same bodies whose processes can be investigated and discovered by the sciences. So the model of the personal now functions to help us conceive of how divine transcendence over and immanence in the world might be consistently held together in a personal model. Perhaps this is one of the multiple senses, much discussed in the long course of Christian history, in which human beings are *imago dei*. If so, then the truest image, or *icon*, we might ever have of God would be through a human person fully open to God so that he or she is, as it were, transparent to the divine life and Being – and thereby embodying that self-limitation of omniscience and of omnipotence which is an expression of God's nature as Love. For there is a self-emptying (a *kenosis*) of God in creation that calls for explicit manifestation.

This modality of God as Creator also points to the self-expression of God's own inherent being as creative Love acting on behalf of the coming into existence and flourishing of something other than God, that is, the created world. Our language inevitably falls short of depicting such a Reality, so we have to say that God is 'at least personal'. Since it is of the nature of the personal to communicate, we come to think of God as self-communicating through his creation, as the Prologue of St. John's Gospel informs us. That Prologue also reminds us that the meanings God intended to communicate through God's Word spoken in creation are uttered to human beings, the creatures capable of reading them. 'In him [the Word] was life, and that life was the light of mankind' (John 1 v.4, REV).

This has certain consequences. The meanings that God is communicating differ for the various levels of creation according to the capacity of those levels both to convey and to apprehend them. So if we believe that God is 'at least personal', can we not hope that in a person, or persons, some time, some place, God might unveil his meaning, express his Word in a fullness appropriate to our human capacity to discern and respond to it?

Before responding to this, we must take a closer look at *HUMAN AGENCY – as a model for God's interaction with the world.*

In the perspective of the sciences human beings are seen as psychosomatic unities, evolving by natural processes, emerging into consciousness and self-consciousness. There seems to be a continuous evolution to the vertebrates and to the higher primates. Then in the *homo sapiens* special features appear that are not entirely discontinuous with those of his and her predecessors – such as a highly developed brain, flexibility, use of language, social cooperation. But in human beings a certain incandescent mix of these qualities appears to have occurred. For the human brain-in-the-human-body displays qualities in mental and personal activities to which we have to apply specific, appropriate and non-reducible language. Human unity is not that of a body plus a 'mind' plus a 'soul'. 'Persons' possess a unity which emerges from a continuous history out of the past but which is, nevertheless, genuinely new. Biblical scholars emphasize that this view of the human being as a psychosomatic unity is indeed that of the Old Testament and also underlies that of the New.

This can give us an important clue to making more intelligible the belief that God interacts with the world to make some things happen rather than others. The various sciences concerned with the human body and brain and their inter-relation all point to our being psychosomatic unities. When we act, total brain states, which we experience subjectively as thoughts, intentions, purposes, etc., are causally effective in the many-tiered levels of our bodies – our muscles, ligaments, nerves and so on. The result is our observable actions within the physical, causal nexus of the world. This action of our brains-in-our-bodies is a holistic one, in the top-down direction and what happens at the 'lower' levels – in our muscles, ligaments and nerves, etc. – is entirely consistent with the known regularities of muscle biochemistry, physiology, neurology, etc. This is but one of the more significant examples of the way in which the state of a whole macroscopic complex system affects and constrains the events occurring at the micro-level of its constituents parts.

It suggests a model for how God might be conceived as interacting with the world, for how God might be causally effective in a top-down way that does not abrogate the known regularities of events at their own distinctive level of description by the appropriate sciences. This would not be an 'intervening' God, in the sense in which he is alleged to have sent lightning to strike a cathedral in which a supposedly 'unsound' bishop was being consecrated, but would be a God continuously interacting with the totality of the world, shaping through his top-down constraint upon the whole both the general course of events and particular ones. God is faithful to the order of his creation and does not act in a way that is inconsistent with the regularities with which he has endowed it. Moreover we now see that God's acts are circumscribed, by the nature of the natural order he himself has created, by the inherent unpredictability and openness of many natural events – including that of the operation of the human brain.

As often in the past, the model of personal agency continues to be fruitful in helping us to conceive of God's interaction with the world. But now it is enriched and nuanced by new insights into the mind-body relation, into top-down causation in complex systems and into the openness and flexibility inherent in the natural world.

HUMAN MORTALITY: the 'Fall' and 'sin'

Like all living organisms, human beings have a finite life and we have come to recognise through the scientific understanding of evolution the biological necessity of the death of the individual. We as individuals would not be here at all, as members of the species *homo sapiens* if our forerunners in the evolutionary process had not died. Biological death was present on the earth long before human beings arrived on the scene and is the pre-requisite of our coming into existence through the processes of biological evolution whereby God creates new species, including *homo sapiens*. So when St. Paul says that 'sin pays a wage, and the wage is death' (Rom. 6 v.23, REV) that cannot possibly mean for us now *biological* death and can only mean 'death' in some other sense, such as death of our relation to God consequent upon sin. I can see no sense in regarding *biological* death as the *consequence* of that very real alienation from God that is a sin, because God had already used biological death as the means for his creating of new forms of life, including ourselves, long before we appeared on the Earth. This means those classical formulations of the theology of the redemptive work of Christ that assume a causal connection between biological death and sin urgently need recasting.

Moreover, the evidence is that human nature has emerged only gradually by a continuous process from other forms of primates and there are no sudden breaks of any substantial kind in the sequences noted by palaeontologists and anthropologists. There is *no* past period for which there is evidence that human beings possessed moral perfection existing in a paradisiacal situation from which there has been only subsequent decline. All the evidence points to a creature slowly emerging into awareness, with an increasing capacity for consciousness and sensitivity and the possibility of moral responsibility and, the religions would affirm, of response to God. So there is no sense in which we can talk of a 'Fall' from a past perfection. There was no golden age, no perfect past, no original perfect, individual 'Adam' from whom all human beings have now declined. What is true is that humanity manifests aspirations to a perfection not yet attained, a potentiality not yet actualized, but no 'original righteousness'. Sin, which is real, is about a falling short of what God intends us to be and is concomitant with our possession of self-consciousness, freedom and intellectual curiosity. The classical conceptions of the 'Fall' and of 'sin' that dominate our theologies of redemption urgently need, it seems to me, re-interpretation if they are to make any sense to our contemporaries.

The human creature that has emerged from evolution exhibits strains that indicate it to be curiously incomplete and having an unhappy 'fit' with its biological, personal and social environment that seems to be unique among living creatures. Only human beings commit conscious suicide. Human beings experience themselves as, as it were, being 'on the way', with increasing aspirations, increasing possibilities of both exaltation and of degradation as human powers over the natural environment increase, Self-consciousness, *ipso facto*, makes humanity aware of its limitations and of its failure to fulfil its highest ideals. Humanity now shapes its own evolution which has itself become psychosocial, internalized and self-directing. With human beings, biological evolution has become 'history'.

We all have an awareness of the tragedy of our failure to fulfil our highest aspirations; of our failure to come to terms with finitude, death and suffering; of our failure to realise our potentialities and to steer our path through life. All of these are realities of the human state. Freedom allows us to make the wrong choices, so that sin and alienation from God and from our fellow human beings are real features of our existence. Our theology will be going on a false trail if it is based on presuppositions of an ideal, perfect past from which we have 'fallen'. Humanity emerges into consciousness with the possession of language and a sense of moral responsibility, an understanding of truth, beauty and goodness – and the freedom to repudiate them. As this self-consciousness comes into existence the possible fluctuations about any norm get bigger and bigger, so that human beings become capable of greater heights and also of greater degradation than any other living creature. With the emergence of self-awareness, *homo sapiens* has the opportunity of both higher achievement and of greater debasement that had his predecessors.

EVOLVED HUMANITY and GOD INCARNATE

Within the processes of creation there has, therefore, come into existence a being capable of self-transcendence, an 'I' which knows itself over against its own body in the natural world and thinks of itself as subject. This human being has emerged within nature by its inherent and inbuilt processes which, by and large, the sciences render increasingly intelligible. Does this not raise the hope that the immanence of God in that part of the natural order which is humanity might perhaps display a 'broken image' of the transcendence as well as of the immanence of God? Because God had brought into existence this human being in and through the process, the transcendence and immanence of human consciousness and bodily experience raises the conjecture that in humanity the immanence of God might one day display, in unique and newly emergent manner, a transcendent dimension to a degree which would unveil without distortion that transcendent-Creator-who-is-immanent.

But humanity is only a broken and distorted image of God. Human beings have misused their freedom by putting themselves at the centre of their lives and of their universe. 'You will be like God himself' (Gen. 3 v.5, REB), said the serpent. Suppose, however, a human being freely chose to be so open to God's immanent presence in the world that his/her life was *totally* God-centred, would not that be the ultimate unveiling of God's being, of God's mode of becoming, and so of the meaning that God is communicating for the discernment and response of humanity? Would it not then be accurate to say that, in such a person, the immanence of God had displayed a transcendent dimension to such a degree that the presence of God in that actual psychosomatic personal unity required new non-reducible concepts to express a unique transcendence in and through immanence? But is not this, in fact, the very concept of 'incarnation'? Thus it is we approach the idea of the possibility of God being incarnate in a human person.

The historical sources in the gospels show that Jesus of Nazareth had an acute sense of his direct and personal relation as a 'son of God' to God as Father, whom he, almost uniquely and distinctively regularly, addressed by the intimate term 'Abba' for 'father'. These same sources show that his was a human response of, in the end, total obedience to God to the point of a death from which he humanly shrank. In so obeying God and consequentially suffering a shameful death through the evil of others he constituted a new kind of humanity (a 'second Adam') in a total obedience and openness to God of which our basic human nature (the 'first Adam') is incapable. The resurrection vindicated him and confirmed him as a revelation of what humanity might become. Furthermore because they perceived the oneness of the human Jesus with God the Father in his relationship continued through his life, death and resurrection, his disciples and the early Christians came to see God as acting in and through him. So totally transparent was Jesus to the loving activity of God, so complete was his relation to, his communion and oneness with, God it also soon came about that the early Christians could not think of the being of God without this person Jesus, now designated the 'Christ' and 'Son of God'. And so it has been for Christians ever since.

Hence it is that Christians are those who believe that the 'incarnation' we adumbrated above, that manifestation of God as transcendence-in-immanence, has actually happened in history in the person of Jesus the Christ. If this *is* so, we still have to ask what is the significance of the life, death and resurrection of Jesus for humanity in its search today for God's meaning in a created world that is increasingly described and rendered intelligible by the natural sciences.

We have earlier been considering how, in the light of the sciences, God as Creator might be coherently be thought of as continuously related to the created order; this now has to be reviewed in the light of specifically Christian belief. I suggested earlier that we had a hint that, if we were going to think of God as creating through the kind of processes the sciences show to be operating, then God must in some sense be regarded as self-offering and suffering Love active in creation. This is entirely coherent with a recognition that in Jesus the Christ we have an explicit manifestation of God as self-offering in suffering love, supremely in his passion and ultimate crucifixion. In the life and death of *this* person we have the supreme revelation of God's own love in suffering in creation.

I suggested above that God's meaning might be more fully made clear, his message more accurately conveyed, his 'information' better transmitted, through the level in the created order of that unique entity, a 'person'. We would then regard 'incarnation' as the word for the new non-reducible concept applicable to this unique person, Jesus of Nazareth, who is the manifestation of God's transcendence immanent in a human life. God's transcendence-in-immanence shines through the image of the person of Jesus, being the perfect vehicle for communicating to us the self-offering and creating Love that constitutes the transcendence and immanence of God, that is, both the divine Being and Becoming.

I described the processes in the natural world as emergent, open-ended and continuous. Jesus was fully open to and obedient to God. He was one with the ever-acting God who brings forth the new in the created order. He was one with God's work in the world, in initiating God's reign (God's 'Kingdom') over all. By virtue of his openness to God as his Father ('Abba') and Creator, Jesus was able to express with a unique originality the freedom of the transcendent Creator immanent in the world process.

I am here concerned not so much with Jesus' nature or what kind of 'substance' does, or did, constitute him (the terrain of the classical debates of the first five centuries of the Church), but rather with the dynamic nature of the relation between God's immanent creative *activity*, unveiled in him, and the *processes* of nature, of human history and experience. There is an activity of God on all the time which is peculiarly and manifestly focussed in the personal life of this Jesus of Nazareth.

I have suggested that God unveils his meaning in and at various distinctive levels in what he has created. In this perspective, Jesus the Christ mediates to us the meaning of that strand of creation which leads to self-conscious personal life. As Emil Brunner once put it, 'The love of God is the *causa finalis* of the creation. In Jesus Christ this ideal reason for creation is revealed'. The meaning which God communicates through the life, death and resurrection of Jesus is the meaning which

God wants to communicate both *about* humanity as well as *for* it. In Jesus the meaning he (Jesus) discerns, proclaims, expresses and reveals is the meaning he himself *is*.

We begin to see that Prologue to St. John's Gospel in a new light. We see that there the Word, the *Logos* of God, the Word uttered in creation, penetrates the whole of what is created. It is perennial, general, implicit – but incognito. When the Word becomes 'flesh', when God is incarnate in the person of Jesus, this activity and presence of God immanent in all that is created becomes focused, historic, particular, explicit, and manifest. All this is a central theme of the Johannine literature, summed up in 1 John, v.1:

> It was there from the beginning; we have heard it; we have seen it with our own eyes; we have looked upon it, and felt it with our own hands: our theme is the Word which gives life. This life was made visible . . . (REB).

This is a perspective in which we can see the significance of the presence and expression of God in Jesus, as both continuous with what went before and as a genuinely new emergent that demands all the special language of 'incarnation' that the Church has elaborated over the centuries to talk about this unique event. But this uniqueness has the potentiality of generality. An evolutionary perspective allows us to recognise both the continuity of Jesus with us – he is human – and the distinctiveness. For the evolutionary process all the time shows emergence of the new out of the old so that new forms come into existence that require new concepts and language for expressing their uniqueness and distinctiveness. Hence we can accept both the continuity and the emergence, both the immanence of God in the creative process of the world and the Incarnation in the sense of a specific and explicit manifestation of God in a unique way – and so, one must also say, in a unique action and communication to humanity of God. In this sense Jesus the Christ is the consummation of the creative work of Love itself in the whole evolutionary process.

But what does this mean for our understanding of what God has done *for* us in Christ? That is what theologians call *THE WORK OF CHRIST*.

The foregoing gives a vantage point from which we can now view the redemptive work of Christ in a new perspective. It has the consequence that what happened to Jesus could in essence happen to all of humanity. God can be embodied in us to the extent to which we open our total selves to God and freely respond to his will. We respond to the Christ-event by allowing our lives to be the locus within which God kindles a love responding to his love shown in that life and death of Jesus the Christ which was vindicated in the resurrection. When we do this, we – as St. Paul puts it – 'take the shape of Christ' (Gal. 4 v.19). Or, again as St. Paul said, 'We are transfigured into his likeness' (2 Cor. 3 v.17).

We become what God intended us to be and our faith is the presence of Christ in us. This is, of course, the whole theme of 'deification', 'divinisation', *'theosis'* that the Greek Fathers emphasized. Christ is indeed the 'second Adam', even if (or rather, especially if) the first was only a projection of our hopes for perfection and a shrewd assessment of what and where humanity actually is. Jesus the Christ is the 'Second Adam' because he has become the primal ancestor, in history, of the new humanity that truly can 'image' God.

Basically what I am urging here is a recovery of that ancient and early strand in Christian theology which is associated with Irenaeus, who, in a compelling phrase wrote. *'Our Lord Jesus Christ,* the word of God, of his boundless love *became what we are that he might make us what he himself is.' (Adv. Haer.* 5, praef.). This constitutes a positive understanding of redemption which, rather than simply seeing it as a reversal of a past collapse from perfection (a 'fall'), as a conferring of a new status by virtue of a past event, instead regards it in a dynamic and positive way as the process whereby God is creating a new humanity by the work of Christ through the Holy Spirit. Redemption and salvation, in this approach, are not the restoration of a *past* original perfection to humanity, that of a perfect 'first Adam', who never actually existed, but an initiative of God which raises humanity into the life of God. Christ is the forerunner, the first realisation and instantiation of a new possibility for human existence. This possibility is made actual for us through Christ's human response of obedience and openness, which was in itself an initiative of God as Holy Spirit immanent within the created world.

But this is not just an item of abstract knowledge. For in the cross of Christ we see God going to the ultimate as suffering Love in the and within the human experience of Jesus Christ in his passion. The same God as Holy Spirit that united the human Jesus with the Father now kindles and generates in us a love for God and for those for whom Jesus died as we contemplate God in Christ on the cross. This action of God as Holy Spirit in us is itself salvific, actually making us whole, making us 'holier' – that is, it saves and sanctifies us, restoring us in our right relationships to God and humanity. 'Through the Holy Spirit he has given us, God's love has flooded our hearts' (Rom. 5 v.5, REB).

Through Christ and in the Holy Spirit, human beings now both know that they can live their lives in and with God through self-offering of themselves in love and obedience to the God and Father of our Lord Jesus Christ – and are enabled to do so by the action of God the Holy Spirit in them as they immerse themselves in the contemplation of the life, death and resurrection of God Incarnate. Thereby we are enabled to share in Jesus Christ's own life of obedience towards the Father, of becoming open to God in the way he himself was. That is our transformation here and now that constitutes our at-one-ment with God and our fellow human beings.

So 'redemption from sin' is seen no more as some rather abstruse transaction within God – not the correcting of some debit in the divine balance sheet, or the inducing of a change of mind in God about what he will do with humanity, as in some 'theories of the atonement'. It is, rather, a manifestation of God's perennial loving, gracious intention to actualize the potential he has given us of a full and enriched personhood by bringing humanity into his own life through the self-offering and suffering love of God himself that he kindles in us through his immanent presence as Holy Spirit. It is a path costly to God and costly to us.

It seems to me that such an understanding of redemption, salvation and (for it is continuous with them) of sanctification is wholly consistent and congruent with both the Christian revelation and an evolutionary-scientific perspective. It affords, I suggest, the Christian faith a way of communicating with a generation to whom the old language, based on other models of atonement and redemption, is often totally incomprehensible and unbelievable – even when they are not morally repulsive, as in the substitutionary theory of the atonement. Those who have been nurtured in the bosom of the Church and steeped in biblical language and models (e.g., that of 'sacrifice') may still be able to appropriate the traditional language of such 'theories of the atonement' and make them their own so that they have a significance for them in their devotional life. But for most of our contemporaries, and especially those who take seriously the scientific accounts of human origins, such language is not accessible and is often totally mystifying and incomprehensible, even for believers in God.

I think that it is imperative that the Church starts talking about salvation and redemption in a believable manner – and still in a way true to Christian insights down the centuries. Salvation is about making whole – about health, wholeness, wholesomeness. It is about living our lives in and with God in such a way that our alienation ('sin' is the classical word for it) from God, from our fellow human beings and from ourselves is overcome by the life God can now live in us as we respond to what God in Christ revealed to us – namely, the gracious, costly, suffering love of God for us and for our fulfilment as his creation. So salvation and redemption are about living our life in and with God; about being taken into the presence of God and being reshaped after the image of Christ so that God creates, as it were, Christ-in-us, and we become one with the resurrected Jesus the Christ who lives eternally in his risen humanity in the presence of God. Such an emphasis seems to me to make intelligible how what happened in Jesus *then* can have significance for us *now*.

OTHER THEMES

Consistent with this perspective, the following theme might be identified for further development.

The Church would be regarded as the community of those who by the action of God in Christ through the Holy Spirit are becoming one with God and in whom the creative act of God in evolution is being brought to fulfilment in community through the creation of a new modality of human existence – one might even dare to call it a new 'species', except that this would be misunderstood as referring simply to the genetically-selected level. The doctrine of the Church should then deal with the new possibilities that are arising for human togetherness in society. Basic New Testament images of the Church might then acquire a new dimension when set in the context of the continuities of evolution.

Matter itself would also take on a new meaning. In the evolutionary perspective we come to realise that matter is not what we thought it was when we talked about it in terms only of Newtonian billiard balls, or, more sophisticatedly, as atoms in the Periodic Table, or, even more sophisticatedly, in terms of quantum physics. We now know that through the evolutionary process matter has become persons. Break us all down and we are just a pile of hydrogen, carbon, nitrogen, oxygen, iron, phosphorus, etc., atoms. But we are also persons: in us matter has *become* persons who know God and who worship. Such an insight into the potentialities of matter has been continuously preserved in the Church by its sacramental language.

When Jesus at the Last Supper said 'This my body, this my blood' and pointed to things of the created order – bread and wine made by human work out of the elements of nature – he was giving a new value and a new meaning to the stuff of the universe. The sacramental tradition of the Church has mercifully preserved in its liturgy the utter seriousness and significance with which we must regard the very material stuff of the created world. This is now entirely consonant with our understanding of how the stuff of the world is in fact the matrix of personality, that which becomes persons. The created world is itself sacramental in this double perspective.

CONCLUSION

If the foregoing has any weight then it seems the Church must re-think its message in today's language for a society deeply impressed by and indebted to science – and that means not only the 'Western' world but everywhere, for increasingly the dependence on, and so the knowledge of, science is permeating all cultures. The old images, although they may still be evocative and meaningful for those steeped in the language and tradition of Christianity, no longer appear at all credible to those outside the churches, which is 90% of those in the United Kingdom, it seems from all the surveys. We need a rebirth of images in continuity with what we have inherited from the scriptures and tradition; we need to revise how we speak of the eternal realities to which we seek to refer and encounter with which we yearn to share our contemporaries. This re-thinking of our metaphors and theological models is the task of the thinking Church in our generation, if the credibility and plausibility of the content of the Church's message is to be recovered. Otherwise the 'Decade of Evangelism' will be stillborn.

For I am convinced that the importance of *ideas*, both in the short and long run, cannot be overestimated. It is our duty to interpret the Word of God uttered in the person of Jesus the Christ in ways intelligible to our contemporaries. That means our received Christian reflections and insights need to be enriched – yes, and corrected where need be – by our knowledge of God's creation that the sciences now reveal to us. Theologians who take no account of the scientific picture of the world are just digging themselves into a deeper and deeper hole and, as they go down, they will be able to talk more and more only to themselves and less and less to other people.

Outstandingly, Peter Baelz has graced the various offices he has held by not being one of their number! For as a theologian he has persistently attempted to communicate across the divide between the study and the pew and to those altogether outside the Church. Our best enduring tribute to him would to be if we went on trying to talk to our contemporaries, and indeed to ourselves, in language – models and metaphors – that are meaningful in the world we increasingly are coming to know: that of the sciences.

References

[1] This chapter is a revised and expanded version of a paper first published under this title in *The New Faith-Science Debate*, ed. John M. Mangum (Fortress Press, Minneapolis and WCC Publications, Geneva, 1989).

RELIGION AND THE ARTS

Peter Walker

The starting point for natural theology is not argument but sharpened awareness. For the moment it is better for us that the arguments have fallen to pieces.

1. *A PRESENT EMPTINESS*

A cry of protest and pain at the impoverishment of contemporary theology from its disengagement, 'all but complete', from imagination ended the opening essay in the Cambridge volume *Soundings* of 1962, the year in which Pcter Baelz and I began the ten years as neighbours for which I remain always grateful. Howard Root's 'Bcginning All Over Again', from which I take my epigraph above, concluded

> The best text-books for contemporary natural theologians are not the second-hand theological treatises but the living works of artists who are in touch with the springs of creative imagination.[1]

Asked, twenty-seven years later, to speak in the same Jesus Lane to the Faculty of Divinity and the Theological Colleges Federation which Peter Baelz had served so faithfully in the heady 1960s, I took Root's cry and, under the title 'Sharpened Awareness', addressed myself to the English poet who speaks to me in Root's dimension. I did so against the background of a Fourth National Conference on Literature and Religion recently attended below Peter Baelz's great Durham Cathedral, at which any such hope as Root had entertained had seemed suddenly precarious. What shall happen when the springs run dry for the creative artist? This was the question I was left with by the accounts successive speakers had given of a numbness, *aporia* – an oppression of spirit in the dimension of Ionesco's cry

> The words in my mouth have gone dead.[2]

Behind the phenomenon lay most obviously the threat of an earth reduced to a desert by a nuclear holocaust, its life gone back into that nothingness which the human mind tries, with a new sense of it as a real possibility, to get itself around. Or, again, this emptiness might be a function of the 'cosmic alienation' felt by men and women here and now as the overwhelming vastness of space comes home to them, or even as they find themselves separated, in the concrete city, from their roots in nature and the earth.

But could the new *aphasia* be perhaps the condition out of which a whole fresh beginning might come? To draw upon the language of a thinker whose death in 1977 was itself a grievous impoverishment to theology and whose touch reminds me much of the theologian whom the present volume celebrates, Cornelius Ernst O.P., the Christian must always be ready to face the moment of darkness, when it comes, in faith that it might prove to be for him one of the 'genetic moments' in which the world will suddenly flower into light and meaning. What was felt as a void turns out to be an emptiness that is 'plenary, superabundant: a radiant darkness', of a piece, in 'ordinary' experience, with 'the hidden God, *Deus absconditus*, who has made his transcendence known in the darkness of a death'.[3]

With this as its question, the method of the present essay will be to take literally Root's plea to let the poets speak, and to do so by allowing two of Geoffrey Hill's poems to speak for themselves. Such self-restraint does not necessarily come easily to the religiously committed (and it is of him or her that I am thinking, and particularly of the Christian church person, in terms of the title given me), tempted always to enlist the artist in his or her own religious cause; and it is good, therefore, that in Hill we have a poet whose work has an integrity which will always resist any such annexation. I take two poems of his, marked by their title as a pair, the

TWO CHORALE-PRELUDES
on melodies by Paul Celan,[4]

and I choose them for their own sakes but also as pieces which incidentally offer us not only the response of this foremost contemporary poet and critic to perhaps the most searching European poet of our century, but also his wave to the poet and critic of the last century whose teaching on the imagination would be bound to command our attention for our present subject, the Samuel Taylor Coleridge who, incidentally, with Archbishop Cranmer, gives lustre to Peter Baelz's Jesus College, Cambridge.

With Coleridge, Celan and Hill, we are at once, as our subject must demand, deep into theology, and there is one more name to mention before we keep our promise of method, namely F. J. A. Hort, the natural theologian (and natural scientist, and prophet) of the 'Cambridge

Three' of the last century. Hort's sixty-page essay, *Coleridge*, in *Cambridge Essays* 1856,[5] is valuable summary still, and, at a point, anticipates remarkably Root's plea from which we began. But a century stands between Hort and Root, even so, just as between ourselves and Root's essay there are now the nearly thirty years in which we have become accustomed to the phrase 'exponential change'. To move forward by way of Hort could offer a perspective.

2. *COLERIDGE AND HORT: AN EMERGENT QUESTION*

Phrases from Coleridge's account of what was to have been Wordsworth's contribution in a shared exercise illuminates, Hort writes, Coleridge's understanding of his own poetic vocation, although his own poetic themes would embrace more widely the 'romantic':

> to give the charm of novelty to things of every day, and to excite a feeling analogous to the supernatural, by awakening the mind's attention from the lethargy of custom, and directing it to the loveliness and the wonders of the world before us, – an inexhaustible treasure, but for which, in consequence of the film of familiarity and selfish solicitude, we have eyes, yet see not, ears that hear not, and hearts that neither feel nor understand.[6]

Hort develops the implications of this 'passage of singular interest and importance' for something which he devoutly desired to see, and saw indeed as already on its way under the influence of the new human sciences, namely a drawing of philosophy and art 'continually closer to each other, and both to simple natural history':

> Perhaps it is not too much to hope that by that time moralists and logicians will have ceased from contemptuous language about the senses; a genuine spiritual philosophy needs no such *bourgeois* self-assertion to maintain its own dignity. Philosophy has denied that it has anything to do with the knowledge of God, and is now being rapidly swallowed up by positivism or science militant, and ancient experience tells of a yet lower deep. *Yet when we shall seem to lie at the lowest point we may perhaps be near the very highest, and the senses themselves may become the very instruments of our deliverance.*[7]

Looking to the poems themselves, Hort quotes from the one to which, as I hope will emerge, Hill looks back past Celan – *Frost at Midnight*. Its theme is simple: the poet, his cradled infant slumbering peacefully at his side, soliloquises in the silence of the winter night, the fluttering 'film' that plays on the hearth providing living company to his imagination. The happy things of nature of which his own city childhood was deprived (he 'saw nought lovely but the sky and stars') will speak to the child

> that eternal language, which thy God
> Utters, who from eternity doth teach
> Himself in all, and all things in himself.

All, including the silent icicles

> Quietly shining to the quiet Moon,

will one day speak *in sweetness* to the child.

Here, for Hort, is the Coleridge who

> undoubtingly believed that the outward world of sense is but the appropriate clothing and manifestation of an invisible spiritual world ... According to him, the first work of imagination is, passively to read this symbolic language of nature; the second, actively to reproduce it faithfully and truly, but so modified as to convey the perceived meaning to all minds endowed with a like passive capacity of interpretation. Of course, such a language ... must proceed from some kind of 'pre-established harmony' of creation: and, what is equally important, the meaning of nature can only be learned by a truthful and affectionate study of nature as she is in herself, and the beauty and majesty in which she is moulded.[8]

A scholar presenting Coleridge for the general reader today is clearly not so sure of Coleridge's *undoubting* assurance. 'One of the great, permanent generosities of Coleridge's work and thought', writes Richard Holmes,

> is his acceptance that if he could not achieve this state of 'blessed' certainty and joy for himself, he would strive to achieve it for those who came after him ... It is this, more than anything, that gives his mysticism its curious quality of human *warmth*, that touches us more closely than many of the chillier contemporary exponents of Being and Non-Being.[9]

Between Coleridge and today there has been indeed, as the passage just quoted recognises – but without perhaps quite allowing the sheer fact of it the *weight* which it demands – the catastrophic century in which such phrases (I take them gratefully from Holmes himself) as 'an apparently alien nature' and man's 'psychic homelessness in the world' have seemed, with all their chilliness, to convey the *truth* of the human condition. We shall look in vain in Hill's *Ave Regina Coelorum*, to which we now turn, for any such touching warmth.

I set out now alongside each other Hill's pair of poems and, in Michael Hamburger's translation,[10] the poems of Celan on which (Hill's note p. 204) he has 'based' each of them.

Paul Celan trans. Michael Hamburger	Geoffrey Hill
	TWO CHORALE-PRELUDES on melodies by Paul Celan
ICE, EDEN	1 AVE REGINA COELORUM Es ist ein Land Verloren ...
There is a country Lost, a moon grows in its reeds, where all that died of frost as we did, glows and sees.	There is a land called Lost at peace inside our heads. The moon, full on the frost, vivifies these stone heads.

It sees, for it has eyes,
each eye an earth, and bright.
The night, the night, the lyes,
This eye-child's gift is sight.

It sees, it sees, we see,
I see you, you see me.
Before this hour has ended
ice will rise from the dead.

Moods of the verb 'to stare',
split selfhoods, conjugate
ice-facets from the air,
the light glazing the light.

Look at us, Queen of Heaven.
Our solitudes drift by
your solitudes, the seven
dead stars in your sky.

KERMORVAN

You tiny centaury star,
you alder, beech and fern:
with you near ones I make for afar, –
to our homeland, snared, we return.

By the bearded palm tree's trunk
black hangs the laurel-seed grape.
I love, I hope, I have faith, –
the little date shell's agape.

A word speaks – to whom? To itself:
Servir Dieu est régner, – I can
read it, I can, it grows brighter,
away from 'kannitverstan'.

2 TE LUCIS ANTE TERMINUM
Wir gehen dir, Heimat, ins Garn . . .

Centaury with your staunch bloom
you there alder beech you fern,
midsummer closeness my far home,
fresh traces of lost origin.

Silvery the black cherries hang,
the plum-tree oozes through each cleft
and horse-flies siphon the green dung,
glued to the sweetness of their graft:

immortal transience, a 'kind
of otherness', self-understood,
BE FAITHFUL grows upon the mind
as lichen glimmers on the wood.

3. *AVE REGINA COELORUM*

Its imagery startlingly reminiscent of Coleridges's icicles shining into brightness as though hung up by the frost to sparkle a greeting to the moon, Celan's *Ice, Eden* presents a dead world glowing into life. It is a lost world finding a resurrection which means a recovery of relationships, of communication, of sight. Here is a dance of speech, the pace of the poem stepping up to an excitement as the verb 'to see' 'conjugates' itself into personal address

It sees, it sees, we see,
I see you, you see me.
Before this hour has ended
ice will rise from the dead.

We rise, as those who died of its cold, from a world lost, cold, and dead, into a Garden of Eden again. The poet holds up a symbol of a world flowering, in Ernst's phrase, into the light: in the words of our modern Coleridge scholar, of Coleridge, here for a moment poet, metaphysician and theologian of hope seem one.[11] It is not an argument, for it is poetry, matching Celan's own wistful description of his poems as 'messages in a bottle', things which someone one day may pick up and read.

Ice, Eden comes from what has been described as Celan's most affirmative collection, 'Die Niemandsrose' (1963). It is indeed a vivid refutation of Adorno's austere observation, that after Auschwitz there could be no poetry written, for Celan, born in 1920 of Romanian-Jewish parents, and dying by suicide in Paris in 1970, had survived a Nazi labour camp and wrote deliberately in the language which was that at once of his mother and of those who destroyed her and his father in such a place. With its 'hiatuses and dislocations' and the 'often violent leaps and elisions' of his 'stone speech' (the phrases are Professor George Steiner's[12]), the poetry, as Celan said of it himself, came out of a 'desperate dialogue', to constitute a 'sort of homecoming' out of the darkness and shadow of death, out of which he had brought with him only one possession, language.[13]

Here, in *Ice, Eden*, then, is indeed a poem presenting words gone dead and come to life: and what our contemporary poet has 'made' of Celan becomes slowly clear as each word of *Ave Regina Coelorum* drops into place.

It is, more explicitly than in Celan, a world *of the mind* that looks to be brought to life in this cry to the moon as Queen of Heaven. It is speech (stanza 2) that is to be brought into play again. But a dead world will look in vain.

The negation of that hope is conveyed, in Hill's poem, by every nuance, by every picking up of a word of Celan to hold it up into a negative. The dance of language, the quickening of a step, the conjugation of a verb into personal discourse, all of these are gone, rubbed out, and the opening of the eyes becomes a stare (with the rigidity of the German cognate 'starren'), its 'conjugation' become one of ice-facets from the air, turning the light into a dead glassiness. And when for a moment the pace steps up into a ballad step 7/6, 7/6 with the cry

> Look at us, Queen of Heaven,

that cry with which Augustine once looked to the stars, and heard them speak to him of their Creator, meets no answering response: the drifting solitudes of the heavens and its dead constellations are only the paradigm of the crier's own encapsulated solitude.

The poem had begun, in fact, in irony, for those alert to Heideggerean echoes, with the very word 'called'. For in that vocabulary to name is to personalise, to make, by the act itself, the earth a dwelling. With irony the poem ends, running out into stony silence with five dead monosyllables. Here is a cosmic alienation and an attendant fracturing of personhood brilliantly – and who is to say not movingly? – presented: and it is not only Celan who is rubbed out here, but the Coleridge for whom the 'outward beholding', 'fixed on the sparks twinkling in the aweful depth, though suns of other worlds', was

> only to preserve the soul steady and collected in its pure act of inward adoration to the great I AM, and to the filial WORD that re-affirmeth from eternity to eternity, whose choral echo is the universe.[14]

What shall the Christian churchman make of such poetry, a hundred years from Hort who commended Coleridge?

4. TE LUCIS ANTE TERMINUM

If the nerve of Hill's *Ave Regina Coelorum* was its refusal of the Celan from which it sprang, by contrast his *Te Lucis Ante Terminum* takes up the same note as Celan's gentle and nostalgic *Kermorvan* but, this time, sustains it. It presents the same affectionate reaching out to the things of the earth, and just as Celan's poem moves towards the quickstep of a grammar of assent in its conclusion (picked up from the little date shell's opening of itself to the world)

> *I love, I hope, I have faith,*

in all the excitement of a message now becoming understood

> I can
> read it, I can, it grows brighter,
> away from 'kannitverstan'.
> (away, that is , from 'can't understand'),

so, too, Hill conveys the message spoken by the creatures of time's covenant in response to the poet's affectionate attention.

It is not an insight given in a moment's flash of inspiration, but rather an apprehension growing almost imperceptibly, as lichen upon the tree in nature's own covenant, to shape a disposition towards the world. Here indeed we might see a Yes to Coleridge, 'poet, metaphysician and theologian of hope' at once, the Coleridge of the 'Treatise on Method'

> Hast thou ever said to thyself thoughtfully, IT IS! heedless in that moment, whether it were a man before thee, or a flower, or a grain of sand? . . . This it was which caused (the nobler minds) to feel within themselves something ineffably greater than their own individual nature.[15]

Yet Hill's lines, with their echo, in the fourth, of Hopkins' 'dearest freshness' (was there a Hopkins echo in Celan's 'I *can*'?), have a tenderness of their own, a poignancy the more searching from coming immediately after the implacable closure of *Ave Regina Coelorum*; more poignant, too, under the rubric of the Compline hymn (Hill's titles always carry weight)

> Before the ending of the day.

5. *RELIGION AND THE ARTS': A MODE REJECTED*

It might seem that at last we have found the affirmative mode for which
we have been groping. And indeed, once set upon it, there are articulate
theologians to encourage us. It is our good fortune, I shall want to
indicate, that the poet whom we have taken for our present study
explicitly refuses a particular annexation.

In the early pages of his *The Poetry of Civic Virtue*,[16] a book noted in
some detail by Hill in his own *The Lords of Limit, Essays on Literature
and Ideas*,[17] Professor Nathan Scott of the Department of Religious
Studies of the University of Virginia offers his readers a glimpse of the
later Heidegger on the distinctive human experience which gives birth
to theological reflection, namely the primal sense of wonder. It is the loss
of this which the Heideggerian sees as the great casualty of our culture,
dominated by the scientific positivism Hort had foreseen and by an
exploitative philosophy of life. So to succumb is to have lost any capacity
for 'reverential awe before the sheer ontological weight and depth of the
world'. It is to be 'alienated from that in relation to which alone human
selfhood can be securely constituted'. And here is to be seen the vocation
of the poet:

> ... it is the poet who presses a relentless kind of quest for intimacy of
> relationship with the various particular realities of experience, not with the
> 'light that never was on land or sea', but with the concrete actualities of the
> world, with the unique historical event, with the unrepeatable personal
> encounter, with all the rich singularity that belongs to 'things' in their
> intractable specificity ... It is the greenness of *this* grass, the poignancy of
> the separation of *these* lovers, the 'moonlit dome' of *this* man's dream, that
> the poetic word seeks to bring into the light of cleansed and intensified
> awareness ...[18]

It is confident writing: and Hill reacts against it with every fibre of his being.

When justice has been done to what this mode is seeking to affirm
(and Hill does exemplary justice always to the work he criticises, and will
here acknowledge the qualifications with which Scott presents this
'Orphic' mode, and confess also that it is not the principle but the
practice on the page that causes him his reservations), Hill will not be
identified with a 'mode of simplistic affirmation of the world' which then
all too easily is 'caught up in its own inflationary language'.

For Hill the critic, the world is a 'dense and complex place', and
although it is possible for good poets to write with luminous clarity about
that density, there can be an affirmation of the dense things (Scott's
'closed possibilities of things') which is in its very assurance and
ebullience a mode that is *heartless*.[19]

With that last word we have, I believe, come to the crux of this whole matter.

6. *RELIGION AND THE ARTS*: A HOPE *DE PROFUNDIS*

The 'genetic moments' of Geoffrey Hill's poetry for me, when it 'flowers into the light', are those when the heart leaps suddenly into assent, most characteristically to the poet's own cry *de profundis*, from the deadness and the chill.

It would be strange if a century which has seen the Shoah, and learnt of the receding galaxies and the black holes of outer space, and knows the desert of the city, and has witnessed the irreversible ruination of fair countryside, and is conscious of living under a balance of nuclear terror, did not know emptinesses of the spirit not experienced by former generations. When, in such a world, Geoffrey Hill sets a triple epigraph on the title-page of his *Collected Poems*, proceeding from *Lamentations 4:1*

> How is the gold become dim! how is the most fine gold changed! the stones of the sanctuary are poured out in the top of every street

by way of Péguy on the modern world's diminishment and travail, to Ezra Pound's:

> In the gloom, the gold gathers the light against it.

The Christian churchman, committed to God's self-disclosure in the darkness of a death, might well see himself as approaching not entirely alien country; and we might ourselves find Hort's words, quoted earlier, about a lowest point near the very highest coming back to us at this point of this essay.

The fact is that we are painfully discovering today, in quite new ways, the vulnerability of our world, and it is the more perceptive spirits (from among whom the creative artist will always be drawn) who will be most sensitive to this, and especially to the hints of the final vulnerability caught classically in our own day in a brief poem of a six-year-old's terror in the night

> At last she leaves her bed and creeps downstairs,
> Trembling a little; whispers, 'I'm afraid.'
> 'Afraid of what?' 'Of Nothing.' When we laugh,
> Saying 'That means you're not afraid,' she cries
> And says, – more loudly, 'I'm afraid of Nothing!'
> Says it again, till suddenly we see it –[20]

In his singularly rich encyclical *Dives in Misericordia* (1980)[21] Pope John Paul II conveyed his own pain at a world in danger of forgetting the meaning of a word deep in the Christian vocabulary, a world 'with no room for mercy'. Yet I believe, with him, that never in the history of humanity could there have been so groping a cry (that yearning *desiderium* with which St. Augustine's *Confessions* are instinct) for a compassion, a *misericordia*, 'from beyond'. It goes up today from a world with a new and deep uneasiness and fear of final emptiness and loss. It is almost as if today for the first time we know the meaning of the Apostle's words about a whole creation groaning and in travail until now.

The conclusion towards which this essay has been moving is that a true poetic vocation, of a Coleridgean dimension but with a new immediacy and shorn of fancifulness (we cannot look at the moon quite as Coleridge did, since man set foot upon it), may have been emerging in the gloom. Can the poet (using the term generically now) so articulate the world's emergent cry as to bring out of us a new and sharpened awareness, indeed a new tenderness – for indeed, to turn some words from elsewhere in Hill,

> When we chant
> 'Ora, ora pro nobis' it is not
> Seraphs who descend to pity but ourselves.[22]

It is surely not simply fanciful today to see humanity as caught up so into the cry of the fragile things of nature, Celan's or Hill's flowers and ferns, or the flowers of the field that Odilon Redon could present 'in all their reality . . . as if we had not perceived them before'.[23]

Yet there are two urgent *caveats*. To annexe a chorale-prelude, or a painting, or any work of a creative artist, so as to make of it a theological argument is certainly to reduce it; worse, it is to risk the killing of it stone dead by the 'cerebralising' of the experience it has been seeking to convey. And this would be particularly bitter irony in a day when the theologians themselves, under insights into language new since Hort and indeed since Root's 'Beginning All Over Again', are concerned not so much to reformulate earlier arguments as to take the measure of the limits of argumentation in itself. At its deepest, this could be part of the recognition, in a wholly new depth, of the truth expressed by one of them in the phrase *'the vulnerability of God's truth'*.[24]

The second caution follows closely. If we have spoken of the articulation by the poet of a cry *de profundis*, we must allow that, in truth to the broken-ness from which it comes, his utterance will often be itself a broken thing, in a measure *in*articulate, the fractured speech of a Celan. But then the utterance 'The words have gone dead in my mouth' *is* utterance. Can we allow ourselves to be addressed not only by Dylan Thomas' articulate cry of protest

> Do not go gentle into that good night.
> Rage, rage against the dying of the light[25]

or the moving protest of Britten's *War Requiem*, but by the abrupt, yet deeply poignant, violence of Tony Harrison's *V.*[26] or of Fancis Bacon's studies of a Pope, the pontifical figure boxed as it were in glass and starting forward in his seat, mouth open in that terrible and silent scream?[27]

POSTSCRIPT

An essay such as this might invite the question have we seen such a disposition towards the creative artist in our time? Born into Hort's world, Bishop George Bell of Chichester (1883–1958) crossed the frontier into our own turbulent century. Newdigate Prizeman once, his devoted patronage of the creative arts was of a piece entirely with his deeply compassionate, deeply engaged, and at moments anguished, outreach to the world. For its theology I would look to his hurried note to his younger friend, Dietrich Bonhoeffer, as the darkness and the separation of war descended on them

Let us pray together by reading the Beatitudes,[28]

and to the young Bonhoeffer's words at the beginning of his *Lectures on Christology* (University of Berlin 1933)

To pray is to be silent and cry out at once.[29]

References

[1] H. E. Root, 'Beginning All Over Again' in *Soundings*, Essays Concerning Christian Understanding, ed. A. R. Vidler (Cambridge 1972), pp. 3–19.

[2] Quoted G. Steiner, 'After the Book?' in *On Difficulty and Other Essays* (Oxford 1978), p. 196.

[3] Cornelius Ernst O.P., *Multiple Echo*, Explorations in Theology, ed. Fergus Kerr O.P. and Timothy Radcliffe O.P. Foreword by Donald MacKinnon (Darton, Longman and Todd, London 1979), pp. 34–5 ('flowering into the light' p. 11).

[4] Geoffrey Hill, *Collected Poems* (André Deutsch and King Penguin, 1985), pp. 165–6 (from 'Tenebrae').

[5] F. J. A. Hort, 'Coleridge' in *Cambridge Essays* contributed by Members of the University, 1856 (London, John W. Parker and Sons), pp. 292–351.

[6] op. cit. pp. 302–3 (qu. from Biographia Literaria, II, 1–3).

[7] ibid., p. 333.

[8] ibid., p. 305.

[9] Richard Holmes, *Coleridge* (Oxford, Past Masters, 1982), p. 59 (and now see his *Coleridge*, Early Visions, Hodder and Stoughton, 1989).

[10] *Poems of Paul Celan.* Translated and Introduced by Michael Hamburger (Anvil Press Poetry 1988), pp. 173, 203.

[11] op. cit., p. 46.

[12] G. Steiner, review of *Paul Celan: Materialen*, ed. Werner Hamacher and Winifried Menninghaus (TLS Feb. 10–16 1989), pp. 135–6 (see also his 'The Long Life of Metaphor, An Approach to "the Shoah"' Encounter, February, 1987).

[13] M. Hamburger, op. cit., Intro. p. 22.

[14] Coleridge, *Biographia Literaria* (ed. G. Watson, 1965), 289, qu. Holmes op. cit., p. 38.

[15] Coleridge, *The Friend* (ed. B. E. Rooke, 2 vols., 1969), I 514, qu. Holmes op. cit., p. 58.

[16] Nathan A. Scott Jnr., *The Poetry of Civic Virtue*, Eliot, Malraux, Auden (Fortress Press, Philadelphia 1976).

[17] G. Hill, *The Lords of Limit*, Essays on Literature and Ideas (André Deutsch, 1984).

[18] Scott, op. cit., pp. 5–6.

[19] Hill, op. cit., pp. 156–7.

[20] Edward Lowbury, 'Nothing', printed in John Press *A Map of Modern English Verse* (Oxford 1969), p. 269.

[21] *Dives in Misericordia*, Encyclical Letter of the Supreme Pontiff John Paul II on the Mercy of God (Catholic Truth Society 1980).

[22] Hill, 'Funeral Music' 5, *Collected Poems*, p. 74.

[23] Phrases from Klaus Berger *Odilon Redon* (N.Y. 1965), p. 90, quoted, on Redon's *Coquelicots et Marguerites*, in a Christie's Catalogue, November 1989.

[24] Vincent Sherry, *The Uncommon Tongue*, The Poetry and Criticism of Geoffrey Hill (University of Michigan Press 1987), pp. 181–3, makes the crux of language the whole 'critical theme' of 'Ave Regina Coelorum' (Hill, accomplished as a symbolist writer, writes here as a post-symbolist, to convey 'how the forms of language obtrude themselves on our experience, not to enrich its significance but to distort our perception of it', as language 'locks phenomena into its own grids'). But why has Sherry, to whose pages on this poem I acknowledge my debt, nothing at all to say about Hill's second Chorale-Prelude? For Hill on what I have called the cerebralised, see his 'Funeral Music', 4 (CP p. 73), on 'Averroism', and his own comment on the poem in *Viewpoints*, Poets in Conversation with John Haffenden (Faber and Faber 1981), p. 98. '. . . the vulnerability of God's truth is central to Christianity's own gospel': Nicholas Lash, Norris-Hulse Professor of Divinity in the University of Cambridge, *Cambridge Review*, December, 1988, p. 174.

[25] Dylan Thomas, 'Do Not Go Gentle into That Good Night', *Collected Poems*, (J. M. Dent and Sons) (included by Peter Levi in his Penguin Book of English Christian Verse, 1984).

[26] Tony Harrison, *V.* (Bloodaxe Books 1985, and Second Edition 1989, with press articles on 'screams of outrage'. The present writer declares an interest: he was born and grew up in the Beeston area of Leeds.)

[27] For Bacon's concern as a painter to give the image 'added depth and poignancy', see Stephen Spender *Journals 1939–1982* (Faber and Faber 1985), p. 249–50.

[28] R. C. D. Jasper, *George Bell*, Bishop of Chichester, (Oxford 1967), p. 243.

[29] D. Bonhoeffer, *Lectures on Christology*, trans. Edwin Robertson (Collins Fontana 1978), p. 27. Hill's brief poem on Bonhoeffer 'Christmas Trees' is to be found in CP p. 171.

WORSHIP AND THEOLOGY

Maurice Wiles

The office of canon-professor combines responsibility for the regular ordering of cathedral worship with responsibility for the pursuit of critical scholarship within a university. It is a combination that cannot always be practised without tension. Can one pursue at one and the same time the kind of commitment inherent in Christian worship and the kind of critical study inherent in the work of theology within a university context, when that study is directly focused on that to which one is committed in one's worship? It was my privilege to share this sometimes awkward dual responsibility in Oxford for many years with Peter Baelz. Through his teaching, his example and above all his friendship during those years he taught me a great deal about how the two parts of the job could fruitfully be held together. This essay seeks to draw upon that inspiration and offer some reflections on the relationship between worship and critical theology.

'He who comes to God must first believe that he is and that he is a rewarder of those who seek him.' So the Epistle to the Hebrews (11:6), and it seems a reasonable enough proposition. Worship is a form of coming to God, of coming 'before his presence with thanksgiving', as the Venite calls on us to do in the invitation to worship at the start of Anglican Matins. That, it may well be claimed, logically requires a prior 'faith in the existence and in the moral government of God' (to use Bishop Westcott's paraphrase of the Hebrews text).[1] But what is the nature of that prior faith? Peter Baelz spoke at length in his Bampton lectures, *The Forgotten Dream*, about the 'half-believer'.[2] The half-believer, as he rightly insists, is a totally different species from the half-hearted believer. The question of belief is one of passionate concern to the half-believer. But he is one for whom the evidence, both intellectual and experiential, will not fall into a pattern that constitutes a settled conviction. There is no way in which he or she can first establish a firm belief in the existence of God and in his moral government of the world and then come to God in worship. Nor is his or her half-belief the kind of thing that is open to a probabilistic calculus, which exceeds 50% one week allowing one to join in worship, but falls to 49% the next forcing one conscientiously to abstain. Faith in God is not like that. The dual format of the Hebrews text can indeed, easily be misleading. There are not two separate questions. Does God exist? and Are his dealings with us and with the world moral? – as if one could answer the first with certainty while still being in doubt about the second. The problematic character of the meaning of the word 'God', as somehow the ground both of existence and goodness, is part of what puzzles the half-believer. And the half-believer's intellectual studies will certainly continue to feed his or her doubts and sense of puzzlement. But few of us, I suspect, would want to exclude such a person from the practice of Christian worship. If there are difficulties about the half-believer's participation, they should more properly arise from the conscientious hesitation of the half-believer him or herself than from exclusivist zeal on the part of church authorities.

Anthony Kenny in the moving close to his book, *The God of the Philosophers*, has pushed similar reflections a stage further. His book displays a more clearly defined understanding of the word 'God' and a more decided agnosticism about his existence, yet one which falls a long way short of convinced atheism; but the book also gives voice to the same insistence on the fundamental importance of the question. In its final pages Kenny argues for the reasonableness of prayer on the part of one such as himself for guidance and illumination from the God who may possibly exist.[3] If such prayer can seem reasonable to the agnostic himself, it should do so even more to any Christian for whom the kind of experience of God claimed to be characteristic of prayer and worship is seen as a fundamental feature of the grounding of belief in God.

In recalling the work of Peter Baelz and Anthony Kenny I have been arguing that the half-believer and the agnostic may wish to participate in Christian worship, and that such a wish should be welcomed by the Christian community. In first century Corinth unbelievers (for whatever motives) seem sometimes to have attended the Church's worship, and in his first letter to the Corinthians Paul even suggests that, if they are not attracted by what they hear, the fault may not necessarily lie with them but may lie rather with the form of worship adopted (1 Cor. 14:23–5). But such an attitude was short-lived. In the case of unbelievers, precaution against possible informers will have played a part. But more theoretical justifications soon played their part too, if indeed they were not part of the story from the outset. Such theoretical justifications were not exclusively Christian in origin. An esoteric attitude was part of the surrounding religious ethos, clearly exemplified in the mystery religions. But soon more explicitly theological reasons became the dominant force. Not only outsiders but fellow-Christians with divergent forms of Christian belief were not to be accepted as fellow worshippers. That attitude is still very much with us. It is wrong, we are often told, a form of dishonesty indeed, to share in eucharistic worship with those who have a different understanding of what is happening in the sacramental service. The Catholic Ecumenical Directory, for example, still requires each individual member of any other Western Christian body, who is without access to eucharistic ministry in his or her own communion, to demonstrate that he or she has a faith in the eucharist in conformity with that of the Catholic Church before such a person can share in Catholic eucharistic worship.[4] Of course there are many issues involved in such a judgement. But set it in the context of what I have just been saying about the participation of the half-believer and the agnostic in Christian worship, and it is hard not to conclude that concern for institutional control over the community may be a more powerful factor in the case than the impropriety of people with different understandings sharing in a common act of worship.

It is interesting to observe the gradual emergence of this exclusivist attitude to Christian worship, and its application to those judged to be deviants in the matter of belief. The fourth gospel tells us that the worship of God must be 'in spirit and in truth' (Jn. 4:24). The earliest Christian exegesis of that text gives a broad interpretation to the word 'truth'. Our worship must pass beyond the level of type and shadow; it must be at the level of the ultimate, the real. As the true light and the true vine belong not to the realm of the senses but to the suprasensible realm, so the same contrast underlies the insistence that worship must be worship in the truth. But by the end of the fourth century a marked change of emphasis has emerged. The earlier interpretation is not completely forgotten. But the main stress has changed. Worship in the truth is, above all, worship in conformity with the dogmatic teaching of the church.[5]

Exegesis of another verse from that same context of Jesus' discourse with the Samaritan woman figures prominently in one of those fourth century debates in a way that bears directly on the issue with which I am concerned. Just before the injunction to worship God in spirit and in truth, Jesus is described as saying to the Samaritan woman 'you worship what you do not know; we worship what we know' (Jn. 4:22). Eunomius, the fourth century Neo-Arian, made much of it in his controversy with the Cappadocian Fathers. That worship in truth was worship in accordance with the dogmatic teaching of the Church was common ground between them. But Eunomius, employing a realist theory of language in which names depict the essence of what is named, presses the point home with rigour. Christian revelation communicates the true name of God. When Moses asked God his name, the answer came back: 'I am that I am. Tell them that I am has sent you to them' (Ex. 3:14). God is the great I Am, ὁ ὤν underived being, Being itself. Christians have been enabled to know the very essence of God. True worship is worship of what we know. Any worship that is equivocal about our knowledge of God's essence is not Christian worship. It is Samaritan worship of what one does not know; it is pagan Athenian worship of an unknown God.[6]

His Cappadocian opponents did not deny that revelation tells us many things about God: about his trinitarian nature and about his attributes. But Eunomius' claim to know the essence of God amounted in their eyes to the ultimate blasphemy of claiming to know as much about God as God himself knows. The highest knowledge of God open to us does not have that kind of clarity. It is to advance with Moses into the dark cloud on Mount Sinai, into the thick darkness where God is (Ex. 20:21); it is to grow in the recognition of our ignorance of what God in himself is, of what it is to be God. Moreover the knowledge about God that is communicated to us is communicated through the indirect medium of finite, human words and concepts. It tells us something about what God does, nothing about what he is. Even the word for God (θεός) is derived from the word to see and indicates God's oversight of the world, not his essence. And even that it can do only imperfectly, because the concepts it uses have their primary location in our human speech.

In that debate the sympathies of all of us lie, I suspect, with the Cappadocians – the sympathies even of those with a special concern to see some righting of the wrongs so often done in the past to the heretics of the early church. For the Cappadocians worship and philosophical reflection on language are more closely integrated into a coherent religious outlook than is commonly to be found in many of their modern counterparts. The two do not appear to be in tension. Both point in the same direction, in the direction of an apophaticism which their work did much to further as an important strain in the subsequent history of Christian thought. They are held back from the more radical agnosticism towards which it might seem to lead by their conviction about the clear and specific content of what is given in Christian revelation.

The problems that face us are not altogether unlike those that they had to face. And there are those who would counsel a return to something like their way of reading scripture as a way out of our difficulties. 'There is . . . no good reason', says George Lindbeck, 'in the present intellectual situation for not once again utilizing this pre-modern way of reading scripture'.[7] It is true that there is much that is attractive in the reading of Scripture as 'a Christ-centred and typologically unified whole with figural application to all reality'[8] (to cite Lindbeck's own summary description of the pre-modern reading of Scripture), and much to be learned from the insights of exegetes of earlier centuries. But their situation was different from ours, and the answer to our problems is not to be found in an attempt to recover a lost age of innocence, masquerading as a form of post-modernity. We have to explore the interrelation of worship and critical reflection, especially the philosophy of language, as an issue that bears directly on the viability of our faith. And if we start to suffer from vertigo in the process, there is no scriptural safety-net.

I have already indicated that there is no way of starting from the end of philosophical reflection and thereby establishing the truth of Christian claims about the existence and nature of God in such a way as to satisfy ourselves once for all about the validity of Christian worship. The problematic character of any such procedure is well enough known, and I restrict myself to one example of the kind of difficulty involved.

One form of such argumentation for the existence of God, which has not only been important historically but which in my view continues to be important philosophically also, is the argument from contingency. But the argument is not really a narrowly intellectual form of reasoning based on the logical status of contingency as such; its real basis is a way of experiencing the fact of contingency, which is closely akin to the underlying attitude implicit in the activity of worship.[9] An orientation towards the validity of the way of worship is already present in the grounding of the philosophical argument. The latter cannot function, therefore, as a logically prior step towards the establishment of the validity of the former.

Nor can we start with the practice of worship and use it to confirm the truth of our particular theological beliefs. The *lex orandi* has often been claimed to establish some specific aspect of the *lex credendi*. But it is usually easy enough to demonstrate that the particular form of the *lex orandi* to which appeal is being made has itself been determined not just out of the experience of praying but as the outcome of some prior theological argumentation. The late fourth century appeal to the language of the Gloria in Christian worship as evidence in support of an orthodox trinitarian belief is a clear case in point. The precise form of the language appealed to was in fact a product of the earlier years of that century, consciously adopted on the basis of commitment to the theological belief in question.[10] There is no such thing as the pure experience of worship which is uninfluenced by some preexisting theological understanding of God and of his relation to the world.

Thus the two, worship and theological reflection, are not to be found in isolation from each other. Nevertheless they are not identical, and it is important to recognise their distinctness and to consider the ways in which they interact on each other. One can draw an analogy with the two commandments to love God and to love our neighbour. For certain purposes we may rightly want to insist that the two are really one commandment – and that to love God and hate one's neighbour is not to fulfil half one's duty; rather it is a logical impossibility, because it is through love of the neighbour that love of God finds its expression. But for other purposes it may be necessary to emphasise their distinct but interrelated character, and seek by concentration on one to enlarge and modify our understanding and practice of the other. It is an approach of that kind that is called for if we are to further our understanding of how our worship and our critical theological reflection may not merely coexist but mutually reinforce one another.

The most obvious difference between the two is in their contrasting styles of language. The characteristic language of worship is poetic with its rich interplay of symbols. The characteristic language of philosophy and theology is a punctilious prose with its careful selection and ordering of concepts. I spoke just now of the 'interplay' of symbols in worship. The word 'interplay' is appropriate. For there the symbols seem often to be at play with a child-like innocence, trailing clouds of glory as they come from the rich imagery of their past in the Bible and in Christian tradition. But the language of playfulness invites the riposte that worship is either a form of sheer projection, contributing nothing to true knowledge, or else at best an epiphenomenon, depending for whatever cognitive validity it may have on the knowledge established by the more serious, if more prosaic activities of the philosopher and the theologian.

The riposte is familiar enough; but it has also enough plausibility and sufficient barb of truth that we need frequently to recall and to refresh our reasons for not accepting it. In so far as the objection is based on the analogy with poetry, it is based on a very superficial view of poetry. 'Poetic metaphor', to cite Frank Burch Brown, 'alters and expands one's ever finite understanding of oneself and of the realities within and by which one lives'.[11] And if that is true of poetry, there seems to me no good ground for denying a similar cognitive role to worship. Such a view is sensitively argued by Dan Hardy and David Ford in their book *Jubilate*. They describe the praise of God as 'a key to the ecology in which right knowledge of God grows;' in the activity of praise 'not only is God known . . . but also God enhances our rational powers'.[12] In the nature of the case there can, of course, be no proof that it is so. The most we can expect to claim is that the style of language that is characteristic of worship appears in other contexts to be a way to knowledge. Imaginative language does not depict only the purely imaginary. As Janet Soskice has argued with such care, the parallel of its use in other areas of discourse (not least in the natural sciences) gives the theist reasonable grounds for regarding the talk of God which it enables 'as reality depicting, while at the same time acknowledging its inadequacy as description'.[13]

It follows from what I have been saying that the radical contrast between the style of language characteristic of worship and that characteristic of critical theology does not reflect a radical contrast of function. For one aspect of our worship is a search for the true knowledge of God, which is the ultimate goal also of the work of the critical theologian. As in other disciplines the reflective exploration of basic images can fulfil an important heuristic role. Imaginative construction is a necessary path towards true knowledge. But it is a form of projection; and even though not for that reason doomed to futility, it is highly fallible. It is therefore in continued need of checking and correction. It extends our knowing through enabling us to see things differently; but we need to be sure that it is genuine sight and not illusion to which we have been brought. It enhances our rational powers; but we need to be able to distinguish between an enhancement and a renunciation.

Thus the practice of worship does not simply tolerate the separate coexistence of critical theology, like the two halves of the Nestorian Christ or as in the practice of apartheid. It positively requires it; it needs its interaction. As Frank Burch Brown puts it, 'the fullest possible understanding of Christian faith . . . is inherently dialogical . . . it moves back and forth between metaphoric and conceptual thinking'.[14] But the movement is not an easy one. Conceptual thought cannot fully encompass the creative implication of the significant metaphor. But it is needed to provide some curb on the other's chaotic fecundity. The fundamental Christian conviction about the transcendence and the unity of God involves on the one hand an acknowledgement of the inadequacy of all our language about him, but also an insistence on the ultimate coherence of the varied affirmations which we are led to make. It is that latter task to which the philosopher-theologian is committed. He or she must pursue it with rigour, but also with a clear recognition of the incompleteness of all conceptual systems, including his or her own.

I have been presenting the philosopher-theologian's distinctive role as the careful corrector of the fecund creativity of the worshipper-poet. And that I believe is a very important aspect of that role. But it claims perhaps both too much and too little. Too much, because it suggests that theology can sit in judgement on the way of worship with the right to pronounce where it is true and where it is in error. But in fact it cannot dispose in that way; it can only propose, because its findings too are fallible, as are those of the way of imaginative projection. Yet also too little, because it suggests that the theological task is a wholly secondary and derivative activity. But it too has a creative role. The process, as Burch Brown says, is inherently dialogical. It is not only the symbol that gives rise to thought; 'the thought, in turn, gives rise to the symbol'.[15] That side of the process can only be a slow and gradual one. But it has happened in the history of the church down the ages, and it is important that it should continue to happen. Its most significant form is not the incorporation of the theologian's formula into the language of the liturgy, but the evocation of symbols or ritual patterns that give expression to, and take further, insights arising from the process of the theologian's critical reflections.

So the way of worship and the way of critical theology belong closely together. It is a conviction with which Hardy and Ford strongly concur in their book to which I have already referred. But they enter a caveat that deserves to be heeded. 'Both the praising and the knowing of God', they write, 'tend to be disconnected from the rest of living and knowing. Just relating them together might only increase their isolation in a religious ghetto'.[16] Has the approach I have been advocating left itself open to that risk? Two factors, I hope, will guard against it. In the course of the essay I have laid stress on the parallels with other disciplines in relation both to the role of imagery and of conceptual thought. The way to theological knowing is not radically different from the ways to other forms of knowledge. Good theology cannot flourish in isolation from the rest of knowing. Secondly one important criterion to be used in the critical task of theological reflection on the possibilities adumbrated by the religious imagination is a pragmatic one. It is not only the logical coherence of the religious visions to which worship may give rise by which critical theology seeks to test them. Another important criterion is their implications for human life and action – a theme much stressed in various forms of contemporary theology such as political, liberation or feminist theology. So once again good theology cannot flourish in isolation from the rest of living. The danger to which Hardy and Ford draw our attention is real enough. But the resources to meet it are already inherent in the structures of theological reflection.

I began this essay by recalling the obligation on a canon-professor to integrate the activities of worship and critical theology. I have tried to reflect on how that can appropriately be done at the level of theory. It is more simply summed up in the command to love the Lord your God with all your mind. The love with which we are to love God is a realistic love, not the blind love of infatuation which denies the evidence of defect or weakness in the object of its love. The Christian does, of course, deny defect or weakness in the object of his or her love; but he or she does not deny defect and weakness in the evidence. We see through a glass darkly. There are defects and weaknesses, not only in ourselves but also in the glass, which obscure and distort what we see. The commitment for which worship calls is not commitment to the vision just as it has been described by those who have gone before us; it is commitment to the struggle to interpret and to live by the confused images that we are enabled to glimpse with the help of what our predecessors have seen. And that calls for a rigorously critical and questioning spirit in theology.

A theology of such a kind is a necessary part of the process whereby we seek to ensure that our worship will be worship in the truth. And it may involve a conflict between the two traditional interpretations of that phrase that I spoke of earlier – worship in accordance with the dogmatic teaching of the Church and worship at the level of the ultimate, of the real. Part, indeed, of the aim of this essay has been to try to provide a context for the better understanding of such conflict when it does arise – and in one form or another it is surely an aspect of the experience of many people to-day. If my account is on the right lines, it may help make it more possible for us to reaffirm our commitment to our specific forms of worship with renewed conviction, while at the same time enabling us to be clear, when conflict does arise between the two senses of 'worship in the truth', where it is that our primary allegiance lies.

References

*A version of this essay was given as the Aquinas lecture for 1990 at Blackfriars in Oxford, an institution which exemplifies in its life the combination of worship and theology discussed here. I am grateful to Dr Janet Soskice for helpful comments on an earlier draft of the essay.

[1] B. F. Westcott, *The Epistle to the Hebrews* (MacMillan 1889) p. 356.

[2] P. R. Baelz, *The Forgotten Dream* (Mowbrays 1975).

[3] Anthony Kenny, *The God of the Philosophers* (O.U.P. 1979), especially pp. 128–9.

[4] See ed. A. Flannery, *Vatican Council II: The Conciliar and Post Conciliar Documents* (Costello 1975), p. 558.

[5] See my *The Spiritual Gospel* (C.U.P. 1960) pp. 68–71.

[6] For this and the following paragraph, see my 'Eunomius: Hair-splitting Dialectician or Defender of the Accessibility of Salvation?' in ed. R. Williams, *The Making of Orthodoxy*, (C.U.P. 1989).

[7] G. Lindbeck 'Ecumenical Theology' in ed. D. Ford, *The Modern Theologians* (Blackwell 1989) Vol. II, p. 267.

[8] ibid., p. 266.

[9] Cf. J. M. Soskice, *Metaphor and Religious Language* (O.U.P. 1985) p. 150.

[10] Cf. my *The Making of Christian Doctrine* (C.U.P. 1967) ch. 4.

[11] Frank Burch Brown, *Transfiguration* (University of North Carolina Press 1983), p. 171.

[12] D. W. Hardy and D. F. Ford, *Jubilate* (Darton, Longman and Todd 1984), pp. 112, 113.

[13] Soskice, op. cit., p. 141.

[14] Brown, op. cit., p. 175.

[15] ibid., p. 177.

[16] Hardy and Ford, op. cit., p. 115.

THEOLOGICAL ETHICS

CAN CHRISTIAN ETHICS BE CREATIVE?

Basil Mitchell

In any discussion of Christian ethics at the popular level – in television programmes or the correspondence columns of newspapers – the charge is commonly repeated that the leaders of the Church have failed to defend traditional standards, have abandoned absolute for relative principles and, in so doing, have surrendered to secular values. Ordinary churchpeople feel that there is a citadel of which the Church is guardian which should be defended, but is all too often betrayed.

But as soon as any ethical issue is seriously investigated – by the Board for Social Responsibility, say – this clear position begins to dissolve. If there is a citadel to be defended, it quickly becomes apparent that it cannot be identified straightforwardly with some position already widely accepted and understood. The members of the Working Party who thought their task was simply to define the Christian view on some disputed issue find themselves involved in a strenuous and exhausting exercise of 'creative' moral thinking. It is almost inevitable that what they eventually produce will not immediately be recognizable as 'the teaching of the Church' and will be repudiated by traditionalists and radicals alike.

Peter Baelz was, as a rule, less disconcerted by this experience than I was, because it was what he had expected all along. He was prepared to be more 'creative' than I was, while insisting that he was at the same time being genuinely traditional. There was, he claimed, no inconsistency here, for it was in the nature of the tradition to be continually renewing itself.

That the simple contrasts of the correspondence columns will not do becomes apparent as soon as the historical record is examined. There are positions which were regarded as traditionally Christian as recently as a century and a half ago which virtually no Anglican would wish to maintain now. They would include the complete subordination of women in marriage, the ban upon contraception, the need for children to be rigorously disciplined, acceptance of a comparatively rigid social

81

hierarchy. In the face of these changes should we say that the Church is responding to secular culture in its contemporary emphasis upon the 'unitive' aspect of marriage, responsible parenthood and respect for the individuality of children, or was it, perhaps, reflecting the secular culture of the time in its earlier attitudes? In any case it is not a straightforward matter to discriminate between Christian and secular movements of thought. It may be possible to determine what, at a particular time, was the official teaching of the Church, but are we entitled to assume that it was always authentically and undilutedly Christian? In a broadly Christian culture what appear as secular trends may well be of Christian inspiration. Indeed, given the conservatism of religious institutions and the need for a national church to make some accommodation with the existing distribution of power, it is to be expected that genuine movements of reform of undoubted Christian inspiration should often originate outside its formal structure. A gap thus opens up between two senses of 'secular': 'originating outside the Church' and 'uninfluenced by Christianity'.[1]

Similar problems attend the contrast between 'absolute' and 'relative' which turns out to be equally ambiguous. There is, indeed, a crucial distinction between the view that moral principles are entirely relative to the culture of a particular time or place and the view that they are absolute in the sense of timelessly true, but the latter claim does not entail that they are absolute in the sense of altogether exceptionless. At the very least it is clear that they may sometimes conflict with one another, so that a judgement has to be made as to which in the circumstances of a particular case is to have priority. To allow, for example, that there are circumstances in which, to prevent a greater evil, abortion may be permitted is not in the least to imply that the Church's view on abortion is or ought to be relative to modern culture and not based upon any unchanging truths about human nature.

It follows that any attempt to determine the Church's view on an ethical issue cannot be a routine matter. It cannot be decided by an appeal to tradition without first considering how true the tradition has itself been to Christian teaching. It cannot automatically reject secular thought, which may in certain respects be more authentically Christian than what the Church has taught. It cannot assume that the relevant principles will be absolute, in the sense of altogether exceptionless, in advance of careful and sensitive enquiry into particular cases. There is, then, a clear need for 'creative' thinking in relation to these ethical problems. In theological terms the Working Party will need the guidance of the Holy Spirit.

The dutiful and devout layman is, however, deeply disturbed by this situation. In place of the familiar and clear directives which he looks for he finds himself offered a series of carefully qualified utterances which seem to him to sell the pass. As he strives manfully in his corner of the battlements to keep the enemy at bay, often at considerable personal cost, it appears to him that his leaders are abandoning one salient after another without a struggle. The growing strength of fundamentalism probably derives to a large extent from a suspicion that the intellectuals, if given their head, will substitute their own private judgement for the truths of Christianity and will produce in the end something virtually indistinguishable from the prevailing secular culture.

It is sometimes suggested (notably by Clifford Longley in occasional pieces in *The Times*), that the problem is a peculiarly Anglican one, arising from that Church's lack of a clearly defined teaching authority. But in point of fact the predicament of the Roman Catholic Church in respect of contraception illustrates the problem from, so to speak, the other direction. Nothing is plainer than that the Catholic Church is, in some sense, officially committed to a ban on artificially induced contraception, but it is equally clear that the majority of loyal Catholics do not accept this ruling, and are supported in this by many theologians. A perusal of the very careful and judicious chapter on *Humanae Vitae* in John Mahoney's *Catholic Moral Theology* must leave the intelligent lay Catholic convinced that there is ultimately no alternative but to rely on personal judgement. The fact that there exists an 'official' view on this matter is more of an embarrassment to the Church than a source of strength. It is as difficult for the laity when the leaders of the Church appear to them to be adhering obstinately to an outdated ethical position as when they seem to be surrendering to secularism. In this case they feel that they are being required to hold on to a salient that has become indefensible.

I have been assuming, up to this point, that those who are charged with discovering the mind of the Church on a disputed ethical issue are committed to a task which is onerous and exacting, but nevertheless in principle achievable. But there are some observers who would draw a quite different conclusion. They would argue that the task is in fact an impossible one, if understood in anything like a traditional sense. Among these are some Christian theologians who adopt a frankly relativist position and argue that 'the teaching of the Bible', even if we can recapture it, is so bound up with the thought-forms of its time (which means, of course, its varying times) that it cannot have any relevance to our contemporary problems. The same applies, they would claim, to the tradition of the Church at intermediate periods. Hence we really have no alternative but to do our own ethical thinking. There is, of course, good reason for us to go through the motions of consulting Scripture and the traditions of the Church since our ethical intuitions will have been to some extent formed by them, but in the process what we shall be doing, inevitably and rightly, is to select those judgements from the past which accord with our current beliefs. This procedure can be glossed theologically in terms of 'listening to what God is saying to us now'. Indeed if we believe, as surely we must, that God can speak to us now, why should we need to attend to what he said to others, differently situated, in times past? Revelation is a dynamic, not a static, process.

There is no comfort here for the conservative layman. If these thinkers are right, there is not now and never was a citadel to be defended. To that extent his suspicions are fully warranted but they are to be dismissed as proceeding from a quite untenable conception of the nature of revealed truth. The layman has to be told that the sort of certainty and security he yearns for cannot be had.

This is not, however, the view that Peter Baelz has taken. Notwithstanding his emphasis on the creative element in Christian moral thinking, he places himself firmly in the Church's tradition and is prepared to learn from it. He does not, however, want to be entirely constrained by it, and the whole tenor of my argument so far shows that he is justified in demanding a considerable degree of independence for the Christian moralist. His claim to be traditional is borne out by the reflection that he is making the familiar four-fold appeal to Scripture, Tradition, Reason and Experience.

This four-fold appeal implies that each of the four has its own independent weight and that the final decision will rest on estimating the weight of each correctly. 'Creativity' comes in at just this point. 'Scripture' and 'tradition' are to count but how properly to interpret them is affected by reason and experience. Reason and experience themselves are to count but they in turn are to be assessed in the light of Scripture and tradition. All four contribute to the formation of a Christian mind, which nevertheless has in the end to judge for itself.

Reason and experience explain themselves. An entirely secular thinker would admit their relevance and would, indeed, regard them as sufficient. Scripture and tradition are more problematic. The secular thinker sees no need of them and Christian thinkers, acknowledging their authority, are bound to ask upon what that authority rests. Is it simply, as I have heard said, that a Christian thinker is by definition one who appeals for guidance to the Bible and the Fathers rather than, for example, to the Koran or the writings of Marx and Engels? The question *why* he looks in that direction rather than some other is to be ruled out as illegitimate. Or is it, perhaps, that experience has shown that these sources are as a rule trustworthy – they do on the whole tend to get things right? Their authority is presumptive; they are to be accepted in the absence of good reason for not accepting them. There is, it is important to note, a crucial difference between either of these views and that of the relativist. Both assume as against the relativist that there is a truth of the matter and that thinkers in the past may well have had access to it, so that we may properly learn from them.

To what extent should our concerned layman be reassured by this account of the authority of Scripture and tradition? To be sure it relieves him of the worst threat, that of relativism. He knows that his leaders stand firm on the distinction between truth and falsehood, and will seriously review the Christian tradition before deciding where the truth lies. But what guarantee is there that when they have completed this review the conclusions they reach will be Christian ones? Is it not open to them to arrive at secular conclusions either by explicitly rejecting what has hitherto been Christian teaching or by interpreting it in a manner conformable to current secular opinion?

Let us take a specific example from the field of sexual ethics. There has developed, in modern times, a characteristically modern conception of sexual relationships. The sexual act is thought of essentially as an appropriate way of continuing a conversation between two people, through which they are able to get to know one another in a unique way. It can, of course, be a serious conversation, a continuous life-long dialogue between a man and a woman, but it need not be. There is no reason at all why it should be exclusive, any more than there is reason why one should talk only to a single individual. In a modern television drama men and women go to bed with one another more or less as a matter of course if they display any interest in one another at all, and it is left entirely open at the beginning how long the conversation will last. This new development gives an extra dimension to personal relationships which in the past they could not have because the fear of conception could never be banished entirely. It is, of course, open to abuse through the exploitation of one partner by the other, but then so is marriage. Those who have experienced this way of life find it entirely natural and claim that it enriches their lives and enables them to flourish in new ways. Why then should the Church not give its sanction to this characteristically modern conception of sexual activity and recognize it as among the purposes of God for the present stage of human development? There have even been some anticipations of it in the acceptance of 'free love' in various Christian sects in the past. Common sense arguments in favour of marriage as the norm would remain valid and the significance of erotic love in marriage would continue to be stressed. Only its exclusiveness would be questioned in the interests of a more generous and flexible life-style.

It is possible to challenge this position on its own terms. Is it, in point of fact, as satisfying as it is made out to be? Can the easy, stress-free approach to sexual relationships in general be achieved without an overall lessening of intensity in particular cases? The troubled layman will see the force of such considerations and be prepared to rely on them, but he feels intuitively that they are not meant to bear the whole weight of Christian criticism. Something essential is missing and it is something structural.

It sometimes happens that a clear-sighted and fair-minded critic has a better idea of the difference Christianity makes to ethics than most of its official defenders, and the late J. L. Mackie is a case in point. In his book *Ethics: Inventing Right and Wrong* he develops a purely secular conception of morality as a human invention. He admits that his account fails to accord with the deep-seated conviction of ordinary people that morality is discovered not invented, that it is, as he puts it, somehow 'required by the universe', but he insists that what we know about man and the world cannot justify this conviction. What would justify it, he suggests, would be a thorough-going theism in a form which he then sets out:

> It might be that there is one kind of life which is, in a purely descriptive sense, most appropriate for human beings as they are – that is, that it alone will fully develop rather than stunt their natural capacities, and that in it, and only in it, can they find the fullest and deepest satisfaction. It might then follow that certain rules of conduct and certain dispositions were appropriate (still purely descriptively) in that they were needed to maintain this way of life. All these ... might be products of the creative will of God which, in making men as they are, will have made them such that this life, these rules and these dispositions are appropriate for them.[2]

Mackie goes on to suggest that men might not be able to discover wholly by their own observation and experiment what kind of life is ultimately satisfying for them and that God, knowing this and wishing them to flourish, might reveal instructions as to how they should live.

This is a recognizable account of what the Church has traditionally taught. In more explicitly theological terms Christian ethics revolves upon the twin poles of divine revelation and natural law, each complementing and interpreting the other. In terms of this account the reliance upon Scripture and the careful study of human nature that are characteristic of Christian ethical thinking became intelligible. Mackie regards it as providing the best foundation for the objectivity of morals. The trouble is only that, as far as he can see, there are no good grounds for believing in God.

In estimating the worth of this model contemporary Christian theologians are subject to anxieties which do not trouble the atheist philosopher. They have to make it work, while he does not. Neither the appeal to Scripture nor the appeal to natural law is unproblematic; each has been understood, and indeed still is, in ways that are patently unsatisfactory. Concerned like all academics to repudiate their own past errors, theologians are frequently more inclined to abandon both these concepts, or drastically reinterpret them, than to rehabilitate them. Revelation cannot be thought of as a sort of divine dictation, and the entire discipline of biblical criticism with its concentration upon the Bible as a set of texts, each with its own historical provenance, militates against any more sophisticated doctrine of divine inspiration. The idea of natural law, as elaborated, for example, in the contraception debate is unacceptably mechanical and insensitive to the nuances of personal relationships.

But, if Mackie is right, the consistency and coherence of Christian ethics depend upon the viability of just such notions, and they provide the structural strength and elasticity which the concerned layman finds to be missing in so many Church pronouncements. In almost all the ethical disputes that at present exercise us there is a broad divide between those who conceive of human welfare in terms of the preferences of individuals or groups and those who regard the natural world, and human nature with it, as having its own integrity which may not be violated. It makes a crucial difference to medical ethics, for example, whether medicine is concerned to give people what they want or whether there is a norm of human health which it exists to serve; whether the foetus is to be regarded as a growth in the mother's body of which she is free to dispose, or whether it is to be thought of as a potential human being and worthy of respect as such; whether people are entitled as autonomous human beings to end their own lives when they no longer find meaning in them, or whether their lives are held in trust; whether the doctor's task is to keep people alive as long as possible, or whether there is a proper time for dying; whether pornographic acts involving children are to be judged by the degree of physical or psychological harm the children suffer, or whether they are intrinsically wrong as inappropriate to their status as children; whether genetic manipulation may in principle be used to improve human characteristics, or whether it should be restricted to restoring normality. In all these instances, and many others, the issue is whether there are, in the nature of things, limits to what human beings may properly choose to make of themselves or the world in which they live.

The division is, in principle, clear enough. To use Mackie's phrase again, it is about whether or not morality is 'required by the universe'. The whole of our earlier discussion shows that it is not possible to read off solutions to contemporary problems from what the Church has taught in earlier times. The concerned layman must be reconciled to this fact. Nevertheless, his unease is justified if it begins to appear that the distinctive character of Christian ethics is being lost. It is one thing for Christian thinkers to argue that the Scriptures have at points been wrongly interpreted or excessively influenced by ideas belonging to their time; it is another to deny them any genuinely independent authority at all. It is one thing to maintain, in the light of accumulated knowledge and experience, that past ideas about, e.g., the place of sexual intercourse in human life, have been distorted by social pressures or infected by poor science. It is another to regard our natural make-up as material simply for the exercise of unfettered freedom.

I wish to suggest that what the concerned layman is, or ought to be, concerned about is the tendency to obliterate this distinction. What makes the present situation so difficult to understand is that two oppositions are constantly collapsed into one. There is, on the one hand, the opposition between a conservative adherence to the ideas of the recent past and a radical readiness to revise these in the light of more thoroughly thought out Christian principles; and there is, on the other, the opposition between adherence to Christian principles and a typically modern tendency to make personal preferences the key to moral decisions (whether this takes a relativist form or not). The layman is very clear as to what he is against; it is this latter secular attitude. Identifying as he tends to do, Christian principles as such with their formulation in the early modern period, he sees the defence of these as the only way of safeguarding Christian ethics against the threat of secularism. There is ample excuse for him in the attitude of same Christian moralists of a liberal temper, for they often fail to observe the crucial distinction also. Justifiably critical of moral attitudes which seem to them insensitive to the needs of individuals and unresponsive to advances in our knowledge of human nature, they come to rely increasingly upon typically modern intuitions which they share with secular thinkers. These they then fail to expose to criticism in distinctively Christian terms because they have abandoned prematurely the attempt to rethink the concepts of revelation and natural law which alone afford the resources for such criticism.

The creative thinking which is needed in order to decide where the Church should now stand is not, then, readily categorized as either conservative or liberal. It is essential to involve in it people of both conservative and liberal temperaments. Left to their own devices conservatives will tend to be insufficiently critical of the previously accepted consensus and not alert enough to genuinely Christian insights emanating from the secular culture. Liberals on their own will tend to overlook or underrate the constraints which Christian understanding of creation must always impose upon human inventiveness. Since what should emerge from their interaction is not guaranteed to coincide with the accepted formulations of the past or the fashionable notions of the present, the layman, in order to judge it fairly, will need to do some creative thinking of his own. There is, however, no reason why he should distrust his leaders to guide him aright so long as he has ground for believing that, when they yield familiar salients of the citadel as he has known it, they are intending to make a stand on a line more defensible than the old one, chosen in accordance with a coherent strategic plan which is recognizably Christian.

References

[1] Cf. John Drury in 'The Archbishop's Hat': 'John McManners referred to the apostate Jean-Jacques Rousseau whose interpretation of the Bible by the spirit of Jesus instead of by individual texts taught the French Catholic Church more than it learned from the aggressive, orthodox eloquence of Bishop Bossuet', *Believing in the Church*, SPCK, 1981, p. 190.

[2] J. L. Mackie, *Ethics: Inventing Right and Wrong*, Pelican Books, 1977, pp. 230–1.

DIVINE AND HUMAN GOODNESS

Brian Hebblethwaite

In his *Ethics and Belief* – still the best short introduction to theological ethics from the standpoint of modern philosophy – Peter Baelz rightly observes that God's supreme authority is 'grounded in God's goodness and grace not in his power'.[1] Very succinctly, he spells this out as follows: 'the Christian command to love is rooted in the conviction that God is love and that he has made man in his image'.[2] God's goodness consists in his nature as love; and his grace is his love in action. This ultimate reality is, of course, for Christian belief no contingent matter. The very source and goal of all there is is, in essence, absolute goodness and love. Whether we learn this from God's self revelation in the story of Christ and his cross, or deduce it logically from the basic premises of theism, God's goodness is necessary goodness, and his triune identity as love given and received and shared still more, is necessarily what it is.

The divine goodness, spelled out in terms of love and of grace, is therefore the basis, the model, and the resource of all the myriad forms of finite, contingent, human goodness. As Christoph Schwöbel has argued, in an article on 'God's Goodness and Human Morality',[3] this is primarily a matter of relation. The divine inner trinitarian love is shared and mirrored by human beings in their relationships with each other (in family, friendship, and society) and with God. In another paper[4] on 'The Varieties of Goodness', I have myself attempted to show how it is the unique pattern of inter-personal relationships in which a Christian stands with others and with God that gives each finite image of the divine goodness his or her individuality, whether of character or vocation, as the white light of the divine goodness is refracted into the myriad colours of the varieties of human goodness.

The suggestion that 'God is love' is not only a revealed truth but also, perhaps, a logical deduction may have struck the reader of my first paragraph as more than somewhat extravagant. In this paper I propose to explore this suggestion, and eventually defend it, through an analysis of the notion of divine goodness. The basic structure of the argument

91

is this: logic constrains us to think of God as necessarily good. But there are problems in predicating goodness of God. Only the concept of God as love fully resolves those problems.

To call God 'good' is a paradigm case of analogical predication. The analogy is from human moral goodness. The problems with the notion of divine goodness arise from the limitations of that analogy. We discover that many important elements in the concept of human goodness cannot be transferred to God. We are driven to qualify the analogy (as we are, of course, with all analogies in our God-talk) but more so in this case, until all we are left with is love.

That the analogical base of talk of the divine goodness is human moral goodness should be clear on reflection. The goodness of God cannot be thought of simply as equivalent to his being, The sense in which 'ens' and 'bonum' are equivalent in their range, as the medieval doctrine of 'transcendentals' has it, is much too wide to capture the notion of the perfect goodness of the source and goal of all there is. As soon as we think of God in personal terms, as we are bound to do when we attribute mind and will to the Creator of the world, we have to think of God's perfect goodness as personal, moral goodness.

I do not intend to devote much space to the first step in the logical argument, outlined above – namely, the necessity of the divine goodness. This is most plausibly derived from the impossibility of an omnipotent and omniscient being doing evil. In accepting this derivation I am siding with Richard Swinburne and Keith Ward[5] against Thomas Morris, for whom the necessity of God's goodness is more a matter of basic theistic intuition.[6] It is surprising that Morris, who has a remarkable penchant for undergirding traditional theism with logical argument, should confess defeat at this point. For surely it must be said that doing evil represents a deficiency in act or intention which omnipotent omniscience necessarily excludes. However, it is the next steps in the argument on which I wish to concentrate. So whether God's necessary goodness is a matter of deduction, intuition – or revelation – we will simply take it as read.

The key elements in human moral goodness which we discover to be inappropriate for analogical transference from the human case to the divine, include libertarian freedom, duty, and virtue. Let us examine each of them.

Where human beings are concerned, our moral language only makes sense in the context of responsibility and freedom. But our freedom is the freedom to choose between good and evil. The condition of our growth in character and virtue is the possibility that we abuse our freedom and take the path of wickedness and vice. The reality, indeed necessity, of such a freedom is integral to any plausible theodicy. God permits wrong choices and the resulting havoc only because without such freedom created persons could not achieve their moral personality and identity. But we cannot transfer any of this to God in our analogical talk of God's freedom. God's freedom is not the freedom to choose between good and evil, if God is necessarily good. So what do we mean by the divine freedom?

God's freedom can only be thought of as the freedom to choose and enact the good, where no one course of action is the only possible good. God's freedom, in creation, in the manner of our redemption, in the innumerable modes of vocation, is the freedom of supererogatory grace. And if, as suggested above, grace is love in action, we are already on our way to supposing that God's necessary goodness must take the form of love.

It is worth repeating that it does not follow from God's necessary goodness and the mode of freedom that entails, that God must act in one way – namely the one and only best possible way. Supererogatory grace is under no such compulsion. There are innumerable ways in which God's grace will act creatively in the world. The necessity lies in *this* being the primary mode of God's free activity, not in the actual choices he makes.

Of course there is an analogical base in human goodness for such a notion of supererogatory grace. Human freedom is not only exercised in choice between good and evil. Human beings image the divine goodness in their own derivative acts of supererogatory grace and love. And we look for an eschatological consummation in which the conditions of our formation are transcended and our perfected freedom approximates eternally to the divine freedom, in no longer being subject to temptation and abuse. So while the freedom which belongs to the conditions of our formation cannot be used in analogically predicated God-talk, the 'true' freedom of love in action which is sometimes glimpsed in human life on earth and is hoped for in the end in heaven, can be used as an analogical base for talking of God.

The second element in human moral goodness that causes problems for our understanding of divine goodness is duty. In our human case, duty is a matter of being bound by obligations which it is up to us to fulfil. If we do our duty we are commended as morally good; if we do not we are blamed. This conception of duty cannot be transferred to the divine case without qualification, since if God is necessarily good, his actions will flow from his perfect nature without any constraint, let alone possibility of failure. The eternal God is not like Wotan in Wagner's Ring, who is torn mercilessly between his will and the treaties he has undertaken. In Wotan's sublime narration to Brünnhilde in *Die Walküre* Act II scene 2, Wotan cries out, 'These are the bonds that bind me. I became a ruler through treaties; by my treaties I am now enslaved'. Not so the Lord God of hosts – whose perfect goodness is expressed in all he wills and does without any conflict or constraint. However, the fact that in the strict sense, God can have no duties or obligations can be over-stressed in a way which leads to a virtual denial of moral personality in God altogether. Thus Brian Davies, in his book *Thinking about God*[7] uses the fact that God is under no obligations as a way of dismissing the problem of evil. As the changeless, eternal and simple source of all there is, God is not to be thought of as a moral agent, to be blamed if he does not prevent the ills he clearly could prevent. God's goodness, on Davies' view, consists in metaphysical perfection, not moral goodness at all. Only if we think anthropomorphically about God do we find ourselves blaming God as Ivan Karamazov does in Dostoevsky's novel.

This type of theology, rooted in the Augustinian and Thomist tradition though it is, has a disastrous effect on our understanding of the moral nature of God. It makes it quite impossible to think of God as love. For one thing, we cannot restrict morality to duty and obligation. As already noted, even in the human case works of supererogation belong to the moral life and afford analogies for our conception of God as love. But even duty can provide a certain analogical base for talk of God's goodness, as T. V. Morris has shown.[8] Morris argues that God necessarily acts in accordance with principles which for us specify duties. In our case a promise binds us with the obligation to fulfil it. God's promise entails necessarily his doing what he says he will do. So we can rely on God's goodness in a way analogous to human goodness, even in the sense of duty. But, of course, God, unlike Wotan, cannot want to do something other than what he has promised to do.

There is a sense in which we can speak of God's supererogatory acts as creating 'obligations' in God. We might say for example, that it follows from God's decision to create a world of persons, that he is 'bound' to act redemptively, to rescue them, if they fall. Many theologians argue further for universalism in this way. Such obligations are not imposed on God from outside, nor is there any chance of his not so acting, given what he has already done. Such necessities are internal consequences of God's nature – perfect goodness. But again, it is only when we spell out that goodness in terms of love that we see how to hold together the analogies from the works of supererogation and the analogy from duty. God's promises which he is 'bound' to keep, reflect his nature as love. The consequential necessities such as promise-keeping, faithfulness, etc. rest on the prior, free, creativity of love and grace. And there is nothing else they could rest on. Again we are constrained to spell out the nature of the divine goodness in terms of love.

The third element in human moral goodness that causes problems for our understanding of divine goodness is virtue. The importance of virtue and the virtues in any account of the moral life has been increasingly recognised in modern moral philosophy. In the human case, virtues are character dispositions, built up and rendered habitual over time, in a way which, as in the cases of freedom and duty, we cannot possibly transfer to our talk of the eternal and infinite Creator. Moreover, when we consider the four cardinal virtues and the three theological virtues, we realise that the majority of these are quite inappropriate for analogical God-talk. I may refer here to the excellent treatment of this matter by Philip Quinn in his book, *Divine Commands and Morality.*[9]

Take the four cardinal virtues, for example – courage, prudence, temperance and justice. It make no sense to speak of God as courageous; for courage presupposes limited powers, real dangers, and genuine possibilities of loss, injury or death. It makes no sense to speak of God as prudent, for prudence again consists in the husbanding and direction of limited resources in the light of long-term goals. It makes no sense to speak of God as temperate, for temperance consists in restraint from yielding to immoderate desire. Only God incarnate can display these virtues, and it is *qua* incarnate, that is to say *qua* human, that Jesus lived courageously, prudently and temperately. Justice of course, is different. Alone of the cardinal virtues can justice be appropriately predicated, by analogy, of the divine. There is a great deal to be said in Christian theology about the nature of divine justice and in particular its relationship to God's love. I will return to this in a moment. But we should note at once that if we are to speak of something analogous to justice in God, it is in respect of God's relation to his creatures that we all call God just. Justice is hardly the right concept for thinking of God as he is in himself, in his inner-trinitarian relations. We do not suppose that Father, Son, and Holy Spirit manifest perfect goodness in acting justly towards one another. And if we are tempted to complain of some forms of atonement theology that the Father appears to be acting unjustly towards the incarnate Son, the answer must lie in correcting our theology of the atonement in ways which show not the justice but the love of God in Cross of Christ.

Even if we may speak analogically of the justice of God in relation to us sinners, this notion, being restricted to God's activity *ad extra*, cannot have the basic and prior status that we accord to the divine love.

Let us then turn to the theological virtues – faith, hope and love. Clearly, we cannot attribute faith to the absolute, infinite, and eternal God. It is controversial how far it is appropriate to speak of the faith of Jesus, God incarnate. I think it is appropriate to see in Jesus' relation to the Father the paradigm of human faith. But again it is *qua* human not *qua* divine, that God incarnate can be said to have exemplified, supremely, the virtue of faith.

Whether we can attribute hope to God depends entirely on whether it is correct to think of God in temporal terms. This is a highly controversial matter. If with Paul Helm[10] we defend the traditional atemporal conception of God's eternity, we can in no way predicate even analogically the virtue of hope of the divine. If, on the other hand, with many philosophers of religion, such as Swinburne, Ward and Lucas,[11] we find ourselves driven to postulate temporality in God in order to speak of him in personal terms and as a moral agent at all, then maybe there is some sense in which even the eternal God, having created an open-futured world, may have hoped that the path from creation to consummation might have been actualised less arduously than we know it to have been so far. Presumably the Holocaust was not inevitable. May we not suppose that God had hoped that his creatures would not persist in their depravity to such an appalling extent? I do not pursue here the questions of theodicy that the Holocaust raises, though I doubt if anything remotely convincing can be said without appeal to an eschatological recreation and restructing of torturer and victim alike, as Rabbi Dan Cohn-Sherbok has recently argued from a Jewish perspective.[12]

But even if we are able to predicate hope of God in some such analogical sense, we are still, as we were with justice, speaking of God's relations *ad extra* – namely to his human creatures and to the future of creation.

With love we come to the virtue which alone can be predicated of God not only *ad extra* but *ad intra* too. Human love, in its varieties and degrees, reflects not only the love of God for us his creatures but also and supremely, the inner trinitarian relation of love given, love received, and love shared still more, that we glimpse through God's self-revelation in the mutual love of the Father and the incarnate Son, and their mutual indwelling by the Spirit, as well as the outpouring of the Spirit upon and in Christ's adopted brothers and sisters. Certainly, the winning and the transformation of God's personal creatures will entail what we can only speak of as the divine justice. Justice is how love is experienced by those yet to be transformed and indwelt by love. But as, Joseph Fletcher has rightly insisted, 'justice is love distributed'[13] (even if Fletcher's own conception of love leaves much to be desired). So we cannot set justice against love, and we must give love the priority

Love is not just a matter of compassion, nor just a matter of self-sacrifice. Certainly, compassion is one of the forms love takes in relation to the suffering of sentient creatures. Certainly we learn from the Cross of Christ that perfect love stops at nothing in the way of self-sacrifice in order to bring about the rescue of the lost and the unlovely from their predicament (whether self-inflicted or not). But love cannot as such consist in compassion or self-sacrifice, since in ideal conditions there would be no suffering, sin or loss, and love cannot depend upon there being such things in order to exist. This is clear even in respect of creation, whose eschatologically consummated state will surely not be deprived of love by the absence of death, mourning, crying and pain. *A fortiori*, when we think of God as being love in God's own, internal, trinitarian, relations, the impossibility of equating love with compassion and self-sacrifice is even more obvious. So both in the case of the communion of saints in heaven and in the case of the blessed and glorious Trinity love has to be *defined* otherwise, in terms of mutual self-giving, sharing, and rejoicing in the other's creativity and joy. As with supererogatory grace, so with its foundation, love, there is an analogical base in human experience – that of every anticipation of the future of creation given to us in ecstasy and mutual joy – but the prime analogue ontologically speaking is the mutual indwelling of the persons of the Trinity.

I return, finally, to the question of deduction and ask again whether and how far it is possible to deduce the fact that God is love – in this strong trinitarian sense – simply from the promise of God's necessary goodness.

Richard Swinburne has recently revived an ancient argument to be found in Richard of St. Victor, to the effect that God *must* be thought of in trinitarian terms.[14] This *a priori* argument, in the earlier Richard at least, has two stages. First it is shown that God's goodness cannot lack the perfection of love, for nothing is better or more perfect than love, and without love there cannot be supreme goodness. Then secondly, the nature of love is analysed as necessarily containing both dilection and condilection. Dilection – dilectio – is love of another, condilection – condilectio – is mutual love of a third. In Swinburne's terminology the values necessary to perfection must include sharing and co-operation in sharing. It is worth quoting Richard of St. Victor, from his *De Trinitate*, on this latter point: 'In mutual love that is very fervent there is nothing rarer, nothing more excellent than that you wish another to be equally loved by him whom you love supremely and by whom you are loved supremely'.[15] There is perhaps a false step, as Swinburne points out, in Richard of St. Victor's claim that a creature would be unworthy of such love. It is better to argue, more generally, with respect to both dilection and condilection, that the picture of God as love, cannot possibly depend on there being creatures for God to love. The creation of a world of persons may indeed express and reveal God's supererogatory grace and love, but the world is not necessary to God, and we have to be able to think of God as containing within himself, prior to that creation, the perfection of love given, love received, and love shared still more.

Both Richards – St. Victor and Swinburne – have arguments against any further proliferation of persons in the Godhead beyond the three necessary to permit talk of both dilection and condilection in God. Without going into this in detail, we may note that the form of the arguments here is that, for Swinburne, there is no reason to postulate yet more persons in God since the necessary values of sharing and co-operation in sharing are secured by the three persons of the Godhead, and, for St. Victor, unless we stopped at three, 'there would be irrationally an infinite processional series'.[16]

To sum up – the more we think about human goodness as the analogical base for talk of the divine goodness, the more we find ourselves driven to think of supererogatory grace and love as the most appropriate elements in perfect goodness for such analogical predication. Even justice, appropriate though it certainly is, cannot be given priority over love; for justice is only one of the forms love takes in relation to finite creatures, who, unlike the persons of the Godhead, are potential competitors. But love can only be predicated of God as he is in himself, if we think in trinitarian terms of God as already love shared and shared again, before ever God creates yet more persons to enjoy the values of both dilection and condilection.

References

[1] P. Baelz, *Ethics and Belief*, London: Sheldon Press, 1977, p. 88.

[2] ibid., p. 108.

[3] C. Schwöbel, 'God's Goodness and Human Morality', *Nederlands Theologisch Tidschrift*, Vol. 43, No. 2 (1989).

[4] 'The Varieties of Goodness'. To be delivered at the Philosophy of Religion Conference at Claremont Graduate School in February 1990.

[5] See R. G. Swinburne, *The Existence of God*, Oxford, O.U.P., 1979, pp. 97–102, and J. K. S. Ward, *Rational Theology and the Creativity of God*, Oxford, Basil Blackwell 1982, chs 6&8.

[6] See T. V. Morris, 'The Necessity of God's Goodness' in his *Anselmian Explorations*, Notre Dame 1987.

[7] London: Geoffrey Chapman 1985.

[8] T. V. Morris, 'Duty and Divine Goodness', in *Anselmian Explorations* (see note 6).

[9] P. L. Quinn, *Divine Commands and Morality*, Oxford: Clarendon Press 1978, chapter VI.

[10] Paul Helm, *Eternal God*, Oxford, Clarendon Press 1988.

[11] See R. G. Swinburne, *The Concept of God*. Ward, op. cit. (see note 5), and J. R. Lucas, *A Treatise of Time and Space*. London: Methuen 1973.

[12] D. Cohn–Sherbok, *Holocaust Theology*, London: S.P.C.K. 1989.

[13] J. Fletcher, *Situation Ethics*, ch. 5.

[14] R. Swinburne, 'Could there be more than one God?' in *Faith and Philosophy* for July 1988.

[15] Quoted from E. J. Fortman, *The Triune God*, London 1972, p. 193.

[16] Fortman, op. cit., p. 194.

HOW IS CHRISTIAN MORALITY UNIVERSALISABLE?

James W. McClendon, Jr.

Are Christian morals moral; is Christian ethics ethical? I do not mean merely to ask whether we Christians are sometimes, even often, morally at fault in our following of the Christian way. Evidently we are. I mean rather to ask whether the pursuit of Christian morality is in itself a moral mismove. Is Christian ethics like hamburger stretcher – the more stretcher, the less hamburger: the more Christian, the less ethics? Universalisability seems to lie close to the heart of morality itself. It says that what is fair for one case is fair for another like it; that what is required of one is required of another; that 'logical impartiality' is a necessary predicate of morality.[1] Rejecting every form of this demand seems to be rejecting morality itself. Does Christian ethics necessarily refuse or inevitably fall short of universalisability, and does it thereby fail to be ethical?

There is a form of Christian moral thinking that clearly escapes this charge. I am thinking now of the view that denies that there is any distinctively Christian ethics. Christianity may still be seen as adding a motive for moral behaviour, or it may be considered a penthouse atop the main structure of common human morality, displaying a characteristic silhouette though not constituting a morality in itself. This way of thinking is common enough, and for it Christian ethics is universalisable if ethics itself is universalisable. Some problems may arise for this sort of Christian understanding, but they are not my problems here.

For I am here interested in a Christian ethics that grasps the whole of morality christianly, a perspective that involves (1) a Christian sense of embodied human selfhood, (2) a Christian concept of community and its powerful practices, and (3) a Christian narrative awareness centrally formed by the resurrection of Jesus Christ from the dead. I have explored such a grasp of morality in my volume, *Ethics*.[2] For example, I take up there the Christian practice of community building. I say that forgiveness, not punishment, is to be the norm of Christian community. Punishment is indeed a coherent concept; it, too, is a device for the rehabilitation of offenders, even within the Christian community. Yet it is forgiveness, not punishment, that is for Christians the characteristic way of restoration. Forgiveness stands as a defining predicate of Christian community.

> Christian community is exactly one in which forgiveness not punishment is the norm. Forgiveness is the healing of a broken church. As such, it is intimately linked with salvation itself – with atonement, with Christ's presence, with the goal of the common life in the body of Christ.[3]

And I go on to provide there an 'anatomy of forgiveness': forgiveness is both transaction and inner attitude; as attitude, it is not forgetting, as some suppose, but a special kind of remembering: It is 'remembering under the aspect of membership in the body of Christ; it is knowing that He who is our body and we, forgiven and forgiver, are one.' Thus forgiving, for Christians, means that one 'takes another's life up into one's own, making the offender a part of one's own story . . .' As transaction, forgiveness is the act of granting pardon, an act normatively exemplified in praying 'forgive us our debts as we [here, now, performatively, in this very act of prayer] forgive our debtors.'[4] But has this account offered in my *Ethics* violated the universalisability principle? To prescribe forgiveness, not punishment, as the way of community maintenance for all the world seems naive and unrealistic; yet to neglect it as the way for Christians seems disobedient to Christ speaking in Scripture and in the Spirit. Does Christian ethics, then, prescribe only for Christians? If so, what about universalisability?

I will show here (part 1) that universalisability means different things in different ethical theories. For Mill and utilitarians, universalisability is attained by concern for the general welfare on the part of any who would think and act morally; we might call it a universalisability of concern. For Kant and for Sidgwick, it is attained by the adoption of a common standpoint, a moral point of view. For Winch universalisability is a matter of sincere and serious moral engagement. Thus universalisability itself differs from system to system – universalisability is not universalisable.

What then (part 2) can test Christian ethics (my own being held to account) with regard to universalisability? I will here argue the case for a universalisability via witness. Christian morality that is faithful in witness is *eo ipso* universalisable. To be a Christian witness involves an encounter with grace and entails life within Christian community, but it is also, necessarily, inclusive, reaching out to each and all, far and near, to share itself with all who will receive it. To fail to practice such sharing is to fail to be a witness; it is thereby to fail the universalisability test in its Christian form. But if we can fail to witness, we can also succeed; therein lies the possibility of a universalisable Christian ethics.

I

Consider first the principle of universalisability as it arises for Immanuel Kant. In the *Groundwork*,[5] a little book whose fame and whose difficulties endure,[6] Kant sets out to uncover a principle of morality that, while found in experience, does not rest upon experience, but is truly philosophical, that is, a priori. If, as Kant believes, the only truly good thing in the world or out of it is a good will, what can possibly be the measure of such a will? Is there such a thing as a command of reason? If so, it must take the form of a synthetic a priori proposition. To ask for this, however, is already to know the proposition that will satisfy it:

> Act only on that maxim [or internal rule] whereby thou canst at the same time will that it would become a universal law.
>
> So act as to treat humanity, whether in thine own person or in that of any other, in every case as an end withal, never as means only.
>
> Act according to a maxim which can at the same time make itself a universal law.[7]

Kant believed these to be three modes of one categorical (as opposed to hypothetical) imperative, one principle of pure practical reason, a principle that can be deduced by a transcendental argument from the nature of reason and understanding themselves. Whether or not Kant was correct, it is important that all three modes be reported if we seek Kant's principle of ethical universalisability. From the third comes the reach of the moral imperative: it must be no less than a universal law. From the first comes the characteristic standpoint from which alone truly moral judgments may be made, the standpoint of one willing to act as a citizen legislator, a member of the kingdom of ends. And from the second comes the only rationale that can guide us in this far-reaching legislative task, namely the absolute dignity of each person.

> Reason then refers every maxim of the will, regarding it as legislating universally, to every other will and also to every action toward oneself.[8]

Why does Kant see the demand of morality in this threefold form, and why in particular does he require his citizen moral legislators each to legislate as though for the entire kingdom of ends and not just for him or herself? One may hesitate here between Kant's practical reasons and one's own. Kant's are well known: we must eschew self-indulgence and self-favouritism. I suggest another: Kant in his quest for Enlightenment autonomy is obliged to overthrow that ancient monarch, the King of the kingdom of ends. God, in the *ancien régime*, gave the law for everybody; shall not the citizen legislators do as much in the new age? For if they do not, then God the moral authority is come again. Kantian universalisability, on this view, is not the constitutional standard so much as it is a revolutionary government seeking *de jure* status, not the archetype of universalisability so much as its somewhat creaky clockwork copy in the 'heavenly city' of eighteenth century philosophy.[9]

In any case, there was more than one Enlightenment philosopher, and one of the more notable arrived on the scene a century late. John Stuart Mill's *Utilitarianism*[10] occupies a scant 63 pages in the familiar Hackett edition, and it is riddled with unresolved (many would say unresolvable) difficulties, yet it has fostered a theory of moral thought whose star is still high in the sky. Mill begins, in explicit contradiction of Kant, by founding everything on consequences. Mill thought the principle of utility, or greatest happiness (of the greatest number) principle, was not to be established by a priori proofs; nevertheless there are considerations that favour it. These include the remarkable breadth subsumed under what Mill finds desirable (or pleasant). The main constituents of a satisfied life, tranquillity and excitement, could be made available to all if only mankind would take up its task in the spirit of Jesus of Nazareth: seeking this welfare of all is the content of morality. The ultimate sanction for the principle of utility, however, is neither God nor custom, but 'a subjective feeling in our own minds,'[11] to which external sanctions of whatever sort can at best only add reinforcement. 'No reason can be given why the general happiness is desirable, except that each . . . desires his own happiness.' From this Mill thought it followed that 'the general happiness' is 'a good to the aggregate of all persons,' i.e., to humanity summed up.[12] If other things are desired, they are desired as means to the end, which is happiness itself. The desirable is the desired is the pleasant, and the happiness of all is (therefore?) the goal of each.

Where, then, does universalisability come in? Clearly not in the particular content of happiness. Some desire 'higher pleasures,' some, alas, only 'lower' ones. One might think that universalisability here lies in the common drive to pleasure not pain, yet that conclusion would miss the grandeur of utilitarianism. This grandeur lies in the outcome or consequence at which it aims, the general happiness, in which each one counts for one, and in the motive that aims at that consequence, namely, benevolence. My aim here is merely to call attention to the very special nature of the universalisability that utilitarianism proffers. One feature of this is that what is held out to each is in no sense an equal share in the general happiness. Indeed, one of utilitarianism's doctrines especially commended by Mill is its demand for sacrifice for the sake of others' happiness. 'The readiness to make such a sacrifice is the highest virtue which can be found in man.'[13] Mill here contemplates self-sacrifice, but there is nothing in the theory to prevent the sacrifice of others as well (or instead!), and tough-minded utilitarians have notoriously acknowledged that this was so.[14]

Another aspect of utilitarianism bears upon the distribution of traits of character. It is right, on Mill's view, for most folk to pursue merely their own pleasure; these have no better way to contribute to the general happiness. There is, though, that 'one in a thousand' in whose power rests the happiness of multitudes. Such a one has a different sort of responsibility, that of the leader. Sidgwick, no enemy of Mill's theory, points out a curious consequence of this feature: while acting contrary to a moral rule may promote the general happiness if done in secret, it may contrariwise set a bad example if known. From this, it follows that a sophisticated utilitarian leader might sometimes do well to follow in secret (or in sophisticated company) practices that if known should not be performed, and even that it is 'expedient that the doctrine that esoteric morality is expedient should itself be kept esoteric.' And Bernard Williams, commenting on this, remarks upon 'the important colonialist connections of utilitarianism,' calling Sidgwick's version 'Government House utilitarianism.'[15] Williams goes on to characterize this as a morality of the few, providing for the 'welfare' of the many, and refers to an 'uneasy gap or dislocation' between the spirit of the theory (concern for the common good) and the spirit that it justifies (elitism in practice). Yet this gap is an essential feature of the universalisability that utilitarianism displays.

At the end of the nineteenth century, the aforementioned Henry Sidgwick, a Cambridge philosopher, sought to reconcile the main features of utilitarian and Kantian ethics, so as to relate these to the deliverances of common sense. Sidgwick's book, *The Methods of Ethics*, went through many editions.[16] For this reason it will be helpful to have before us his statement of the universalisability principle:

[W]hatever action any of us judges to be right for himself, he implicitly judges to be right for all similar persons in similar circumstances.

And, Sidgwick adds, a 'corresponding proposition may be stated with equal truth in respect of what ought to be done to – not by – different individuals.'[17] Here universalisability appears in Kantian fashion in universalising judgments, only these take the form of case law rather than of legislation – the evaluation of (contemplated or actual) deeds rather than the promulgation of laws.

It was just this feature of Sidgwick's version of universalisability that was challenged by Peter Winch, a generation ago, in his influential *Monist* paper, 'The Universalizability of Moral Judgments.'[18] There is a significant difference, Winch believed, between judging in my own case and judging in another's, whereas Sidgwick wrote as if the question of who judged was 'of no logical interest.' The difficulty here, Winch believed, is that in making judgments about another's action, we very often imaginatively put ourselves in the other's place, asking, 'What would I think it right to do in such a situation?' Yet I may be a very different person than the one who did actually act, so that what each of us did would differ, and still that difference need not exclude either of us from the realm of genuine moral action.[19] Winch illustrates this by his reading of the deeply moving sea tale by Herman Melville, *Billy Budd*.

That story in brief is as follows.[20] Billy, a competent seaman and a splendid human being, with but one defect, an occasional inability to speak at all, has been impressed by a British man-of-war commanded by Captain Vere. The satanic master-at-arms, Claggart, persecutes Billy, and then falsely accuses him before the Captain. Billy's speech impediment prevents his answering; in frustration he hits Claggart, who dies of the blow. In the ensuing trial, Vere is torn between the demands of the military code and the order it maintains, over against the evident injustice of punishing the innocent. Melville, telling the tale, emphasizes the demands of morality (and not merely sentiment or law) on each side of the case. As Winch reads the story, 'Vere is faced with a conflict between two genuinely moral 'oughts', a conflict, that is, within [the one?] morality.'[21]

In the story, Captain Vere opts for punishment, and Winch shows that Melville means this to be a moral, not merely a legal, decision. The 'ought' to which Vere has responded when caught between two 'oughts' is itself a truly moral 'ought.' Winch, however, believes that he himself would in that case have acted differently, even though he would have felt the same problematic constraints, the same conflict of 'oughts,' that Vere did. Captain Winch could not in those circumstances have condemned a man 'innocent before God' to suffer for his deed. Yet Winch does not deny that Captain Vere acted morally. Winch would have decided differently because he was a different man, and this different 'agent's perspective' must enter into the moral balance. Somewhat cryptically, Winch holds that in the very act of deciding how to judge in the case, Vere found (and Winch, had he been there, would have found) what was right, since who one is affects what one must do.

What, then, of universalisability? Winch quotes R. M. Hare to the effect that it is 'nearly always presumptuous to suppose that another person's situation is exactly like' our own in relevant ways, and then adds that in the cases Hare contemplates, 'the universalisability principle is idle.'[22] Perhaps inconsistently, Winch concedes that Sidgwickian universalisability applies to each spectator's moral judgment, so that anyone who judges that A has done right (wrong) in such and such circumstances must judge that B would have done right (wrong) to do the same in those circumstances.[23] But though the judgments issued by each moral subject must be consistent with one another, they need not, to be moral, be consistent with those of other moral subjects, as the difference between (fictional) Captain Vere and (hypothetical) Captain Winch makes evident. Thus Winch felt that there was no conflict between his belief that Vere acted morally (obeyed the ultimate 'ought' in judging between two 'oughts'),[24] and his belief that he, Winch, would have acted morally by acting differently than did Vere. In such cases, he believed, moral judgments are not subject to the universalisability principle.

Yet it seems to me that Winch too readily excludes the sort of case he presents from the realm of universalisability. For by now it begins to appear that the principle has no single, fixed form. So I would prefer to say that Winch's principle reckons that while he and Vere would have acted differently, they are importantly alike. In each case, in Winch's words, the agent did act (or would have acted) 'rightly.' What sort of threshold, he asks, might there be beyond which one would not have acted 'rightly'? He offers three tests, of which only one concerns us here: this is the case where the other's ideas of right and wrong differ so profoundly from our own that we are unwilling to accept the claim that the other acted rightly.[25]

So Winch's circle of genuine moral behaviour is not infinite, but it is nevertheless large enough to include agents who make contrary decisions in cases significantly alike. It is this wide circle that leads me to the view that for Winch it is morality itself, morality and not just particular judgments or concerns, that is universalisable. One remembers his concurrent interest in the differences between 'primitive' societies and our own.[26] Here he seems to be at the opposite pole from the 'Government House' morality that knows what is best for the human species. Winch cannot guarantee specific rules that apply to all cases, for the cases simply aren't alike, and the differences pertain not only to the situations in which agents act, but also to the character of those who must by acting create a morality. So if we were coining names, we might call Mill's a universalisability of concern (for the greatest number), and Kant's (or Sidgwick's) a universalisability of legislative (or judicial) standpoint, while we would not be wrong to call Winch's a universalisability of moral engagement.

II

Some forms of Christian ethics nearly resemble the ethical theories of Kant and Mill. Here the demand for universalisability is likely to assume the modes of universal concern or identity of standpoint that characterize these theories.[27] Other versions of Christian ethics, especially from the 1960s, are likely to display with Winch the mode of engagement. They will be able to say little or nothing about the content of others' morality, but must content themselves with pointing to a somehow recognised analogy between other's morality and one's own. My own understanding of the moral task is certainly different from that of Kant and Mill; it is different, as well, from Winch's. Perhaps the best brief description of my *Ethics* is that it seeks to discover, interpret, and renew a moral perspective comprising (1) a particular sense of creaturely selfhood, shaped by its drives, needs, and capacities, but shaped as well by the narratives and underlying convictions that make Christians the people that we are. The perspective also includes (2) a certain sense of community, and of a particular community, one that incorporates characteristic (God-given) practices (e.g., community formation via forgiveness) and that exists in tension with the practices of still other communities (e.g., those incorporating the 'practice' of war). The perspective includes as well (3) a narrative awareness of both self and community being not only formed but transformed by the recreative power of God in Christ Jesus, a power destined to make all earthly things new, so that this is a 'resurrection' ethics.

Is such a morality universalisable? Universalisability by analogy is probably the dominant view among thinking Christians. Typically it sees Christianity as a species of the genus religion: Christian morality is appropriate for Christians just as the morality of Buddhism is appropriate for Buddhists, etc. This view may posit a core or essence of religion, accompanied and paralleled by an essence of morality.[28] In this way, while starting from Winch's view, universalisability by analogy may acquire some affinity with the theories of Kant and Mill. Yet the philosophical arguments against this analogical path are powerful.[29] For example, George Lindbeck argues that an 'essence of religion' approach to the religions has failed to capture their structure and character as these are observed by social scientists (we recall Winch again), and in particular such an approach neglects their narrative shape and their internal dynamic, or their changing relation to one another. There are also theological arguments against this analogical path. These begin with the failure of analogy to take seriously the claims of Jesus Christ upon his followers.[30] Since these negative arguments can be found elsewhere, I will not repeat them here. Instead I will take a look at the witness path, hoping to show that it leads to a universalisability that I fear the path of analogy cannot.

How does the universalisability demand arise for Christians who take seriously the task of witness? Note first that the concept of witness takes the perspectival situation of Christians much more seriously than do its rivals. (Here appears its own kinship with Winch.) Not everyone is a qualified witness – either at law or in Christ's kingdom. The good witness is one who knows at first hand and who tells exactly what she or he knows. To be a witness (to be a Christian?) involves an encounter with grace, a collision of one's own story with Another's story, a re-vision of vision by another light than one's own light. Second, the Christian witness is by its own nature corporate, it is solidary not solitary. We may become Christians one by one, but to remain Christian is to maintain a solidarity with the fellowship and with its present Lord; it is to share one Spirit; it is to engage in communal practices of prayer and ministry and mission. The Christian witness on a lonely assignment is still supported by these continuing engagements.

Third (and here the weight of my argument must fall), Christian witness is characteristically inclusive. No snug sectarian exclusiveness and no smug cultural imperialism, no deadening doctrine of divine determinism and no arrogant doctrine of human adequacy, no narcotic theory of human religiousness and no disabling theory of human depravity[31] must be allowed to overrule the plain command of Jesus Christ in Scripture: 'You shall be my witnesses in Jerusalem and in all Judaea and Samaria and to the end of the earth' (Acts 1:8b). It is this inclusive witness, I hold, that constitutes the universalisability of Christian morality and that is the necessary presupposition of a proper Christian moral theology or ethics. Christians cannot consistently expect that non-Christians while remaining non-Christians will follow the way of Jesus of Nazareth as they know they themselves must follow it; cannot, for example, take it for granted that forgiveness not punishment will be the norm of non-Christian communities as it is the norm of Christian community. What Christians must nevertheless do is serve as witnesses in the power of the Holy Spirit, from Jerusalem to the far margins of earth and at all intermediate points, in the belief that God intends to put that witness at the service of all.[32] There are some philosophical difficulties to be reckoned with here, but most of them are addressed to caricatures of the Christian mission (regrettably some of them caricatures in practice not just in theory) rather than to the doctrine itself. To unfold the full concept of witness is beyond the scope of this paper; to illustrate it briefly is a task best undertaken by way of another story.

Mine is a true story, authenticated by an old chronicle. The time is the middle of the sixteenth century; the place is the south of Holland, at Asperen, territory in Catholic control, as it happened. Dirk Willems, a resident, fled from a 'thief-chaser' who was set upon him because Dirk was (correctly) suspected of 'Anabaptism', the deadly doctrine abhorred by Catholic and Protestant alike. There had been a hard freeze, and Dirk Willems ran across the ice, followed by the thief-chaser. He was making good his escape when he saw that the thief-chaser had fallen through the ice and was in deadly peril. He turned back and rescued his pursuer. Whereupon the thief-chaser would have released him, it is said, but for Asperen's Burgomaster, who 'sternly called to him to consider his oath.' So Dirk Willems was seized, confined, tried for his crimes, convicted, and sentenced to death by burning.[33]

Why shall we not read this story by the light of the categorical imperative, the maxim of the universal citizen moral legislator? Or why not according to the hedonic principle and its calculus, maximizing the general pleasure? That theory, as we have seen, provides for self-sacrifice. Or why not as a Winchian narrative of moral dilemma resolved by moral decision? Is not Dirk a better sort of Vere, confronting now not innocent but somewhat tarnished life? But for the story these are the wrong questions. The flaw in each is this: it does not grow from the story, but is brought to it, imposed upon it, requires a standpoint or a calculus or a choosing of which the story itself knows nothing. Who are these 'Ana-baptists'? What are their models of selfhood, their understandings of community, their life-shaping narratives? Is it thought among them that to be like Jesus is normative for Christian character? Is love of enemies (and related to that love, forgiveness) determinative for them? Is there here a Great Narrative, turning upon the resurrection of Jesus Christ from the dead, that must shape the participating narrative of each community, each believer? And finally, is their witness, their 'outreach', a mode of universalisability?

Yet if these questions are the right ones, they must return us to the story itself. Whence comes this flight, this turnabout, this sacrifice? Let us begin, as does *Martyrs Mirror*, with Dirk Willems' flight. Not seldom in this heritage, withdrawal is a kind of witness.[34] Joseph withdrawing from seductive enticement (Ge.39:9), Israel withdrawing from Egypt in an exodus (Ex.14), Elijah withdrawing from the wrath of Jezebel (I Ki.19:1–8), the holy family withdrawing from Herod's infanticide (Mt.2), disciples withdrawing from towns closed to their tidings (Mk.6:11) – each constitutes a kind of witness to those who reject their purity, their worship, their prophecy, their holy presence, their gospel, their way. In their eyes, it is not they but their persecutors who are 'sectarians'. They universalise their claim by illuminating for those whom they leave behind the consequence of its rejection. Dirk Willems departing Asperen in winter's cold flees it may be to save his life and perhaps as well to save his persecutors from a bloody sin. Yet his flight echoes, too, the old biblical pattern, repeats its witness, renews that Great Story by reliving a part of it.[35]

The second moment of witness is return. The ice broke; Dirk Willems turned back. Again life was at risk; now the persecutor's life rather than the victim's. And again the witness rendered was more than the calculus

Figure 1.

of life weighed against life. The turn back was spontaneous; there was no time for tortuous 'deciding'. Rather, that turn followed a long pattern of faithful returns: Jacob returning to face his older brother Esau in Canaan (Gen.32–33), Elijah returning from his cave of hiding (I Ki.19:15–18), Hosea returning to seek Gomer in the marketplace (Hos.3:1–3), Jews returning from Babylon to a shattered Jerusalem (Ezra 1:1–2:2), Jesus returning to his home synagogue in Nazareth (Luke 4:16–30), the disciples returning to confront their Master's executioners (Acts 2:23, 36; 3:13; 4:1–13), Paul the Apostle returning to Jerusalem (Acts 20:22). Dirk Willems' return to aid his pursuer (to love his enemy?) was no bravado, no laughter in the face of fate. As the printmaker draws the scene in *Martyrs Mirror* (see Figure 1), when the thief-catcher breaks through the ice, the Burgomaster waits in safety on the shore. He will not risk his life. (Thief-catchers, we are told, did not as a class belong to society's higher social strata.) As the artist conceives it, the thief-catcher is a pitiful figure whose last hope has become a hunted Christian. Again the Christian note of inclusiveness sounds: 'Inasmuch as you have done it unto the least of these . . .' (Mt.25:40).

The third moment of witness is suffering in the 'name' (i.e., in the character) of Jesus (cf. Mt.5:11). The judicial machinery of the seventeenth century was slow. (Some things do not change.) After months in prison, Dirk Willems was brought to trial. There was no denial of the facts. In any case, the evidence was clear: he had practiced the despised faith. His life of witness – believer's baptism, sheltering fellow believers, hearing their forbidden teaching, consenting to their [ana]baptism – became now (in another, legal sense) the witness that betrayed him. He was condemned; he was taken out to the stake. The fire was inexpertly laid, so that he suffered a long, long time. He died. Succumbing with cries to his Lord so strong that they were heard and reported back at the village, Dirk Willems, *martus*, witness, by dying committed the particularity of his life to public scrutiny. Was it not once again the case that 'Wherever the gospel is preached in the whole world, what [he] has done will be told . . .' (cf.Mk.14:9)? The circle of public testimony has become a circle without limits as the tale is told and told again by other witnesses.

The universalisability of witness does not require that the witness be endorsed or adopted by those to whom it is in each case addressed, only that we be in position to tender it and do in fact tender it. The Burgomaster need not have regarded Dirk's withdrawal from Asperen as a moral act; the thief-catcher need not have seen his return to rescue him as anything more than stupid folly; the judges who condemned him need not have taken his oral testimony or his death-testimony as a witness of God's grace to them. It is enough that Dirk, or Dirk with his community, or Dirk with his community and its Lord, should recognise the authenticity of witness in a given case. Nevertheless, it is widely demonstrated in world history that the multiplied instances of this witness carry much weight; without them, the church would not be the church; if they should cease, Christian morality would no longer stand in need of justification, for there would no longer be any Christian morality. And on the other hand, it is by this witness that Christians find their way, by it that the church becomes the church, by it that the world knows itself to be world and to face the decision of faith.

It could even be argued that Dirk Willems' universalisability via witness captures as well the limited truth of universalisability via analogy, since his story, retold, reaches across lines of community to find its counterpart in other tales of faithful love. It seems to me too much to go further and say that he displayed, that winter's day on the river, a Winchian engagement with moral dilemmas, or a Millsian calculus of the greatest good, or a Kantian willingness to act as a universal moral legislator so that no Higher Legislation need prevail.

The Christian doctrine of mission and Christian 'sectarianism' are often singled out as twin moral offences in Christian conduct, the first because of its bold universal claim, the second because of its narrow particularism. If the idea of this paper is correct, these objections cancel one another, and these two aspects of Christian life and thought require one another in a universalisable Christian faith. To see this, however, it helps to know that witness is the form of universalisability Christians require for their morality to be moral, their ethics ethical. Nonetheless, some defences of Christian ethics have invoked other forms of the principle, not this characteristic Christian form. How, then, are we to choose between versions of the principle? Such a choice may require choosing not merely between ethical theories, but between forms of life.[36]

References

[1] Peter Baelz, *Ethics and Belief* (New York: Seabury Press 1977), pp. 17–19.

[2] See especially James Wm. McClendon, Jr., *Ethics: Systematic Theology Volume I* (Nashville; Abingdon 1986).

[3] ibid., p. 224.

[4] ibid., pp. 224–230. Quotation, Matthew 6:12 and parallel; for a transactional interpretation of this utterance see *Ethics*, p. 227.

[5] Immanuel Kant, The *Grundlegung zur Metaphysik der Sitten* (1785) is translated as *Fundamental Principles of the Metaphysic of Morals* and published in Thomas Kingsmill Abbott, editor, *Kant's Critique of Practical Reason and Other Works in the Theory of Ethics*, (6th ed., London: Longmans, 1909). I will refer to it as the *Groundwork*, and cite pages from the Abbott edition.

[6] Bernard Williams, in *Ethics and the Limits of Philosophy* (Cambridge, Massachusetts: Harvard University 1985), calls the *Groundwork* 'the most significant work of moral philosophy after Aristotle,' and then adds, 'and one of the most puzzling. . . .' (p. 55).

[7] Kant, *Groundwork*, pp. 38, 47, 55.

[8] ibid., p. 53.

[9] The allusion is to Carl Becker's *Heavenly City of the Eighteenth Century Philosophers* (1932), in which he argued that the *philosophes* of that century, though they sought to abolish medieval concepts, yet replaced them with recognisable counterparts of their own construction. Kant seems the perfect example of that tendency.

[10] John Stuart Mill, *Utilitarianism*, published in 1861. My references are to the Hackett edition, edited by George Sher (Indianapolis 1979).

[11] ibid., p. 28.

[12] ibid., p. 34.

[13] ibid., p. 16.

[14] See e.g. J. J. C. Smart, in Smart and Bernard Williams, *Utilitarianism: For and Against* (Cambridge University Press 1973), pp. 69–71.

[15] Williams, *Ethics and the Limits of Philosophy*, p. 108, citing Henry Sidgwick, *The Methods of Ethics* (London: Macmillan 1907), p. 490.

[16] Henry Sidgwick, *The Methods of Ethics*, 7th edition, 1907. My citations are to the University of Chicago edition, reprinted 1962.

[17] ibid., p. 379. Sidgwick notes that in the latter form, the principle is very close to the Golden Rule.

[18] Peter Winch, 'The Universalizability of Moral Judgements,' in *The Monist*, Number 49 (April, 1965), pp. 196–214.

[19] ibid., p. 198.

[20] Herman Melville, *Billy Budd, Sailor (An Inside Narrative)*. This posthumous manuscript of Melville's has been often republished; I have used the authoritative text of The Library of America edition (1984).

[21] Winch, p. 22.

[22] Winch, p. 213, citing Richard M. Hare, *Freedom and Reason* (Oxford: Clarendon, 1963), p. 49. I have steered clear of reporting Hare's 1963 views directly, since they involve complex distinctions between logical and moral judgments – distinctions that have not weathered well. Winch provides a fair illustration of the British philosophical ethics of the 1960s.

[23] Winch, p. 199.

[24] ibid., p. 206.

[25] ibid., p. 210.

[26] See Peter Winch, *The Idea of a Social Science and Its Relation to Philosophy* (New York: Humanities Press 1958); and 'Understanding a Primitive Society,' *American Philosophical Quarterly* 1/4 (1964), pp. 307–324.

[27] I take the formal standpoint of Peter Baelz's ethics to belong to this class, and specifically to be deontological or Kantian. See chapter 2, 'A Moral Point of View,' in his *Ethics and Belief*. It is part of Peter Baelz's own moral and Christian substance that he will not only accept but welcome being thus challenged in this volume by his affectionate former colleague.

[28] See e.g., Friedrich Schleiermacher, *On Religion: Speeches to Its Cultured Despisers*, trans. John Oman, 1st German ed., 1799 (New York: Harper & Row 1958), and ibid., *Introduction to Christian Ethics*, trans. John C. Shelley, from the German ed. of 1826/27 (Nashville: Abingdon Press 1989).

[29] George Lindbeck, *The Nature of Doctrine* (Philadelphia: Westminster, 1984), pp. 30–72.

[30] See Karl Barth, *The Doctrine of the Word of God (Church Dogmatics I/1)*. Trans. G. T. Thomson. (Edinburgh: T. & T. Clark 1936). See also Hendrik Kraemer, *The Christian Message in a Non-Christian World* (1938).

[31] These six pejorative phrases ('snug sectarian exclusiveness . . . theory of human depravity' are intended as mere reminders that the great Christian doctrines of (1) the church, (2) the Christian life, (3) predestination, (4) human freedom and dignity, (5) human need for God, and (6) original sin) must not be so construed as to cancel (7) the equally great Christian doctrine of mission. Curiously, this last doctrine is much neglected in systematic theologies – presumably relegated to 'practical theology', or simply omitted in snug, smug Western thinking.

[32] See Gen. 12:3 and its echoes in Old Testament and New.

[33] Thieleman J. Van Braght, compiler, *The Bloody Theater or Martyrs Mirror of the Defenseless Christians* . . . trans. Joseph F. Sohm. 5th English ed., from the

Dutch edition of 1660 (Scottdale, Pennsylvania: Herald Press 1950), pp. 741–2. See also N. van der Zijpp, 'Dirk Willemsz,' in *Mennonite Encyclopedia*, ed. Cornelius Krahn (Scottdale, Pennsylvania: Mennonite Publishing House, 1956), II, 66f.

[34] On flight from persecution as the model for Christians, see Athanasius, *de Fuga*, 22. On the general history of the 'Anabaptist' (or as I prefer to write, 'baptist') movement, see first Donald Durnbaugh, *The Believers' Church* (New York: Macmillan 1968), recently reissued by Herald Press. A carefully researched history of one sixteenth century leader is C. Arnold Snyder, *The Life and Thought of Michael Sattler* (Scottdale, Pennsylvania: Herald 1984); the primary Sattler documents are translated and annotated in John H. Yoder, *The Legacy of Michael Sattler* (Scottdale, Pennsylvania: Herald 1973). A valuable interpretation of the sixteenth century movement is Walter Klaassen, *Anabaptism: Neither Catholic Nor Protestant* (Waterloo, Ontario: Conrad 1973). Revisionist historiography of radicals in that period is found in Hans-Juergen Goertz, ed., *Profiles of Radical Reformers*, English editor Walter Klaassen (Kitchener, Ontario and Scottdale, Pennsylvania: Herald 1982).

[35] On the typological hermeneutics that is here presupposed, see my *Ethics* (op. cit.), ch. 1.

[36] I am grateful for assistance in preparing this paper given by Nancey Murphy, James Smith, and John H. Yoder, and for the session of the Society of Christian Philosophers gathered at Loyola Marymount College, Los Angeles, where an earlier draft was presented and discussed, and especially for the critical response of Tiina Allik at that session.

THEOLOGICAL REFLECTION

Peter Sedgwick

The relationship between theology and questions of public policy is a problematic one. Despite the growth in the attention which the media gives to Christian comment on public affairs, especially when uttered by ecclesiastical leaders, the reasons why theology should be interested in social affairs are not clear. There is a vast amount of comment by the Churches on public policy, but comparatively little on the basis for this utterance.[1]

A second area where theology finds itself in uncertain waters is where theological reflection is invited on the practical problems of church life. There are whole libraries on the traditional questions raised by ecumenism, such as the validity of orders, the nature of ecclesiastical authority, the understanding of the sacraments, etc. Yet it has been recognised for some while now that the major difficulties faced in ecumenism are sociological and cultural, rather than theological. There are of course profound differences which remain within churches on, say, their understanding of priesthood – as the difficult reception within the Church of England of the document *The Priesthood of the Ordained Ministry* produced by the Church of England's Faith and Order Advisory Group made clear – but nevertheless at local, regional and national level the primary stumbling blocks are cultural. Why do regional ecclesiastical leaders find it easier to achieve a modus vivendi, albeit in fairly cautious terms, while at other levels ecclesiastical relationships will be either rather bleak or impatient of traditional practices and regulations? The answers will again be given in cultural or sociological terms.[2] What is the place then of theology in reflecting both on these sociological realities (the lives of men and women in a particular culture) and on the explanations, however tentatively offered, of their behaviour?

Ecumenism is one obvious area where traditional theology is ill at ease in dealing with the practical realities of church life. Let the experts sort it out on ARCIC, or in the Anglican – Lutheran conversations, and then the ecclesiastical hierarchy can seek to implement their findings in a process of reception. Yet perhaps such a model no longer fits the ecclesiological understandings found in contemporary Christian practice. There are similar difficulties in ordering the sacramental discipline of the church. Should children be allowed to receive Holy Communion, and what is the relationship of baptism, confirmation and the reception of Communion? Who should be baptised, and what discipline should the church administer? What of second baptism, which is a familiar demand in the fast-growing charismatic wing of the churches? Again the theological literature on the sacraments is extensive.[3] What is far more problematic is the relationship of this to the practical problems of Church life. What place is allotted to the experience of congregations? Is that experience, in turn, taken on its own, or is it placed within the social and cultural context of the congregation's life?

There are many more examples which could be given, from questions of the place of women in the leadership of the church, to discussions of the relationship of Christianity to other faiths. In each of these areas the role of experience, and theological reflection on that experience, becomes crucial. So one of the initiatives which Peter Baelz took as Dean of Durham was to remodel the job description of the Theological Consultancy to the North-East Churches. He drew together a small group from the denominations represented in the regular meetings of the North-East Church leaders, known as the North-East Ecumenical Group (NEEG). This group was made up of ordained and lay members, men and women, academics and parish priests. Peter chaired this group from 1982–1988, and it was this group which appointed me as its full-time officer in 1982. Its task was to assist the Churches in their theological interpretation of North-East society, and the life of the Churches within that society.

II

In January 1987 the Consultancy met with Peter Baelz to discuss what might be meant by theological reflection. A tape-recording was made of the conversation. Peter suggested that doctrine was a reflection upon, and out of, the fundamental concrete elements of biography, story and historical event. The convictions which make a person, by which they stand, and which contribute to the assumptions by which they live are better explained in terms of historical contingency than rational convictions, although of course there is a subtle interplay between the two explanations. However if the contingent basis of a particular life is allowed, and a complex determinism predisposes us to certain convictions, then it will be no surprise that some people will hold convictions in one way, and some in another. Convictions will arise when in the contingency of a particular historical event, perhaps repeated on many subsequent occasions a person is grasped by something perceived to be more fundamental than the fleeting succession of events. The language of vision is used, and a belief is expressed that whatever else is true, this must be the case. Such a conviction is built into a person's history thereafter. Once sufficient new convictions are built up and interwoven, a person so changes their outlook, and in turn modifies their behaviour, that they speak of a conversion. What then becomes at issue are the criteria by which convictions can be assessed as truthful, even if this truth is always expressed in and through historical contingency. Once such criteria are established, and the authority for employing those criteria vindicated in discussion, then a corpus of beliefs will come to be expressed as doctrine.

The manner by which a corpus of beliefs is established is a complex one. Beliefs do not arrive from nowhere. There is first a prior interpretative scheme, which is then related to particular historical events and to experience which will be both individual and collective. The interaction of interpretation, event and experience will create both new criteria for assessing the truth of particular convictions and vindicate the authority for assessing those criteria. Only when authority and criteria are established can a new framework arise, which will cause a particular community to create a set of beliefs which it will call doctrine. Such a process finds its paradigm expression for the churches in the response to the incarnation and resurrection of Jesus Christ.

So Brian Hebblethwaite in his careful discussion of the appeal to experience in Christian doctrine works out clearly the interplay of these factors of interpretation, event and experience.[4] The experience does not create the interpretation, nor the other way round. It is through the interplay of the two elements that reality impinges on human beings. The transformation of the faith of Israel by the events of the life, death and resurrection of Jesus Christ made possible a new experience of salvation. The developed Christian doctrine – the new framework of interpreting the convictions expressed by human beings which is held by Christians to be true – turns on an identification of God's self-revelation and God's offer of reconciliation. The revelation of God as one who comes to us and to our situation is shown in the contingent historical events of the life of Jesus, and such a revelation also in the same act achieves a reconciliation. Knowing who God is implies statements about the nature of the love of God.

Such a brief account of the development of Christian doctrine as a framework for assessing the contingent convictions which human beings come to hold depends on an awareness of that reconciliation. It is not, and never has been, simply an intellectual exercise. Thus the importance of devotion and spirituality looms large in any account of theological reflection. However it is not as though devotion, spirituality and the practice of the Christian life are opposed to the rational judgements which may be made about the Christian faith. Spirituality is not irrational, while theology is rational. Rather spirituality is a 'pre-rational' condition of theological thought.

Spirituality, as a pre-rational element in the Christian faith, will include many elements of human nature. In Anglican theology, the moral element has been especially stressed, following the influence of Butler and Newman. Mystical apprehension, as the direct knowledge of the transcendent independent of moral considerations, is not a feature of Anglican, English spirituality. Nevertheless, the pre-rational is wider than spirituality itself. It is interwoven in Anglican apologetics with the entirety of all human experience, whether religious or not. It is a characteristic of English Anglican theology that it appeals to the existence of 'the basal conditions of human cognitional activity', where faith is the elemental, primal confidence in the reliability of our experience of the world. Yet faith is also for Scott Holland the term for communion with God.[5] Thus spirituality is placed within what might be called the pre-rational: the basal conditions of cognitional activity. Therefore doctrine, which provides the interpretative framework in Hebblethwaite's words for interpreting experience and the convictions which contingently arise within and through experience, is itself nourished by spirituality, which for many Anglican theologians is closely related to a pre-rational condition of existence, including feelings and an awareness of reality. Doctrine therefore is not just the means by which we reflect theologically on experience: it is continually informed by spirituality and moral sense which is itself interwoven with the life of the self, and its daily experience.

How has Anglican theology handled this appeal to the pre-rational in its account of theological thought? The chief advocates of this appeal are influenced by Butler, and before him by the Cambridge Platonists.

Charles Gore in *Can We then Believe?* argued that the self-disclosure of God could not be excluded a priori. Appealing back to Bishop Butler, Gore claimed that divine revelation 'vindicates itself, he would show, by being close-knit into the fabric of natural experience which all admit. It is wanted to complete it.'[6] However human experience is both inherently complex and difficult of assessment. The primary stress in our understanding of experience must be of its fragmentary nature.[7] Likewise Newman cites Butler, when in *The Grammar of Assent*, he speaks of the formation of rational judgement in the conscience: 'to a mind thus carefully formed upon the basis of its natural conscience, the world, both of nature and of man, does but give back a living reflection of those truths about the one living God which have been familiar to it from childhood.'[8] Cumulative and converging indications of the truth awaken feelings of certitude in the enquirer, which is an informal inference resting on the totality of the evidence.[9] So too Peter Baelz in *Ethics and Belief* discusses Butler's description of conscience, which can be called 'moral reason, moral sense, or Divine reason; whether considered as a sentiment of the understanding, or as a perception of the heart; or, which seems the truth, as including both'.[10] Equally in his discussion of Schleiermacher Peter Baelz appeals to the significance for Schleiermacher of 'religious feeling, which although non-conceptual, embodies a kind of pre-conceptual, intuitive apprehension. An awareness through participation of that which transcends the individual's own consciousness ... there is here the suggestion of a structured unity of apprehension which underlies and conditions the ordinary distinction between subjective and objective'.[11]

Such an analysis of the pre-rational appeals closely to the fabric of common human experience, however complex and fragmentary that experience may be. It is inherently a moral dimension, where psychological fact is transcended by an assertion of intrinsic value or 'moral fact'.[12] The importance of the personal is a constant feature in this argument. However the pre-rational can itself become introverted, and lose its clarity of vision. The intellect is always needed to purify the pre-intellectual in its activity of searching and questing (spirituality) for its understanding of ultimate reality. Nor is this pre-intellectual sense immune from moral failure. While Newman may have placed great store on the deliverance of conscience, speaking of the enormous power of 'holiness embodied in personal form ... the silent conduct of a conscientious man',[13] a more characteristic note in Peter Baelz's writings is that of the conflict of interests. The conscience witnesses to the nature of potentiality, of the freedom of human nature to decide for itself what it may become. And in this lies the possibility of conflict.[14] Newman issues a stern call to obey the inward law of conscience as the first step in the life of faith, where we believe when we have 'no proof of its truth', but quieten 'the murmurs of Reason, perplexed with the disorders of the present scheme of things.'[15] However Peter Baelz suggests that as well as the purification of the intellect, there is also a need for art, and nature, to take one out of oneself. Through art and nature, it is ultimately God who takes one out of oneself, although the paradox is that in the process of creation a person has to become oneself before one can be taken out of oneself.

Thus spirituality, as a part of the pre-rational element in theological judgement, may itself become pathological, introverted and unhealthy.

Hence the strong importance in Peter Baelz's writings on the value of aesthetic experiences which might take a person out of themselves is striking. He speaks of the conversion of the imagination by art. Clearly aesthetics is not to be confined to this role, and there is much to be said for its intrinsic value, but nevertheless its sheer objectivity is crucial over against the potential introversion of pre-rational experience.

The recognition of the centrality of the contingent in forming the convictions by which we live is an integral part of unpacking what theological reflection might mean. However such contingent convictions must be assessed as true or false, and at this point there will be the need of a framework of interpretation. This doctrinal framework will spring out of the interplay of prior interpretative patterns of belief, certain historical events, and experience, both individual and collective. The doctrinal framework is itself nourished and held in being by the practice of spirituality. Such practice takes us back to the familiar Anglican appeal to the pre-rational which is an awareness of moral experience and of reality itself. Therefore any development of spirituality which loses touch with that moral sense will be suspect. Equally in this tradition there is a valuing of the world in and for itself, and of human goodness and human creativity within the creation. The construction of a doctrinal framework for interpreting the convictions which spring out of human experience itself draws on a spirituality and pre-rational awareness of the potentiality of human beings for goodness in daily experience. In spite of all the reality of moral evil it is fundamentally an optimistic assessment of the world, as created by God. Theological reflection thus includes within itself an awareness of the affirmation of the world by the self in its most basic experiential life.

III

At this point an objection may well be lodged. Is not this model of theological reflection, with its appeal to human stories, contingent events and pre-rational experience, conceding too much to the realm of the personal? Even if there is an interplay between doctrine and spirituality on the one hand, and human experience as subjective states, feelings and impressions on the other; even if spirituality, as the nourishment of doctrine, takes us back into the world of experience – is there not also a world of societies, institutions, and structures, both ecclesiastical and secular? Are we not far removed from the events of 1982–1988 in the North-East, such as the miners' strike and the continual round of factory closures? How does the personal and the subjective figure here? There is also the fact that ecumenism is a matter of the relationship of denominations, which carry their doctrinal framework within properly guarded traditions. Neither the political and social events of the 1980s, nor the Christian denominations with congregations scattered across the region, are to be reduced to human experiences as an aggregate of individual life-stories. Such a move would destroy the possibility of a social theology or any reflection on the practical hopes and problems of church life, which is where we began.

Let me take the question of social theology first. Why should a theologian seek to say something about the political and social realities of North-East life? The starting point should be simple. Human beings exhibit a variety of desires, aspirations, and wants in their daily life. Behind and through all of these will be the articulation of certain basic needs. It is notoriously difficult to discriminate between needs and desires, yet some account of human flourishing may be given, which is necessary if human beings are to communicate with each other, and to be in relationship with one another. While these will still remain enormous areas of conflict and choice between human beings, nevertheless it will be possible to see how certain societies promote human relationships and others gravely impede them. So in reflecting on the run-down of the coal industry in County Durham, Jim O'Keefe, the Pastoral Director at Ushaw College, Durham wrote: 'To walk around the streets of Easington and Horden, to drink in the pubs and listen to the people, is to be filled with the very clear feeling that the future of the area is decided by people living way beyond its boundaries. Decisions regarding housing, jobs, education, wealth and social services are all made elsewhere, with little or no attempt at consultation with the people.'[16] Repeatedly in this document the despair of those living in the area was articulated in terms of fear, hopelessness and antagonisms one with another.

This is a clear indication of the grave impairment of human relationships in society. Wants can vary in quality and intensity, but needs are more objective than wants. 'They do not depend upon the presence or absence of conscious desire. They arise out of the condition in which human beings find themselves. Thus we can speak of basic human needs in so far as there are needs which all human beings share as human beings. These needs include physical, psychological, social and spiritual needs.'[17]

What is distinctively Christian in this account of human well-being is two fold. First, I have argued throughout this essay that convictions arise out of the contingency of historical events. Any doctrinal framework which interprets such convictions must itself be aware that it is nourished by a spirituality, which in turn is part of common human experience. Part of that human experience, however fragmentary and complex it may be, is the awareness of moral sense or conscience: the intuitive apprehension of the world as a reality which impinges on us as human beings. Pastoral sensitivity to a situation where people no longer have any elemental, primal confidence in the reliability of their experience of the world will demand the formation of a spirituality which can become genuinely reconciling and healing within those relationships. Therefore the doctrinal framework which interprets convictions, arising out of events which may be profoundly dehumanising, will need to be aware that its interpretation of the truth of those convictions will continually stand under judgement. The judgement will be based on whether or not a true spirituality has been developed or not.

Secondly a Christian account of well-being will be forced in the end of the day to answer the question as to what it means to be truly human. Here the familiar discussion of 'middle axioms' come into play, outlining the directions in which Christians would seek to move the society in which they live. As often as not, such contributions by the moral theologian will be made in the development and implementation of programmes and policies, on which he or she will be invited to comment. Such 'middle axioms' have often been developed by theologians since Temple on the economic system, the sanctity of the individual, education, etc. Middle axioms are developed by forming general ethical principles out of Christian doctrine, and then holding these alongside the concrete decisions which must be made.[18]

There can be no escape from the provisionality of 'middle axioms', but it is important that the attempt, however controversial, is made. In a pluralist society any attempt to articulate truths about human nature will be inevitably unable to command wholehearted acceptance. Furthermore, if the attempt is made while the church is itself involved in social action, the possibility of mistaken views and disagreement is heightened yet further. Nevertheless the obligation to formulate Christian views on a fulfilled human existence is inescapable.

Once the attempt is made, the theologian will find that consideration of social institutions presses upon any analysis of human well-being. Societies can be analysed in many different ways, using interdisciplinary subjects which may be technical, organisational, cultural or scientific. At this point theological reflection can no longer be confined to the realm of the personal. Personal experience, in terms of desires, wants, interests and needs may be the starting point of such reflection; but theological reflection cannot simply stay with the realm of subjectivity. Just as doctrine as an interpretative framework must always be pressed back to the pre-rational awareness of reality found in spirituality and basal experience, so too it must become aware of what is more than personal: the cultural, technical, scientific and organisational worlds of the modern era. There are many difficulties here, for it is not easy to see how these different worlds interconnect.

Niklas Luhmann has pointed to the role of religion in still preserving meanings which are common to society as a whole.[19] Although society is now comprised of functional systems of politics, the economy, science, law, education, etc., which are relatively autonomous one of another, nevertheless religion enables human beings to cope with the necessarily contingent nature of the systems of meaning which press in upon us. 'The need for conscious reflection on the grounds of all meaning persists.'[20] Politics works with power, science with truth, the economy with money, and so on. Religion however combines symbols in a distinctive pattern not shared by other special media of communication, such as love, power or money.

Therefore theological reflection will move beyond the realm of the personal to the mediation of the Logos of God in creation: the presence of Christ in creation, which Peter Baelz has spoken of as enlarging the natural order. Grace is present within the social order, releasing its potentiality and challenging it. 'Morality needs to be rooted in a vision of what truly is and what truly might be. Thus the Christian vision of the Kingdom of God gives another dimension and a profounder motivation to the search for prosperity along with justice and peace.'[21]

Finally, there is the place of the Church as Christian community, in furthering the flourishing of human beings in the ways revealed in God's reconciling act in Christ. Perhaps I might quote from the final report of the Theological Consultancy which Peter Baelz presented in 1988 to the North-East Church Leaders. I wrote in the foreword:

> The reason for the existence of the Theological Consultancy has always been to work with particular issues which arise both for the Church and in society. The particularity or concreteness is important. The aim has been to say something worthwhile theologically about these issues. The Church is the concrete place where certain human beings accept a call to associate with Christ, the reality of Him who is the expression and embodiment of divine love. This association is for the rest of humanity. Thus at the heart of the Consultancy is the Church as the body of Christ. In the Church Jesus Christ, Son of God and our saviour, can be said to take form and achieve present reality for the world. The importance of Christ's significance for the world is a practical one. As the Church is taken up into the love of God it becomes that love for the world.

Therefore the relationships within the Church are themselves a proper subject for theological reflection. The Church must learn to be corporate, while also serving the mission of God as a corporate agency. Hugh Melinsky in his essay has drawn attention to Peter Baelz's contribution to the development of a new vision for theological education and the training of the ordained ministry. The Church represents in its life the new social order which the reconciling act of God in Christ has called into being. It only represents the new reality very imperfectly and the task of theological reflection must be to discern the glimpses of that new reality in the contingent realities of its all-too-human life. Such a task demands patient unravelling of the sociological, cultural and theological factors which determine the existence of a particular denomination in one locality.

IV

Theological reflection remains an untidy discipline. It is pressed one way into the realm not only of the personal but of primary human experience, and so the underlying spirituality which undergirds doctrine is crucial. Spirituality is always concerned both with a relationship with God and with basal human experience. At the same time theological reflection will also be concerned with the realm of institutions, structures and social change. Here the emphasis is on the discernment of the constraints and support which such structures offer for human flourishing. Beyond the question of human flourishing lies the very possibility of finding meaning in a complex industrial society, with its many sub-groups each with their own world of meaning.

Between the different levels of personal experience and social structures the interpretation of convictions formed in the contingency of human events will continue to be the task of theological reflection. In his writings on the very personal world of the desires expressed by childless couples, and in his interpretation of the complex world of economics, Peter Baelz has taken much further the work of theological reflection. However it is his role as Chairman of the Theological Consultancy, attentive to the varying demands of ecumenism, church schools, medical ethics and the future of work that I shall most remember with gratitude for his inspiration, and sensitivity.

References

[1] D. Forrester, 'Social Theology' in ed. M. H. Taylor *Christians and the Future of Social Democracy* (G. W. and A. Hasketh 1982) p. 33.

[2] C. Lewis, 'Unity A Sociological Perspective' in ed. R. Davies *The Testing of the Churches 1932–1982* (Epworth Press 1982) pp. 145–58.

[3] ed. G. Muller-Fahrenholz . . . *and do not hinder them*. WCC Faith and Order Paper No. 109 (WCC, Geneva 1982) *Communion before Confirmation?* (CIO Publishing 1985).

[4] B. Hebblethwaite, 'The appeal to experience in Christology' in ed. S. W. Sykes and J. P. Clayton *Christ, Faith and History* (CUP 1972) p. 270.

[5] S. W. Sykes 'Faith' in ed. G. Wainwright *Keeping the Faith* (SPCK 1989) p. 10.

[6] C. Gore, *Can We then Believe?* (John Murray 1926) p. 151.

[7] C. Gore, *The Philosophy of the Good Life* (Everyman 1935) p. 295.

[8] J. H. Newman, *An Essay in Aid of A Grammar of Assent* (Longmans 1947) p. 88.

[9] ibid., p. 139.

[10] P. R. Baelz, *Ethics and Belief* (Sheldon 1977) p. 44. citing ed. J. H. Bernard, *The Works of Bishop Butler*, vol. 1 (Macmillan 1900) p. 287.

[11] P. R. Baelz, *Christian Theology and Metaphysics* (Epworth 1968) pp. 45-6.

[12] *Ethics and Belief*, p. 80.

[13] J. H. Newman *University Sermons* (SPCK 1970) Sermon V p. 92.

[14] *Ethics and Belief*, pp. 54 and 73.

[15] Newman, op. cit., pp. 19-20.

[16] *Coal Church and Community* 1986 p. 66.

[17] *Choices in Childlessness* (Free Church Federal Council/British Council of Churches report – Chairman Peter Baelz – 1982) p. 21.

[18] Forrester, op. cit., p. 42.

[19] N. Luhmann, *Religious Dogmatics and the Evolution of Societies* (Edwin Melten Press, New York, 1984).

[20] J. A. Beckford, *Religion and Advanced Industrial Society* (Unwin Hyman 1989) p. 84.

[21] *Perspectives on Economics* (CIO Publishing 1984) p. 75.

CHURCH AND SOCIETY

GOD AND THE FORM OF SOCIETY

Daniel W. Hardy

In the General Synod Debate on 'The Church and the Bomb', Peter Baelz described the pacifist vocation, to which he stood very close, as 'a willingness to respond to the way of our Lord whatever the consequences and not to believe that it is the duty of the Christian Church to manage the affairs of the world'.[1] His own response was centred on the issue of being, and becoming, fully human; this was an issue which was as much one of social responsibility as of individual well-being. It could be described as a response made in 'open faithfulness', as – in the many important contributions he made to debates about ethical issues – he sought for ways of faithfulness which would soften the aggressive postures of those who claimed to possess the truth, and which would overcome conflicts of interest.

His concern in Christian faith was always with the transformative effect of faith on human beings. It was always, therefore, a social one, at least in part: the question was how people were to be brought together to a fully human life. But he also realised that the means to this end had to be societal, both governmental and ecclesial. On the one hand, the complexity of modern social life, so reliant on the interdependence of services and technology, had to be controlled by government: 'in the future there is likely to be much more control of our social life through Government action'. On the other hand, while it was not the business of the Christian Church 'to manage the affairs of the world', it might provide symbols of fully human existence; the question for Christians is

> whether there is any way in which we can understand the form of our society so as to give us a new orientation and a new impetus . . . Are there any symbols of hope, symbols of community, symbols of individuality-in-community, which transcend both the system of a warring conflict of interests and the system of central planning of society by the state? Are there here any resources for hope? Since sooner or later we shall run short of that fundamental human emotion and outlook, are there any resources in the

131

Christian tradition which, recognising man's creativity as ambivalent, nevertheless help us to promote not only individual salvation but also the future well-being of mankind?[2]

It is to that question, of giving a new orientation and impetus to the form of our society, that this essay is directed. But the answer to be offered is not so much symbolic as social-structural. In the highly developed societies of present times, Christians cannot offer only transcendent symbols while illuminate and inspire; to do so is to remain in the realm of ideas which do not relate very well to the structures by which social life is organised. They must respond by developing social structures in which people may become fully human in interaction with God. In fact, they must learn to 'manage the affairs of the world' in their relationship with God, not in order to take over the affairs of government, but to give practical form to their life with God, and thus provide a more concrete manifestation of what this might mean for human affairs in general.

The argument which we shall present is that there is an inevitable interaction between conceptions of social structure and those of God. Indeed, social structures are, properly speaking, relative to the nature of God. But, as we shall see, modern conceptions of social structures have tended to make them more relativistic (as distinct from relative), probably in reaction to the absolutism which has continued to infect theology; and theology has tended to conspire in this by adopting a relativistic understanding of social institutions and of God. A more satisfactory reconception of social structures therefore requires a recovery of their relativity to a God who is seen himself to be relative to the world he has created and redeemed. This conception of the relation of social structures is far more consonant with traditional Christian understanding.

SOCIAL STRUCTURES AS RELATIVE TO GOD

The relativity of social structures to God is well expressed in an illuminating aphorism by the English poet-philosopher-theologian S. T. Coleridge:

> He who begins by loving Christianity, better than truth, will proceed by loving his own sect or church better than Christianity, and end in loving himself better than all.[3]

Where there is no recognition of the relativity of social structures to the truth of God, there will be a natural tendency to move in a negative spiral from greater to lesser preoccupations, from universal truth to self-regard. Preference for anything less than the truth (which is by definition universal and for all) leads through varieties of sectionalised identity and ultimately to self-isolation. And the only way of avoiding the spiral is to attend fully to the truth, and to find one's social or personal identity in that.

A like problem can be found amongst those who place love for a particular social order above that for truth. It is possible to parallel Coleridge's aphorism with another describing the state, social groups and the self. It would read:

> He who begins by loving the nation, better than truth, will proceed by loving his own group better than the nation, and end in loving himself better than all.

This would suggest that in the social sphere also, where there is not full attention to the truth, there is the same negative spiral from universal truth to self-regard; preference for that which is less than universal leads through preference for varieties of sectional identity (social groups or classes, for example), and eventually to a priority given to individuals.

When Christianity and the nation are viewed in this way, there is much to be learned from this parallel. It suggests a higher point to which both Christianity and the nation must be answerable, without which each will descend to lesser forms of coherence. But, particularly to the eyes of people in the 1990s, the form of the higher truth – the love of which would bring the highest form of social coherence – seems obscure. Is it – as some have claimed of the Kantian thinking which interested Coleridge – an imaginary ideal, 'an empty signifier of that total knowledge which the bourgeoisie never ceases to dream of ... the phantasmal possibility of a knowledge beyond all categories, which then risks striking what it *can* know meagrely relative'?[4] It need not be, though it will always run the risk of becoming an ideology, a reified emptiness.

The higher point to which Christianity and particular nations are answerable may be a real goal, the goal of true social coherence which is anticipated in societies as they actually exist. And such a goal – genuinely but only partially realised in particular societies – would relativise both Christianity and particular civil societies to the position of instruments which may, or may not, support societies in the achievement of that true social being. In effect, reference to this goal of true social being would 'put them in their place', making each instrumental to universal social coherence.

To relativise Christianity and nations to true social being is not to suggest that they have no value, but that their value is proportionate to their particular contribution to the achievement of true social being. And this, of course, will vary according to what they are. Both Christianity and nations contain within them different kinds of social unit. In each, we can identify 'formal units' with well-developed notions of membership and well-structured distributions of responsibilities, 'informal units' with less well-developed commonality and distribution of responsibilities, and 'fragmented units' made up of individuals with little notion of commonality where responsibility is assumed only by individuals.[5]

But if we follow the line of argument presented so far, each such unit has its value not in itself, but through its contribution to true society; each in its own way should contribute to the achievement of true social coherence. 'Formal units' with their advanced organisational structure, 'informal units' with less well-developed polities, and 'fragmented units' with little commonality and mutual responsibility: all have true social coherence as their goal, and are to contribute to its achievement.

Interestingly, if this is so, there is a profound co-ordination of purpose between the different kinds of civil social units and the different kinds of religious ones. Each is in its own right to contribute to 'true society' in a way which is appropriate to the kind of social unit which it is. This suggests a fruitful relation between states (as the bodies with constituted responsibility for civil social units) and Christianity, or between informal units and sects, or between individuals as social and as Christian. If at each level both are obligated to find true social coherence, they meet in their common purpose. To take one implication of this, the state cannot conceive itself in quasi-religious terms, as if it alone knows or performs 'true society'; it must open itself to criticism. Nor can Christian bodies see themselves as quasi-states, with civil power derived from their knowledge of the truth; they must be reformed through their interaction with the truth.

If this position is right – that Christianity and the state, together with the variety of social units which they incorporate, are relativised by their obligation to contribute to true society – we have an important vantage-point from which to view current social structures, and from which to consider the contribution of theology to social structuring.

If we measure the modern social situation by the standards we have been considering, there are two features of modern societies which stand out. Both are kinds of relativism. The first is the movement toward simpler self-contained social structures and, underlying it, a movement towards a simplification of human relationships. The second is the movement from the position in which social structures are relativised by the obligation to promote true social coherence to the more extreme relativistic position in which certain kinds of social structure are taken to be exemplary forms of social coherence, and therefore important in their own right.

THE RELATIVISING OF SOCIAL STRUCTURES

Despite the notable increase in the complexity of modern societies, it seems to be the case that modern societies in the Western hemisphere – civil or religious – have not maintained the range of social units mentioned before. In place of the formal, the informal and the fragmented units mentioned before, most social practice in the modern West has drifted towards a polarisation of the formal (the civil state or the large-scale religious organisation) and the fragmented (the individual, whether as citizen or as faithful), with a correlative de-emphasis of units more informal and local.

Hence there have typically been two conflicting tendencies, on the one hand that of states or churches which take it upon themselves to control their peoples, through the techniques of administration for example, and on the other hand that which attempts to safeguard citizens against the excesses of states or churches in doing so. Each has given rise to its own philosophy and practice.

In the one case, modern states have been concerned with the 'mass' of human beings and have various devices, including those for social administration (e.g. statistics) and the management of wealth, as instruments to bring about social well-being. In the other case, there is an opposing movement to limit the excesses of states, and to do so through appealing to the notion of human beings as 'individuals' who by nature are endowed with rights to secure their own interests; in this case, the very existence of states is seen as the result of individuals freely contracting with each other to ensure the well-being of individuals, and they need to be restricted by constitutions and laws to prevent the arbitrary exercise of their power.[6] Similar tendencies are found amongst the churches, where there is a like polarisation of large-scale 'institutions' which are regarded with great suspicion by those who emphasize the personal character of religious belief and life.

The 'intermediate' – more informal – social units have tended to suffer. In practical terms, the supposition that society maintains itself in informal units, with strong customs and customary values, has been increasingly displaced. Referring to the like situation in the United States, one writer said:

> The influence of the democratic state has today become so pervasive, and our customary value sources so fragmented, that the process-oriented values of the Constitution that 'inform and limit' the governmental structure are thought by some scholars to be the 'values that determine the quality of our social existence'. As a result we live in something of a value vacuum. The 'megastructures' of society (which may include corporate conglomerates and large labour unions as well as large government bureaucracies) have overpowering influence – yet they do not typically seek to tell us what our lives really mean.[7]

What has largely displaced these more informal social units, however, is as much the notion of the individual as that of the state; the proponents of each of these have subsumed the notion of society into their own conception. It is either 'Societé, c'est nous!' or 'Societé, c'est moi!' Society *is* the state or individuals, not such informal units.

RELATIVISM IN RELATIONSHIPS

When we look more closely at the prevailing emphasis on the formal and on the individual, whether in civil or religious forms, we see that both incorporate a notion of human relationships which is in some ways very surprising, and also quite different from the relationships which often mark informal social units. This is best seen in the way by which those concerned with the state and with the individual define human beings. Neither of these defines human beings by reference to others; the relation of human beings to others is considered extrinsic to them. The chief difference between the two is in how these extrinsic relations take place.

In the case of the modern managerial notion of the *state*, the relations take place indirectly; the assumption is that human beings can be treated as 'externally related' by reference to some property or process which is common to them. The historical antecedent to this was the notion that people were related by the 'property' of being governed. Insofar as governance was not only by a monarch but also through those appointed to governship under him, people were related as 'classes' through the property of being governed by these appointees. Despite the required subservience to the governor, the positive feature of their situation was that people in each class were related to each other by the personal property of being governed; it was their common lot, which actually gave them their commonality. But now, where people are more likely to be seen as units (e.g. statistical units), they are 'related' only in a more 'factlike' way, their explainability (and manipulability) through some identifiable characteristic or process; hence, social improvement happens through controlling this characteristic or process. The most obvious example is wealth, where in the modern state people are explained in terms of their wealth, and social improvement is thought to happen through wealth creation and control. But much the same can be seen in the use which is made of education; people are explained in terms of their educability, and it is thought that the 'right' education 'socialises' human beings and ameliorates problems of social relations, such as those which arise from the class structure of society. Throughout, people are seen as related to each other through the characteristic or process by which they are 'managed'.

In the case of the notion of the individual, which is usually called the 'liberal' conception, the relations – also extrinsic to those involved – take place directly, in the sense that one individual is related directly to others. But directness of relation does not imply obligation, or relations which are necessary to the individual concerned. The view is based on several premises: (1) the human being is ontologically prior to society, and is defined ('externally') without reference to other human beings; (2) each human being is only contingently related to others (in the sense that this relation may or may not obtain), either through accidents of contact or through choice; and (3) each human being is only historically related to others (these relations arise only in, and last only so long as they are maintained in, finite existence). On this view, each individual is seen as a distinct being, and endowed with certain rights such as the liberty to seek his/her well-being through the enhancement and preservation of life, property or anything else seen as conducive to this well-being. As such, human beings are considered equal in their freedom to secure their own well-being. While this by no means excludes the possibility of a sense of responsibility for others, and the importance of conditions which would be conducive to universal happiness, the main thrust of the notion is the maximisation of the freedom of the individual. Society then arises through the actual, contingent historical relations of such individuals. The civil state is constituted by individuals when they freely hand over certain natural rights, renouncing their right to punish intrusions upon their life, freedom and property; but it exists for the sake of individuals. From this vantage-point, the notion that human beings exist by their membership of a whole (such as a given society, state or church) is discarded as potentially, if not actually, totalitarian.

These are some of the main ways in which societies have been simplified in modern times, through preference given either to states or to individuals as the basis of society and thereby (even if not by design) de-emphasizing the informal ways in which societies maintain themselves. And what has accompanied them is favour shown for the notion that human beings are only related externally or extrinsically. Both these preferences deserve to be tested against other possibilities, that societies are as much maintained through informal units and through the intrinsic relatedness of human beings, whereby they are actually defined by relation to each other. Such possibilities do not imply that they may not also be related as states or as individuals, and through properties or processes or by their own choice, but may yield a stronger notion of how it is that human beings are related.

THE RELATIVISATION OF THE GOAL OF SOCIETY

Accompanying the 'simplification' of societies and human relationships just described has been a movement away from the relativity of social structures to truly social coherence – from the position in which social structures are relativised by their obligation to contribute to true society. What appears to have taken its place is a more extreme relativistic position in which certain kinds of social structure are taken to be important in their own right, and present themselves as ideal. On the one hand, this has often brought states to present themselves in quasi-religious terms:

> The wholesale aestheticisation of society had found its grotesque apotheosis for a brief moment in fascism, with its panoply of myths, symbols and orgiastic spectacles, its repressive expressivity, its appeals to passion, radical intuition, instinctual judgement, the sublimity of self-sacrifice and the pulse of the blood. But in the post-war years a different form of aestheticisation was also to saturate the entire culture of late capital, with its fetishism of style and surface, its cult of hedonism and technique . . .[8]

On the other hand, Christianity has tended to present itself as a divinely ordained, and therefore ideal, form of civil power.

The 'ideal societies' thus presented, whether by states or by Christianity, employ the notion of extrinsic relations discussed earlier. True society is not seen to arise from the essential relatedness or coherence of human beings; instead, it is to be achieved through the extrinsic relations in which human beings find themselves.

Where the focus is on states or large-scale societies, it is thought that the ideal will be achieved by appealing to human beings in general and securing their approval through an appropriate form of political process. If, for example, it is thought that states are best conducted on the principles of market philosophy, the implicit suggestion is that this is the most equitable way of securing the interests of most of their citizens and is therefore most likely to succeed in securing their approval. Where the focus is on individuals, true society is seen best to be achieved through securing a greater sense of responsibility on the part of individuals. Adherents of each often fault those who follow the other for their inadequate view of society.

It is interesting to watch proponents of the state or of individualism attempting to relativise each other, while supposing that their own position incorporates the possibility of a more ideal society. Hence David Jenkins, as an exponent of individualism, suggests:

> It should be noted that there is a close connection between a growing awareness of the reality of exploitation and a developing understanding of human freedom and responsibility. To be able to point to exploitation as a feature of present human societies and of the world situation as a whole we must also hold that human social reality is a social construct and not just a reflection of some ordered reality which has its divisions and relationships built in by something like divine fiat or law. Justice then shifts from being a

matter of attempting to see that everyone receives what is due according to their status and position in the ordered hierarchy, with the acceptance of vast differences between these 'dues', to a matter of concern for equality – in participation, in consumption and in enjoyment.[9]

In other words, the correct strategy for the development of true society is to undercut the features of traditional notions of the state, that is a simple causal relationship which is supposed to hold between the 'divine' act or law, the structure of human societies and the social exploitation which results from such structures. We are to relativise existing social orders as 'social constructs' and instead – as the individualist position requires – develop understanding of human freedom and responsibility. As people become more concerned for equality, a truer society arises:[10]

> Thus the pressure of God and his kingdom upon us at the present time is particularly to be seen in the rapid spread of the discovery that everybody is human and even more particularly in the rapid growth of the awareness of everybody that they too are human.[11]

It seems, however, that neither the modern view of the state nor that of the individual has a strongly developed notion of true society. A fairly common view of justice is that it has to do with 'the distribution of rights and privileges, powers and opportunities, and the command over material resources'.[12] But the definition of what is fair distribution and command is made by those who maintain control over the processes and characteristics by which people are related to each other. Their position is protected. It is therefore rather sanguine to claim that justice is actually being achieved.

It seems that states and individuals have reduced the notion of true society to what they can manage without threatening too much the interests of those in a position to control the processes by which human beings are related.

THE MARGINALISATION OF 'GOD'

We have now seen the two kinds of relativism to which modern understandings of societies seem to be subject. We first considered the movement toward simpler social structures, based respectively on the primacy of the state and that of the individual. Accompanying this we found the supposition that human beings are related only extrinsically. Secondly we saw the movement from the position in which social structures are realtivised by their obligation to contribute to true society to the more extreme relativistic position in which certain kinds of social structure are, in their own right, the proper form of social structure.

Though they are often presented and accepted as such, these movements are not theologically neutral. Historically, they have emerged alongside a marginalisation of the Christian understanding of God; it is no longer considered necessary, whether in state or church, to consider the form of society theologically. But conceptually also, they require the marginalisation of God as Christians understand him; to suppose the normalcy of these kinds of relativism undercuts the presence in human social structures of the social coherence which is embedded in God's very being and work, together with the deeper and more varied form of human relationality which that presence implies.

How is that ostensibly Christian societies and churches have marginalised God in such ways? Strangely enough, they seem to do so by revising – or domesticating – the conception of God so that he is seen to be marginal, one who is by nature disinvolved from social structures and human relationships. That is, they do so by relativising God, allowing him only extrinsic and occasional relations with social structures and human beings.

Historically, the disengagement of states and churches from their obligation to promote true society, replacing that by their own ideality, reflects the supposition that God is disengaged from the world. That is the premise of the 'natural religion' which has been widespread in the West since the eighteenth century. There God is thought only to be extrinsically related to the natural world, not defined by his relation to it any more than it is defined by its relation to him. Instead, there are processes or characteristics through which he is related to human beings, such as the natural 'infusions' of energy by which God is seen to operate in the Newtonian universe or amongst human beings. Hence his relation to them may be mediated through an historical process in which he and they are engaged, for example; this is a fairly common position for late twentieth-century theologians. Or he may be thought to be related to them, and they to him, by direct choice; this is an alternative common in theology also. But there is no intrinsic relation between God and the natural or social orders.

In this view, it is possible to satisfy religious people by maintaining the sovereignty of God, through what can be called a magical view of his operation, in which he is occasionally related to the world when it pleases him. For example, he can be seen as providing a justice which modern states cannot.

It often seems that God is pictured as doing more perfectly what the state is failing to achieve. In an age of civil disobedience he was 'the author of peace and lover of concord' who is able to give 'that peace which the world cannot give' ... Today God is thought of by many people in the North Atlantic nations as the celestial grandmother, indulgently handing out benefits and performing more satisfactorily the role which an under–financed welfare state tries vainly to fulfil.[13]

Conceptually also, modern relativistic views of society and the individual require the domestication of the Christian understanding of God. But, strikingly, this distorted form is then transferred to modern views of society and the individual.

First of all, the movement toward simpler social structures reflects an inability to comprehend the complexity of God's own life and relation with the world. This is often characteristic of the strongly monarchian view of God which prevails in the West. There, God is seen above all as absolute and simple, related in the self-same way to all his creation as its ultimate explanation. Because such a view disallows all diversity or particularity as fundamentally unreal, the complexity of nature and humanity is unintelligible. When this view is extended to social structures, what results is that simpler ones are considered preferable, and this authorises the preference for either monolithic states or those based on solitary individuals. In effect, the *monarche* of God is transferred to states and individuals.

A further result of the wish to explain everything by reference to the simplicity of God's being is the supposition that human beings are essentially alike, repetitions of God (or his will) in finitude whose destiny is to be reincorporated in an absolute unity with each other and with him. Since likeness is so strongly the norm, the manifest difference of people is puzzling, and both the complexity of their relations and the unity which might occur in this complexity are unthinkable. Human beings are too different to be intrinsically related; they can be related only extrinsically to each other and to God.

When the *monarche* of God is transferred to states and individuals, it follows, secondly, that social structures are themselves the arbiters of social coherence; they are no longer relativised by their obligation to promote an ideal true society which is beyond them. Those agencies (governmental or individual) and processes by which a society achieves or retains its unity are preferred. By contrast the complexity, pluralism and changeability of the society are regarded as alien, as aberrations. Furthermore, justice is seen as conformity, as requiring a return to the norms of the society, its identity and its enduring character. Whether in large societies or small, the transference of such a notion of God to states or individuals promotes something approximating to a totalitarian view of society or the individual.

If current understandings of social structures are as deeply interwoven with the domestication and transference of 'God' as we have suggested, a more satisfactory reconception of social structures will require a recovery of their relativity to a God who is seen himself to be relative to the world he has created and redeemed. This conception of the relation of social structures is far more consonant with Christian understanding.

THE FORM OF SOCIAL STRUCTURES AND GOD

The development of more adequate social structures is correlative with uncovering the presence and activity of God in them. That will mean turning away from the 'simple' social structures in which the conception of God's activity was domesticated and transferred, and acknowledging the diversity and change which are found in modern society as the location of the presence and activity of God. It is clear that the processes by which society structures itself are inherently non-linear and randomly variable (stochastic), that they are relatively unstable and unpredictable, and that they are too complex to make it possible to construct models adequate for dealing with all their characteristics.[14] On the other hand, they can be deal with as self-organising fields of relations, through which 'operating units' of society arise, and in terms of the energy which they require as they do so. In similar fashion, God's presence and activity in society can be discussed in terms of the fashion in which order arises through energy.

Human social life in the world appears to be a complexity of interrelated human beings, whose identity and relations change through their regular interaction. Each individual life is to some extent a self-producing and self-maintaining structure which is capable – given the energy and power – of constituting and maintaining its unity and distinctness, chiefly through structuring its components and their relations and conditioning its interactions with other lives. In so doing it orders itself by restricting changes in its structures and relations. But such lives, singularly and together, are also defined by their relations – they are internally related to others. And such relations are structured by existing forms of societal structure (formal, informal and individual). Each of these forms of social structure is in turn – given the energy with which to do so – self-constituting and maintaining through change, and for better or worse. Each is benevolent, in the sense that it promotes the possibility of moral formation for those involved, or harmful where it does not. No social structure is neutral.

If we consider God in these terms, we see him as self-structured (in accordance with his own self-determined conditions) and self-identified in a complex and dynamic unity which rests on his energy to structure and restructure himself in self-sustaining cohesion. He is in a structured dynamic relation with his world, and capable of restructuring himself and his relations with the world insofar as constructive or destructive perturbations arise in the world. Hence he is seen as an energetic unity (the Holy Spirit) which is true to its initial conditions (the Father) through ordering its interactions (the Son). But this is to be regarded not so much as a 'state of affairs' in God as an energetic faithfulness maintained in his dynamic relation to the world.

Seen in these terms, both the nature of society and of God may be uncovered without supposing that diversity/complexity and dynamics/change are alien. On the one hand, society is seen as its structured interrelations which are developed through the dynamics of its life. On the other hand, God is seen as a dynamic structured relationality in whom there is an infinite possibility of life.

If this is traced out more fully, the Trinitarian life of God may be seen to inform the structuring of social life, through it bringing about that 'unity in holiness' which marks God's own life. It also helps us to see how the self-structuring of God is to be seen as a self-structuring which occurs in an ongoing 'relation' with human life in the world. In this relation all the characteristics of the divine interact ongoingly with those of human life in the world. This 'interaction' suffuses human participation in the interaction, both as individuals and in the dynamic relationality which occurs in their social structuring. It can and does occur without their awareness, preconsciously so to speak, but it occurs to best effect when, in various ways appropriate to them, human beings interact with the Spirit through their own social structuring.

It is in the energising of his relationality that God reaches his fullness, and in this ordered relationality interacts energetically with human beings to enable them to structure their life together. In their turn they exist in a relationality whose form is derived from God: their self-relationality is also their sociality, both together being structured by the presence and activity of God ('love the Lord thy God . . . love thy neighbour as thyself'). But their relationality (self-relationality and sociality) is also given its dynamic energy from God; their moving toward themselves and towards others are energised by God. They need not attempt to 'possess' their relationships, by relativising particular forms of social structure and by domesticating the notion of God and transferring it to themselves. They need instead to rediscover their own relativity to God in their relativity to each other, and thereby find new social life from God.

References

[1] *The Church and the Bomb:* The General Synod Debate, February 1983, London 1983.

[2] Peter Baelz, 'The Ethics of Strikes in the Caring Professions'. Crucible October–December 1975.

[3] S. T. Coleridge, *Aids to Reflection*, London 1825, p. 101.

[4] Terry Eagleton, *The Ideology of the Aesthetic*, Oxford 1990, p. 77.

[5] See R. N. Adams, *Energy and Structure*, Austin 1975, p. 57.

[6] A useful analysis of the major tenets of each position is found in Dag Österberg, *Metasociology:* An Inquiry into the Origins and Validity of Social Thought, Oslo and Oxford 1988.

[7] Bruce C. Hafen, 'Law, Custom and Mediating Structures: The Family as a Community of Memory' in R. J. Neuhaus, ed., *Law and the Ordering of our Life Together*, Grand Rapids 1989, p. 103.

[8] Terry Eagleton, *The Ideology of the Aesthetic*, Oxford 1990, p. 373.

[9] David Jenkins, *The Contradiction of Christianity*, London 1976, p. 71.

[10] This individualist view frequently sets itself up against a view which it calls traditional, while failing to realise that such a position is by no means normal now. To be sure, examples of the 'traditional' view are still found in places where absolutist states still survive; the view which prevails in the Western nations, however, is not such a 'traditional' one, but rather one which suggests that states have an obligation to develop for the betterment of their citizens. The main problem arises from those who sustain the 'givenness' of their relatively privileged position, by their ability to maintain control over the processes or characteristics by which they are related to others. They may do this either by maintaining such control in a 'betterment-orientated' state or through an individualist position. Both have proved relatively defenceless against the manoeuvres of those who are bent on protecting their position.

[11] ibid., p. 117.

[12] Brian Barry, *A Treatise on Social Justice*, London 1989, Vol. I, p. 292.

[13] David Nicholls, *Deity and Domination:* Images of God and the State in the Nineteenth and Twentieth Centuries, London 1989, p. 30.

[14] cf. R. N. Adams, *The Eighth Day*, Austin 1988, p. 4.

MORAL DEMANDS AND MEDICAL PRACTICE

Michael Langford

1. INTRODUCTION. THE RELEVANCE OF LIBERAL ANGLICANISM FOR MEDICAL PRACTICE

For a number of reasons the practice of medicine is under a new kind of scrutiny, not only within the health care professions, but within society as a whole. One reason is the emergence of a whole range of medical techniques, each of which forces us to ask: 'Ought we to make use of this technique?'; and (if we decide that we should use it and if resources are limited): 'How should we balance the competing claims of other valuable techniques or of competing patients?' It is likely that among the other reasons for the new scrutiny of medicine is a change in the attitude of many doctors towards the nature of their profession. For example, fewer doctors than in the past regard their profession as a 'vocation'; for more it is a career, primarily undertaken for the satisfactions and rewards that it is likely to bring. This is evidenced not only through the explicit statements of many doctors, but by a change in public attitudes towards them.

In the context of the contemporary debate on medical practice, and bearing in mind the overall theme of this collection of essays, I want to begin by asking what insights the tradition of liberal Anglicanism might contribute to the current debates on the nature and function of medicine. If this essay stood on its own I would have to preface the discussion with a statement of what I mean by 'liberal Anglicanism', but in the context of the collection of essays gathered in this volume I think that the term is sufficiently clear. Also, I shall offer a brief reflection on the nature of liberal Anglicanism when I come to refer to Sir William Osler.

It is important to see that the contribution of liberal Anglicanism to medical practice might be of at least three different kinds. First, it might relate to the specific content of Medical Ethics in that it could help to show that certain particular answers to some of the moral dilemmas that arise in medicine are right, or at least, better than others. I shall argue that this is not where we should look for the primary impact of liberal Anglicanism. Second, it might relate to the impact on the medical profession of individual, Anglican physicians. The impact here would not be in terms of the content of Medical Ethics, but on the character of the *profession* of medicine, and on the extent to which it is seen as a vocation. These things may be particularly significant when we recall that medicine is an *art* as well as a science. I shall suggest that we can find a definite contribution here. Third, it might relate to the way we should understand the nature and significance of medical practice. I shall argue that this is where liberal Christian thinking (whether or not it is Anglican) has had, and can continue to have, a significant contribution. Further, notwithstanding the generally negative response that I give in the next section to the question of specific content, I shall argue that there will be occasions when the insights that Christianity can give do have an impact on the answers that may be given to questions in Medical Ethics.

2. CHRISTIANITY AND THE *CONTENT* OF MEDICAL ETHICS

Can any specific content for Medical Ethics (or any other area of applied ethics) be derived from Christian sources? In order to respond to this question we must first distinguish two senses of the word 'derived'. In one sense a content may be derived from a particular source in that a moral insight was first expressed in that source. In a second, and much stronger sense, a content may be derived from a source in that this source is itself the reason for the content.

There is little difficulty with the first kind of derivation. Religious traditions, Christian and non-Christian, have often 'blazed a trail' for moral thinking, a trail that has been followed by all kinds of people, including those with no religious commitments. For example, Jesus' concern for the dignity and welfare of children has been one of the sources for a gradual discovery, by people of different faiths and of none, of our responsibilities to children. However, derivation in the stronger sense raises grave problems. It suggests, for example, that those who do not accept the authority of the source cannot have the moral insight. But the liberal, Christian tradition, has generally denied this conclusion, and this is a point of such importance that the reasons for the denial must be indicated.

To those who hold religious beliefs it is always tempting to derive the content of morality from the expressed will of the gods or of God. It is tempting because, once a suitable authority for the interpretation of the divine will is accepted, the content of ethics becomes knowable, and there is no need for the agonized soul-searching that characterizes much ethical reflection. However, following a seminal discussion of the issue in Plato,[1] many thinkers have realized that if we identify what is good with the will of God, then there appears to be a kind of 'arbitrariness' in the good. Moreover, it becomes trivial or vacuous to say that God is good. It is much better to say that God wills what is good *because it is good* than to say that something is good *because God wills it.*

For a number of reasons, one of which will become apparent in the last section, this is an oversimplification of the issue.[2] Nevertheless, the importance of this insight, at least as a first approximation to the truth, can be seen by observing the history of extraordinary things that have been alleged to be good on the grounds that they represented the will of God, as mediated by some prophet or some grotesque interpretation of a sacred text. The alternative is to insist that the *content* of morality is essentially the same for all human beings. This is the implication of St. Paul's condemnation of the gentiles for not obeying the moral law that is known 'by the light of nature'.[3] If such an unwritten law is to be significant it must be, at least in principle, rationally discernible. This is a central claim of the natural law tradition, a tradition that does not deny the importance of religion for morality, but that sees the primary importance of religion, not as a provider of specific content (except in the sense of 'blazing a trail'), but as a provider of significance to morality, and as a source for a grace that can help us to live in accordance with morality.

Since the time of Richard Hooker's reaffirmation of natural law,[4] the mainstream Anglican tradition has tended to see ethical issues in natural law terms. Although some thinkers on ethics who could be classed as liberal Anglicans have written from a different perspective, such as Joseph Fletcher in his *Situation Ethics,*[5] there is little doubt that they too generally share this 'secular' approach to the question of content. In most contexts, if we are arguing in favour of a certain practice, we need to give reasons of a kind that carry weight for both Christian and non-Christian.

3.   MEDICINE AS A VOCATION

Sir William Osler, in an essay on Sir Thomas Browne, describes the *Religio Medici* as 'an attempt to combine daring scepticism with humble faith'.[6] This quotation serves not only to introduce the theme of medicine as a vocation, but also to indicate what 'liberal Anglicanism' might be considered to stand for in the context of medical practice. There is a 'scepticism' that is not afraid to challenge, for example, the doctrine of the verbal inspiration of Scripture, but that is, at the same time, committed to a personal Christian faith. In the seventeenth century the Cambridge Platonist, John Smith, provides a typical example of this blend, and my contention is that within the history of the medical profession we can find a significant number of Anglican physicians who display an analogous mixture of the scepticism that makes for good science, and of faith.

A glance at the genealogy of medical practitioners in England suggests a strong connection between the clerical and medical professions until fairly recently, and hence one of the strands in the influence of the Anglican church on medicine. Further evidence comes in a recent study of medical practitioners in sixteenth-century England which refers to 'the close connections between the clerical and medical professions', and (as *one* illustration of this connection), refers to the commonly found 'priest-physician'. Some priests, it appears, studied medicine as a safeguard (in case they lost their livings), and some in order to assist their work with the sick poor.[7]

A later, and interesting example of this tradition can be illustrated by the life of the country parson, Stephen Hales (1677–1761), one of the leading scientists of his day and a pioneer in work on blood pressure (though it does not appear that he was very active as a physician). A biographer writes: 'For Hales, science was more than the avocation of a country minister: it was the natural extension of his religious life. He was a devotee of the mechanistic world view and held that the living organism was a self-regulating machine . . .'[8]

Stephen Hales exemplifies the important point that the 'secular' attitude of Anglicanism to science in general and medicine in particular, far from being in tension with faith, was an aspect of it. (Hence the combination of scientific scepticism and faith.) The more one stressed the argument from design, the more the pious mind would tend to expect the mechanical perfection of nature. Indeed, this is virtually what Hales affirms in the preface to his most famous work.[9]

Several historians have noted that the Anglican tradition has tended to see medical practice as a *secular* occupation, and to distance it, for example, from faith healing techniques, which, at least in England, were more common among the dissenting churches.[10] This secular emphasis has its negative side, notably in the risk of undervaluing the spiritual component in overall health,[11] but as the example of Stephen Hales indicates, the secularism was not the result of indifference, but of a positive philosophy about the way God characteristically works within the natural order.

If we move into the nineteenth century we still find a close personal connection between Anglicanism and secular medicine, even though the 'priest-physician' is now less common.[12] The connection can be illustrated by Sir William Osler, whom I quoted at the beginning of this section. Osler was born in a Canadian parsonage in 1849 and died in Oxford in 1919. Both as a practising physician and as an academic we find in Osler an integration of medicine and Christianity that was, I think, quite common. Osler was especially attracted to the writings of Sir Thomas Browne, whom he described as a man 'who mingled the waters of science with the oil of faith',[13] and of John Locke, on whose medical writings he wrote a long essay.[14] If we take a combination of daring scepticism and humble faith to be a hallmark of liberal Anglicanism, then both Browne and Locke can be considered part of the tradition within the field of medicine. (I do not mean to imply that non-Anglicans cannot combine daring scepticism with humble faith, but that it was especially *typical* of a particular Anglican tradition to combine these two things.[15] In the twentieth century, liberal Anglicanism, at least with respect to moral philosophy, may well have become intermingled with a more general 'liberal Christianity'.)

As already suggested, one reason why these references to individual physicians are important is because medicine is not only a science but also an art, and the nature of the art, and the way in which it is understood, is in large part the result of particular individuals who have helped to build a tradition. Congruently, a recent study of medical education refers to one 'dimension' of this education as 'the shaping of the personal and professional character of the physician'.[16] Although the continuing influence of liberal Anglicanism is probably much less marked today, the practice of medicine is what it is, in part, as a result of the contributions of physicians such as those mentioned here.

4. THE NATURE AND SIGNIFICANCE OF MEDICAL PRACTICE

If it is true that Anglicanism has tended to stress the secular nature of medicine, and if it is also true that the specific content of ethics is the same for all rational agents, then the significance of any rational, Christian tradition for medical practice might seem to be limited to three elements that emerged in the previous section. These were, first, the influence of physicians like Osler on a sense of vocation in medicine, second, the influence of such physicians on the character of medicine, especially in terms of the physician-patient relationship (and hence on the *art* of medicine), and third, a general support for the *science* of medicine because of a theological belief in the *order* of nature.

In this section, while maintaining the basic position already defended, I want to suggest that the overall way in which medical practice is perceived can be profoundly influenced by a religious perspective, and that as a result of this perspective, the way that a balance is made between conflicting values may sometimes be affected. Consequently, liberal Christian thinking may have an effect (though an indirect one) on the content of Medical Ethics.

Before I try to suggest some elements of the Christian perspective that bear upon the practice of medicine, I need to expand upon this theme of seeking a balance between competing values because it is only within this context of a 'balance' that my suggestions concerning the effects of Christian thinking can make sense.

Consider the following, realistic case of a moral dilemma in Medical Ethics. Helen is in a coma and is being kept alive by a life-support system. The attending physicians have seen Helen's living will, according to which, once in a coma, all measures to keep her alive should be withdrawn as soon as it is likely either that she will die, or that if she survive there will be considerable brain damage. However, Helen's immediate family do not want the withdrawal of the life support system. The physicians are unsure about what is the right thing to do. On the one side there is the feeling that Helen's clear request should be followed; on the other side there is the desire not to cause more pain and grief to the relatives than is necessary. In addition there are some general misgivings about withdrawal of life support systems. (At least from a psychological point of view it is easier to refuse to provide life support systems in a case that seems hopeless than it is to withdraw them once they are in place.) Finally (and this is typical of ethical dilemmas within the actual practice of medicine), the prognosis, though bleak, is not absolutely certain, and the physicians are unhappy about accepting Helen's request in these circumstances.

A purely utilitarian approach to this dilemma would be entirely concerned with the consequences of different courses of action. I do not propose to argue against this approach here, but it is clear that most ethical physicians would not be happy with it. The consequences of different actions may well be a relevant consideration, but to make them *the only* consideration tends to undervalue the physicians' concern with the *rights* of persons such as Helen. However, if, as an alternate ethical approach, we accept a pure deontological[17] principle, such as 'respect for persons', in typical cases it is still not at all clear what is the right action. In this case we have a tension between respecting the rights of Helen and respecting the rights of concerned relatives. Also, we have to ask whether we really respect Helen most by following her request when the prognosis is unsure.

Another way of describing the dilemma is to say that while there may be (and for the Christian there almost certainly are), ethical 'absolutes', the best candidates for absoluteness are very *general* principles or rules, such as 'love your neighbour'. Absolute, *specific* rules, such as 'Do not kill, period', are hard to defend. (We may note here that the book of Exodus commands the killing of witches and blasphemers,[18] so that the sixth commandment is better translated as 'Do no murder' than 'Do not kill'. But, of course, we are then back with a dilemma, for we have to decide what should count as 'murder'.)

The upshot of these points, I suggest, is that in this case there is no 'right' answer to the physicians' dilemma, but there are a number of relevant principles, such as the autonomy of Helen and the need to do no harm (either to Helen or her family), and the ethical physician attempts to strike an appropriate *balance* between these principles. This can be a thoroughly *rational* process, akin to what Aristotle says about *phronesis* (practical wisdom),[19] and an analogous example of striking such a balance is provided by the deliberations of a wise judge when weighing what sentence to give. A familiarity with the relevant facts and moral principles, experience in using the principles, and a knowledge of appropriate precedents, indicate a *range* in which a reasonable balance can be made. Outside this range a decision would be clearly wrong (so that there is an element of 'objectivity' in the judgement), but within the range there may be room for a 'creative' ethical response.

If this way of looking at ethical dilemmas in medicine is accepted, or at least, viewed sympathetically, then we have a context in which the influence of a liberal, Christian perspective can begin to be appreciated. Perhaps the most important example of the influence of a religious perspective is furnished by the doctrine of Creation. For the 'liberal' Christian (whether Anglican or not), the doctrine of creation poses no obstacle to the 'secular' study of evolution, but it may well influence the degree to which 'interference' with the natural order is thought to be appropriate.

This point needs to be made with great care, since the word 'natural' is highly ambiguous. At one extreme we can imagine a position in which what is 'given' in nature is 'natural', and as such should not be tampered with. But this would exclude all kinds of medical (or other) intervention! At the other extreme, any interference with nature that fulfils some human good is deemed legitimate. In between is a natural law view that starts with Aristotle's definition: 'the "nature" of things consists in their end or consummation . . .'[20] This approach demands that we consider the appropriateness of, say, *in vitro* fertilization, in the context of questions such as: 'What is the "end" (i.e. purpose), of sexual relations?' A Christian answer to such questions does not need to be in explicitly religious terms, and indeed it must not be if it is meant to be of influence in a debate with non-religious people, but this does not mean that it is not illuminated by religious insights. As the present Archbishop of York writes: 'There are times when Christian insight, say into the role of suffering in life, or the significance of death, may differ sharply from the received wisdom of secular society.'[21] Also, I am reminded here of Basil Mitchell's suggestion that metaethics is not entirely independent of moral judgements.[22]

Let us stay with the example of *in vitro* fertilization (IVF), and refer to a thoughtful discussion of the practice by the Anglican academic, Oliver O'Donovan.[23] It is clear that O'Donovan's doubts about the practice of IVF stem from a belief in the *creation* of the natural order by God, and a consequent hesitation about the limits of human 'making' and human techniques.[24] However, this does not prevent much of the argument from being expressed in a way that can (and I think should) have force for an agnostic. For example, it is argued that the use of IVF as an answer to infertility is a case of 'compensatory' rather than of 'curative' medicine.[25] (The latter would cure the tubal blockage, or whatever else caused the infertility.) This point is not used as part of an argument to show that IVF is necessarily wrong, but that it should have a lower priority than a 'curative' procedure in the overall context of medical care. In the same section it is stressed that childlessness is not a 'pathological' condition.[26] Later, the principal argument is summarized thus:

> ... when procreation is not bound to the relational union established by the sexual bond, it becomes a chosen 'project' of the couple rather than a natural development of their common life. Sexual relationship, correspondingly, loses the seriousness which belongs to it because of our common need for a generation of children, and degenerates into merely a form of play.[27]

I am not suggesting that these arguments prove that the practice of IVF is always and necessarily wrong (and neither does O'Donovan), but that they illustrate three things. First, the arguments might affect a decision in Medical Ethics by altering one's view of the *balance* between competing values. For example, one's doubts about IVF might lead one to fund more preventive medicine rather than another IVF clinic. Second, the arguments merit attention (not necessarily agreement) by those whose approach is purely secular. For this reason they are perfectly congruent with the natural law tradition. (For example, several negative implications for human well-being are claimed to follow from the adoption of a general policy of 'making' human beings.) Third, the source of the 'insight' that underlies the arguments is clearly a Christian faith.

In using the word 'insight' in the last sentence I may seem to be assuming too much. However, we know, from both science and philosophy, that the notion that we simply see 'reality' as purely given data is absurd. What we 'see' is necessarily coloured by our perspective. Slightly modifying the quotation from Osler, we can say that the liberal Christian perspective involves a combination of scepticism, belief in the integrity of the 'order' of nature, and faith in a creator God. Part of what it means to have faith is to believe that this perspective involves an 'insight' into the way things really are!

References

[1] *Euthyphro* 10a ff.

[2] See the discussion of this matter in Basil Mitchell, *Morality: Religious and Secular*, Oxford, 1980, ps. 146 ff. Also, from a Christian perspective, one does not want to imply that there is a metaphysical reality, corresponding to the 'good', that is 'above' God. The 'good' may well be, in some sense, identical with the nature of God, but insofar as one can separate the notion of God's *will* from his nature, then his will, far from being 'arbitrary' (as that term would normally be understood), is conditional upon the divine nature.

[3] Romans 2, 14 NEB translation.

[4] In the *Laws of the Ecclesiastical Polity*, Book I (1594), V-IX.

[5] J. F. Fletcher, *Situation Ethics; the New Morality*, Philadelphia, Westminster Press 1967.

[6] Reprinted in *The Collected Essays of Sir William Osler*, ed. J. P. McGovern and C. G. Roland, The Classics of Medicine Library, Birmingham, Alabama 1985, vol. III p. 381.

[7] M. Pelling and C. Webster, *Medical Practitioners*, p. 199, in *Health, Medicine and Mortality in the Sixteenth Century*, ed. C. Webster, CUP 1979.

[8] H. Guerlac in *Dictionary of Scientific Biography*, ed. C. C. Gillispie, Scribner's Sons, vol. VI p. 43.

[9] *Haemastaticks*, London 1733, p. XIX.

[10] See, for example, J. Barry, *Piety and the patient: Medicine and religion in eighteenth-century Bristol*, p. 147 and A. Weir, *Puritan perceptions of illness in seventeenth-century England*, ps. 56–7; both in *Patients and Practitioners*, ed. R. Porter, CUP 1985. Also, M. MacDonald, *Religion, Social Change and Psychological Healing in England, 1600–1800*, p. 119, in *The Church and Healing*, ed. W. J. Shiels, Blackwell 1982.

[11] See M. MacDonald, op. cit., ps. 102–3.

[12] Sydney Smith, 1771–1845 provides one example of a nineteenth-century 'priest-physician'. For a time he doubled as country parson and village doctor.

[13] Quoted in E. G. Reid, *The Great Physician*, OUP 1931, p. 191.

[14] Reprinted in *The Collected Essays*, (see earlier reference) vol. III ps. 186–225.

[15] Thomas Percival, author of the famous *Medical Ethics*, published in Manchester in 1803, is an example of a non-Anglican with a similar perspective.

Concerning him Edmund Pellegrino writes: 'He retained his Christian faith and successfully reconciled it with the liberty of conscience and the critical intelligence preached by the philosophes.' (Intr. to the facsimile of *Medical Ethics*, p. 15 The Classics of Medicine Library, Birmingham, Alabama 1985).

[16] D. W. Shriver Jr in *Medicine and Religion*, ed. D. W. Shriver Jr, U of Pittsburgh Press 1980, p. 14.

[17] Meaning a principle reflecting a *duty* that should be followed, regardless of the consequences.

[18] Exodus 21, 12–17; 22, 18.

[19] N. E. VI, 5 1140, Cf. I, 4 1095.

[20] Aristotle, Politics 1252b, tr. E. Barker.

[21] J. Habgood, *Confessions of a Conservative Liberal*, SPCK 1988 ps. 138–9.

[22] Basil Mitchell, op. cit. p. 99.

[23] O. O'Donovan, *Begotten or Made?*, Oxford 1984.

[24] O'Donovan p. 12.

[25] O'Donovan p. 68.

[26] See V. Love, *Childless is not less*, Minneapolis, Bethany House, 1984.

[27] O'Donovan p. 74.

NEIGHBOURLY BENEVOLENCE OR ARROGANT MANIPULATION: ON ARTIFICIALLY ASSISTED HUMAN REPRODUCTION

Ann Loades

1982 was the year in which the UK government set up a Committee of Inquiry into Human Fertilisation and Embryology, chaired by Mary Warnock. Christians are sometimes accused of lagging behind politicians in their response to matters of the most crucial kind. As it happens, in 1979 the Free Church Federal Council and the British Council of Churches had set up a working party on childlessness, 'because of a concern in the churches of England, Wales and Scotland about the ethical implications of A.I.H., A.I.D. and other medical procedures related to conception and childbearing.' Peter Baelz was then the Dean of Durham, and he acted as chairman, and collated and edited various chapters of the report which came out in 1982, entitled *Choices in Childlessness*. It remains one of the most rewarding of the documents which have been produced by church groups on the very painful and difficult matter of childlessness because it attends with care to the experiences and emotions of the childless, and to wants, needs, limits and limitations, possibilities and moral constraints, in a manner elegant and perceptive. It allows reflective moral sensitivity on the Christian tradition to address one of the most difficult issues facing us, and rightly attempts an evaluation of the technology, research, resource and power which can so easily be ignored in perplexing discussion of the moral status of the human embryo, a topic all too often pursued in isolation from consideration of a range of relevant considerations. This present essay is written after the publication of the report of the Committee chaired by Mary Warnock in 1984, and is written in greeting to Peter Baelz, but also out of a sense that women's voices have been too little heard in formal discussion of the hazards into which these new developments may precipitate them. My essay is designed to consider a cluster of issues which I think are neglected in the discussion of so-called artificial reproduction. It expresses my disquiet about the pressures upon women especially, in trying to think about these new developments, and is I think, an expression of my view that an incarnational understanding of women should both celebrate their embodiment with all its problems and difficulties, should these arise, but also offer them the strength which flourishes in celebration, and a new sense of the asceticism proper to it. As *Choices in Childlessness* comments at one point (p. 43) 'There is more than one kind of creative transcendence'.

My overall topic is artificial reproduction, or more precisely, artificially assisted reproduction. Strictly speaking, we do not reproduce artificially, but we can now assist human reproduction by artificial means. Assisted reproduction as such is not a recent phenomenon, but its application to human beings is relatively recent and it is connected of course primarily with the very real distress of human infertility. This is a characteristic of a species which produces a low number of offspring per pair of parents compared to many primates, and a very low number as compared with the rest of the animal world.[1] Our socio-economic pattern in this country has changed too, from the days when a significant proportion of the population remained unmarried and childless, to one in which the majority of women expect to marry and have children, with fertility now a social issue involving a higher proportion of the population.

Taking married couples as the least controversial case, it has been calculated that some 10% of married couples are infertile. Of those 10%, some 40% are infertile because the male is infertile, and about 33% are infertile because the female is infertile, with a 'don't know' label for the rest of the problem. Artificial insemination not merely from the husband but by donor (now referred to as DI rather than AID) may have resulted in at least a million children born worldwide. The practice has grown up unregulated, for perfectly understandable reasons. And given the basic presumption that a child born in a marriage will be the issue of the marriage, people have coped with DI without genetic screening, hoping that the resulting child will not need a reliable medical history. Most people have to manage without that anyway; and it is arguable that anonymity and secrecy play down the emotional stress involved. The donor is not of course taking responsibility for his offspring, but there is nothing new about that in human sexual relationships.

Even here, however, but not only here, we need to attend to the issue of 'informed consent', as Samuel Gorowotz recently argued at the 1988 Leeds conference on *Philosophical Ethics in Reproductive Medicine*.[2] He pointed out that consent in the context of human reproduction is a particular challenge since it requires, because of its subject matter, a higher degree of self-knowledge than is required in most other contexts, higher perhaps than can be achieved. Of his two examples (one being a 'surrogate mother') the second was concerned with one of the more vigorous participants in a sperm bank programme where he was a medical student:

He went to Medical School in a community that was limited in size and he was suddenly beset, some years later, by the perception that the young couples that he saw in the park, engaged, one Spring, in the sort of behaviour that young couples engage in parks in the Spring, for all he knew, might well be both of them half his. By his retrospective calculations, there were many adolescents around who were products of his entrepreneurial approach to financing his medical education. He was very upset by the thought that half-siblings, who did not know that they were half-siblings, were making sport, unaware of their genetic inheritance.[3]

They indeed needed information, as he had come to see, about their biological inheritance, to protect them, against a highly undesirable risk. So what had he consented to? What do donors of gametes consent to?

Consent apart, and thinking only as far as DI, the word 'father' can now vary in meaning. To a more limited extent, that was true even before artificially assisted human reproduction, we should note. Recall to begin with that in the traditions of many non-Christian cultures as well as Christian ones, 'paternity' has meant that the father has the primary, essential and creative role in reproduction. A child was held to originate from only one source,[4] and a very common analogy is that the man plants the seed and the woman is like a field; he impregnates, she is fertile or infertile. This fits nicely with monotheism, and the analogy that woman is to man as the created, natural world is to God. It makes some sense of polygamy, and of substitute spouses, misleadingly called 'surogate mothers', a well-known phenomenon in some parts of the ancient as well as the present world.

And in the nineteenth century legal system in England, for instance, paternity used to mean that children were 'his', so that after divorce, for instance, a woman might never see her children again.[5] What happened in the first third of the last century to make a significant modification in the meaning of the word 'father' was confirmation of what had only been suspected, that is, that the woman was also a pro-creator, in that she contributes the ovum/egg, half the genetic constitution of a child in addition to its nurture in the womb, its birth and its suckling. So modifying the meaning of 'father' is not entirely new, but what is new is changing it not only on the basis of accurate knowledge, but above all by the application of new techniques.

So now we can distinguish between three meanings of 'father', that is, between the *genetic*, the *nurturing* and the *complete* father.[6]

(1) The *genetic* father is the one who provides the sperm whether for internal or external fertilisation.

(2) The *nurturing* father is the one who helps care for the baby after the birth, assuming that is what fathers do in any meaningful sense in our cultures, given prevailing gender constructions and social and economic arrangements.

Hard-pressed professionals, including workaholic academics, know the problem. One of my former students had made a lot of money by the time he was thirty, but decided to change tack. His boss said to him, 'Why did you become a lawyer if you wanted to see your family?' Nurture is not exemplified by the provision of cash in lieu of normal presence. Nor, presumably, are crèches and nursery places solely women's responsibility, unless children are seen only as appendages of their mothers, rather than of their parents.

(3) Then there is the *complete* father, the one who combines the gentic and nurturing roles, which is presumably what many men think they do.

The really big development in artifically assisted human reproduction has come about with external fertilisation, external not merely to the man's body, which is always the case, but to the woman's body, which is new. The first so-called 'test-tube' baby was Louise Brown in 1978, her birth associated with the names not only of her genetic and nurturing parents, but with those of Robert Edwards and Patrick Steptoe, the experts who achieved her conception. Since Louise Brown, it is calculated that there have been 12,000 such babies born world wide, 1,250 as a result of treatment at Bourn Hall, and 2,000 altogether produced in the UK ('produced' is the word used by the Interim Licensing Authority).[7] What the phrase 'test-tube' refers to, rather misleadingly, is the fertilisation of sperm and egg outside the female body, *in vitro* in glass, and it may be used as a 'test fertilisation where there is unexplained infertility or mild problems of one kind or another.

Of course it makes available 'spare' embryos for a number of other purposes – and we might note here the questions, 'spare from what?' and 'available to whom?' For instance, in one major centre outside the UK, in 1983–4, 4,215 eggs were collected and 157 babies were born. By the end of 1985 there were 402 frozen embryos at this centre, of which 396 were thawed, 150 discarded and the rest were transferred to 144 women, resulting in sixteen successful pregnancies. In the UK in 1986[8] 4,687 patients (women?) underwent 7,043 IVF treatment cycles, resulting in 605 live births, less than 0.1% of live births.

Having discovered the female egg, the problem for a long time has been how to get access to it. What was needed were the right hormones to stimulate the growth of the egg or eggs over a 5–7 day period, response to the drugs monitored by chemical means and by ultrasound. Needed also were the right hormone to ensure that thirty-two hours later the eggs are ripe for removal from the woman's body; and the appropriate medical team available to carry on with the next stage of the process – and access to a theatre. Also needed was the development of laparoscopy, the introduction under anaesthetic of a light which is part of a hollow needle, inserted through the woman's abdomen into the ovary, to suck the eggs from the nest on the surface of the ovary. This has been replaced more recently by ultrasound scanning, a local anaesthetic and a probe. In assisted reproduction, next required is the right medium in which the eggs mature for five to six hours before being mixed with sperm so that fertilisation occurs. Some sixteen hours later, there can be a check for the appearance of the pronuclei, and later again for the condensation of chromosomes. When the fertilised eggs reach the four to eight cell stage after forty to sixty hours, they may be returned to the woman's body. This is the only point at which 'egg recovery' has anything to do with the woman concerned. The phrase usually refers to the initial removal of eggs *from* her body.[9]

Calculating 'success' from the point of view of a married couple, there is a 10% success rate with one embryo (and this is not likely to improve in the near future) – i.e. which implants and results in a baby carried to term and born alive; and perhaps a 35% success rate with three. And here some more problems arise, since IVF results in more multiple pregnancies: 20.6% will be twins (5–6 times higher than in ordinary pregnancies) and 3.4% will be triplets and 'higher order' pregnancies (a hundred times higher). Twins may be just manageable – triplets and beyond are arguably disastrous, as Dame Mary Donaldson, who chairs the ILA has pointed out. Assuming that they survive, they may cause extra problems for hard-pressed neo-natal services, not to mention the problem of bringing them up with little, if any community support. (The perinatal mortality for 'singletons' is 10 per thousand; for twins 60 per thousand).[10] Such a prospect has led to a practice of very doubtful legality, that of selective survival, or selective reduction, or more honestly, selective feticide, by injecting a lethal dose of potassium-chloride into the foetal heart, using an ultra sound image of the foetus as a guide. Selective reduction has to be considered in relation to section 58 of the Offences against the Person Act of 1861 and with the 1967 Abortion Act.[11] The pregnancy continues, but some (at least one) foetus has been killed. It's a serious problem, since IVF and another procedure, GIFT, produced nearly 40% of all triplets and quadruplets born in 1987.

GIFT is short for gamete interfallopian transfer, a procedure in which the eggs are collected, placed unfertilised but adjacent to sperm in a catheter, and reinserted into the Fallopian tube. This technique was developed by those who thought it was important to mimic natural functioning as closely as possible, and not surprisingly, is much more successful than IVF, with a 40% success rate – including those multiple births. The sperm may be collected by sexual intercourse for those for whom masturbation represents a problem of conscience, using a condom minus spermicide, obviously, and in a clinic financed by the Roman Catholic church, using a perforated condom, to allow for the possibility that fertilisation might occur naturally. So far as I know, this is the only use for a perforated condom that even theologians have been able to dream up. A variant on this procedure is Low Tubal Ovum Transfer for women with blocked Fallopian tubes.

So what can the word 'mother' mean, apart from 'the one who give birth'? There are seven possible meanings,[12] beginning with the one that recalls the discovery of the nineteenth century.

(1) The *genetic* mother – the one who produces and matures the egg.

(2) The *carrying* mother – the one in whose uterus the embryo implants and develops, and who gives birth to the baby.

(3) The *nurturing* mother – the one who cares for the baby after birth. If nurture is an important aspect of mothering/fathering, rather than genetics, then prospective parents could seek mutuality in adopting babies if they were available. That would depend upon social, political and economic policies which do not exist, affecting the provision of adequate maternity grants, support for those who are single and pregnant, improvements in the way in which women give birth, and in the handling of adoption choices.

(4) The *genetic-carrying* mother is the one who supplies the egg and the uterus, but who does not care for the child after birth, one version of the surrogate spouse in other words. We do not like the phrase because it suggests a 'marital' relationship which does not exist, but if we continue to say 'surrogate mother', who is surrogate for whom?

(5) The *genetic-nurturing* mother is the one who produced the egg and will care for the baby after birth, but who does not carry the pregnancy. There was a case reported in *The Times* on 1 March 1990, accompanied by a photograph of an embryologist and one of a pair of enchanting twins, whose birth-mother was a 'stand-in' for a woman who had ovaries but no uterus. The babies were conceived by IVF from the genetic parents, and handed over to them at birth, but the genetic parents have to adopt them to have legal rights to them.

(6) The *carrying-nurturing* mother is the one who carries the pregnancy and cares for the baby after birth, but who does not supply the egg.

(7) Finally, there is the *complete* mother, with whom we are most familiar, the one who individually combines all three roles, genetic, carrying and nurturing.

These are the possibilities, and it is all too obvious that the women involved must necessarily bear the brunt of the impact of the new techniques and technologies. This begins for the infertile with the humiliation and stress of acknowledging the problems faced by a couple who want a child. Producing a sperm sample to order may be difficult and embarrassing for a man, but hardly compares, I suggest, with a hystosalpingogramme (hsg) X-ray – a radio-opaque dye inserted into uterus and Fallopian tubes – which *may* be painless, or acutely uncomfortable. There is little chance of knowing which in advance. Egg recovery involves an invasive technique of some kind, and there may be an even higher degree of medical control of the pregnancy and birth than is usually the case, with extensive monitoring of the pregnancy. Yet pregnancy, whatever its possible complications, is not a disease, any more than is infertility. A higher proportion of the resulting children may, especially in the USA, be delivered by Caesarian section, of which the USA has a much higher rate than elsewhere. As an American surgeon recently commented, 'If you can avoid surgical techniques, you basically make the process a lot more palatable to patients and less expensive.' He was referring to GIFT by fine catheter, without surgery, but the general point applies. And for 'patients' read 'women' and for 'palatable' read 'freer of pain' or even 'painless', cash limits aside.

But cash matters, inevitably, and there are cost, class and race issues to attend to here, in thinking about the users/consumers of the new technologies.[13] Treatment may cost between £1,000 and £2,000 – two cycles, one might say, adds up to the price of a decent car – but not everyone can afford a decent car. In Australia, the cost will run to some $A40,500 per baby for a couple,[14] added on to the $A17m from the federal budget. This item in the budget added up to $A30m in 1988, a year in which $A10.1m had been allocated to the national AIDS campaign, and $A32.9m for the whole of the national community health programme. In the USA the cost involved is not likely to be less than $50,000. These costs are the costs to each couple, including the *un*successful ones – the 85–90% who will need to negotiate their lack of success to move on with their lives. What are the implications of the American cost, for example, in a society where *existing* children now form the poorest age group[15] – more poor children in the USA than at any time since 1965. What are the implications for the UK, given the recent public acknowledgement that there is not the 'trickle down' of wealth from rich to poor which was supposed in part to justify recent economic policy?[16]

And what are the likely implications of remarks in the Explanatory and Financial Memorandum of the Human Fertilisation and Embryology Bill, where under the heading 'Financial effects of the Bill' it is said that the balance of the costs associated with setting up the Human Fertilisation and Embryology Authority 'will be met by fees charged to licence holders'? And under 'Effects of the Bill on Public Service Manpower' it is added that 'No significant effect on National Health Service manpower is expected'. Waiting lists at some NHS clinics are already four years long. An estimate for treating 275,000 infertile couples has been calculated at some £7 billion.

Of course, no one can dispute the joy of the couple whose child is recompense for all they have gone through. As one father said (reported in *The Sunday Times* of 21 May 1989) 'We have fourteen childless years and this was our last hope. The strain of waiting was appalling. But David is everything we could have hoped for. If we had ordered him made-to-measure, he couldn't have been better.' Apart from the concerns I have already expressed, there are a lot of problems to be thought through here, one of which is indicated by the question, 'Why do people have to have their "own" children?' – granted that people on the whole do not want to adopt or foster half-grown, half-socialised children, who may in any case be the wrong sex, or colour, or who are not 'perfect', whatever that means in societies obsessed with performance indicators and quality control. The answers to this question are astonishingly variable, and still include the male need to transmit 'his' own lineage or whatever. Even Baroness Warnock seems to be convinced to judge from remarks attributed to her in the press during the Easter vacation of 1990: 'Hereditary peers should be allowed selective in-vitro fertilisation for male heirs to continue family lines.'

And if sex-linked inherited diseases can be prevented by determining the sex of an embryo before implantation; and destroying the 'affected' ones, why not opt for sex-selected babies? That in some contexts may already be happening. There is a report from the USA of a couple with several existing boys hiring a 'surrogate' in the hope of having a girl. When twins were born, one boy and one girl, they took the girl into their family, putting the boy in an institution, from which he was mercifully rescued by his birth-mother.[17]

We may indeed be operating with a very mixed bag of motives here, only one of which for women may be the problem of achieving an acceptable identity, as Susie Orbach remarks of women's attempts to change their bodies as they enter a society 'in which they are told that not only is their role specifically delineated' but that success in that role relates in large part to the physical image they can create and project.'[18] She made this remark in connection with her discussion of anorexia nervosa. Another example might be the phenomenon of breast enlargement.[19] In a newspaper report about the possibility that since silicone gel causes cancer in laboratory animals, it might, also in women's bodies, we could attend also to the remarks attributed to some of the 'medics' involved. A nurse for a plastic surgeon is quoted as saying, 'Breasts are "in" again . . . the fitness craze slowed us down, but now . . . breast augmentation is on the increase.' A plastic surgeon is reported as saying that 'We live in a breast oriented society', in his interests presumably, since in the USA the cost is between $3,000 and $4,000 at present, and an estimated two million women have had these implants since they first became available more than twenty years ago. The director of a 'modelling' agency is quoted as saying that a lot of 'models' are doing it, 'And the surprising thing is that they are doing it so young. I'm seeing 16, 17 and 18 year olds having it done.' And according to one writer, 'the "ideal" breasts women want don't typically come naturally.' If a women had thought that she could control her body by workouts and diet, then she discovers that the 'ideal' body of her dreams is now different. 'And what's needed to reach that ideal can't be done by women alone.' Whose dreams and ideals? In whose interests? Breast enlargement has nothing to do with nurturing a child who may die without breast feeding, but it has everything to do with making oneself acceptable. The analogy, like most analogies, is problematic, but the basic problem of achieving one's identity remains, and how we understand infertility, and the 'remedies' we propose for it, manifests our preoccupation with 'acceptability'.

Leaving all those problems on side, however, let me turn at this point to the questions of what we think the techniques to alleviate the distress of infertility have to do with what have been thought to be the purpose of medicine,[20] – such as, healing the sick, intervening to repair a system not working properly, or restoring it to its proper state. This is done by administering medication or treatment or by intervening surgically or technically. That would cover GIFT and giving hormones to correct non-ovulation, and unblocking Fallopian tubes occluded by infection. Medicine in those ways may well be deemed to treat infertility as a malfunction of a biological process or of an organic system. It seems to be of a different order of interference if a woman receives a zygote made up from donor egg and donor sperm by either IVF or GIFT. She remains infertile, and donor gametes are not exactly analogous to say, insulin, or even a donated kidney.

We might want to say that medicine is not required to resolve childlessness, though social policies may be, unless there is to be an insistence on one's 'own' child. And even where medicine may overcome childlessness by its techniques, is infertility, childlessness, the sort of accidental contingency that we ought to try to remedy medically? It's a hard question to face. Appeal to the 'right' to have children, as in the Declaration of Human Rights, functions primarily in a negative way, that is to say, it is the right not to be forcibly sterilised, or to have one's children aborted because they are the 'wrong' race or sex, or because there are 'too many' children already. No one may prohibit one's efforts to have a child, or to interfere with those efforts, but having the capacity to try does not mean that we, or our representatives in medicine, have to do *everything* to secure the conception and birth of a child to a particular couple.

So this is one of the points where we need to back off, and if so, why? On the one hand, nature left to its own less than enchanting devices presents too many problems for us not to welcome many of the technological and scientific developments from which we may all benefit, so why not welcome the discovery of medical, rather than social means, to help the childless? (not pursuing for the moment more than a very rough and ready distinction between 'medicine' and 'society'). Yet on the other hand, as one theologican wrote in connection with genetic manipulation some twenty years ago, it may be important to learn again the renunciation characteristic of maturity.[21] How vital it is, he wrote, for humanity to develop resistance to the fascination of novel possibilities, those things with which one can *not* have a preliminary run through in order to gain experience for the next occasion and become wise through trial and error. We can no longer think we are the kind of beings who can do the sort of mischief which does not matter very much.

The unease he expresses could be said to be reflected in a publication three years ago by the Vatican Congregation for the Doctrine of the Faith's 'Instruction on respect for human life in its origin and on the dignity of procreation' of 22 February 1987.[22] It received wide publicity and is explicitly mentioned in the Council of Europe Legal Affairs document on *Human Artificial Procreation* of 1989 which noted also, the work of the Parliamentary Assembly of the Council of Europe Recommendation 1046 (1986) on 'the use of human embryos and foetuses for diagnostic, therapeutic, scientific, industrial and commercial purposes.'[23] It is precisely because many of us may disagree with some of the positions and arguments of the Instruction that a particular feature of it has not received the attention I nonetheless think it deserves, that is, the demand it makes for us to try to evaluate our technology.

At this point, it is worth attending to an extended quotation from the Instruction:

> Science and technology are valuable resources for man when placed at his service and when they promote his integral development for the benefit of all; but they cannot of themselves show the meaning of existence and of human progress. Being ordered to man, who initiates and develops them, they draw from the person and his moral values the indications of their purpose and the awareness of their limits.
>
> It would on the one hand be illusory to claim that scientific research and its applications are morally neutral; on the other hand one cannot derive criteria for guidance from mere technical efficiency, from research's possible usefulness to some at the expense of others, or, worse still, from prevailing ideologies. Thus science and technology require for their own intrinsic meaning an unconditional respect for the fundamental criteria of the moral law: That is to say, they must be at the service of the human person, of his inalienable rights and his true and integral good according to the design and will of God.[24]

The Instruction reminds us that no one, simply by virtue of scientific competence, may decide on people's origin and destiny. 'This norm must be applied in a particular way in the field of sexuality and procreation, in which man and woman actualize the fundamental values of love and life.' The document of course is predictably exasperating (like Durham University documents) in its incapacity, except occasionally, to use inclusive language, and it would be too much to expect that its authors would understand how a feminist critique of the new procedures might lend strength to their case. Women worth their salt in any case have no interest in substituting one form of paternalism for another, any more than in allying themselves simplistically with the gender constructions of the Christian churches. But we can appreciate, I believe, why it is that this aspect of the Instruction has been virtually ignored, since the new technologies to do with artificially assisted human reproduction have been associated with medical therapy, with much publicity being given to the cases of successful treatment, that is, to the newborn children and their properly delighted parents, the lucky 10–15%.

To have children of one's own is still a powerful religious and cultural value, and freedom to exercise one's reproductive rights are centrally important values. Even in very litigious societies such as the USA, those who work in medicine have enjoyed much freedom of professional action, because we trust that they want to benefit patients. And 'progress', and 'turning one's back on progress' is powerful rhetoric. That apart, we must certainly also reckon with the genuine goodwill of those who will agree with Professor Bob Williamson, as reported in *The Times*, 7 December 1989: 'Our objective is to permit families who want it to have a prenatal diagnosis as early and humanely as is possible, and to permit families who continue a pregnancy to term and have an affected child to get the best treatment.' Once one sees IVF/GIFT as a possibility for couples known to be at high risk of having a child with Duchenne's muscular dystrophy or cystic fibrosis, then we might think that we should simply organise the most sane balance of advantages we can.

So are we to argue for 'neighbourly benevolence' on the grounds that these technologies enhance the natural course of marital life, as we might say that bottle feeding enhances suckling and Caesarean section aids birth and saves lives in the cases where it is actually necessary?[25] Or do we need a form of radical resistance to 'arrogant manipulation' here-as for instance, represented by the organisation whose literature I have so far neither obtained or read, the Feminist International Network of Resistance to Reproductive and Genetic Engineering? The writers of the Instruction are rightly in my view concerned with the point that societies can and do authorise the direct suppression of the innocent.[26] They urge conscientious objection to 'morally unacceptable civil laws' and of passive resistance to the legitimisation of 'practices contrary to human life and dignity'.

Whatever we think of that recommendation, it is surely right to think that 'recourse to the conscience of each individual and to the self-regulation of researchers cannot be sufficient for ensuring respect for person rights and public order', for we have plenty of evidence in our own century as to why that point is of central importance.

The bogy here is *not* the 'mad' scientist or Frankenstein, as Michael Banner has properly reminded us.[27] It is rather our own blindness to the possibility that what will be taken to be part of mainstream medicine may exhibit a lack of moral foundation. Those who work in medicine are no less vulnerable than the rest of us to the subtle undermining of conscience, fudging our way along with euphemisms, and under the pressure of impossible expectations. As disquiet grows, so inflated claims for the benefits may grow too. On the other hand, as Helen Oppenheimer remarks, 'In the decisions we have to make we cannot always be on the safe side, even when we are sure which the safe side would be.'[28]

So let me conclude by quoting from the work of the author of the phrases 'neighbourly benevolence' and 'arrogant manipulation', a Roman Catholic moral theologian, Professor Jack Mahoney, critical in his response to the Vatican Instruction. He comes down on the side of 'neighbourly benevolence' and what he recommends as 'the enterprising and inventive nature of human interpersonal love seeking ways in which to express itself'.[29] Yet also, at the 1988 Leeds conference he suggested that *if* religion can take a positive attitude to human enterprise and ingenuity in its remedying of human deficiencies, such as infertility and the incapacity to reproduce, 'it can also locate the phenomenon of infertility in a wider context and de-absolutise it'.

> By providing a religious context of ultimate trust in a loving creator, it can remove the psychological burden of considering that fertility and having a child are a human and social absolute which must be achieved at all costs, or that infertility is somehow a stigma or a reproach. It can offer the satisfaction of the parental urge through acceptance and through its channelling into the service of others. And it can place a radical question mark against the idea of individuals, whether women or men, somehow possessing a natural, or God-given 'right' to have a child.

Religion apart, at the least it seems to me that people need to find the inner freedom to back off from some of the pressures upon them, and which they may internalise. And that inner freedom might well find its expression in the affirmation of a fully achieved adult sexuality which is *not* construed primarily as a means to the propagation of the species. That in itself might do as much as anything else I can think of to cheer up large numbers of people.

I am grateful to audiences at the College of Wooster, Wooster, Ohio; York and Durham Universities; Shotley Bridge Hospital and the Cambridge Medical Forum; and the members of the Anglo-Scandinavian Theological conference at Visby, Sweden, in 1989 – all for their comments on versions of this lecture. I am specially grateful to Dr Jill Robson for her help, though remaining errors are of course mine.

References

[1] J. B. Stewart, 'Surrogacy from a genetical point of view,' *University of Leeds Review* 32 (1989–90) 168–73, p. 168.

[2] S. Gorovitz 'Informed consent', in D. R. Bromham, M. E. Dalton and J. C. Jackson, eds., *Philosophical Ethics in Reproductive Medicine: proceedings of the first international conference on philosophical ethics in reproductive medicine,* University of Leeds, 18–22 April 1988, Manchester: Manchester UP, 1990, pp. 228–35.

[3] Gorovitz, p. 233.

[4] C. Delaney, 'The meaning of paternity and the Virgin Birth debate', *Man* 21:3 (1986) 454–513.

[5] See, for instance, M. Forster, *Significant Sisters,* Harmondsworth: Penguin, 1984, p. 16.

[6] T. A. Shannon, *Surrogate Motherhood: the ethics of using human beings,* New York: Crossroad, 1988, p. 80.

[7] *IVF Research in the UK: a report on research licensed by the Interim Licensing Authority (ILA) for human in vitro fertilisation and ebryology 1985–89,* November 1989, p. 4.

[8] *Institute of Medical Ethics Bulletin* 38 (May 1988) 4.

[9] J. Murphy, 'Egg farming and women's future' in R. Arditti, Dr D. Klein and S. Minden, eds., *Test-Tube Women: what future for motherhood?* London: Pandora, 1984, pp. 68–76, p. 70.

[10] *IME Bulletin* as in note 8; and 50 (May 1989) 3–4.

[11] *IME Bulletin* 35 (February 1988) 10. See also the article by W. Varley, 'A process of elimination', *Guardian,* Tuesday, 28 November 1989, p. 38 which recounts some of the experiences of women who have had selective feticide.

[12] Shannon, p. 80 as note 6.

[13] T. A. Shannon and L. S. Cahill, *Religion and Artifical Reproduction: an inquiry into the Vatican 'Instruction on respect for human life',* New York: Crossroad, 1988, pp. 99–101.

[14] *IME Bulletin* 38 (May 1988) 5.

[15] National Conference of Catholic Bishops, *Economic Justice for All: pastoral letter on Catholic social teaching and the US economy,* Washington: United States Catholic Conference, 1986, p. 87.

[16] *The Observer,* Sunday, 8 April 1990; 'Revised figures show that the incomes of the poorest 10% rose at only half the rate of the whole population, not double, as previously thought'.

[17] J. B. Stewart as note 1, p. 171.

[18] S. Orbach, *Hunger Strike,* London: Faber 1986, p. 104.

[19] Des Moines, *Sunday Register,* 29 January 1989, p. 3E.

[20] Shannon, p. 84.

[21] K. Rahner, *Theological Investigations* IX: Writings of 1965–67 trans. G. Harrison, London: Darton, Longman & Todd, 1977, on 'The experiment with man' and 'The problem of genetic manipulation'.

[22] Reprinted in Shannon and Cahill, pp. 140–74.

[23] Council of Europe, *Human Artificial Procreation,* Strasbourg: Council of Europe, 1989, p. 6. See also *IME Bulletin* 51 (June 1989) 13–17 on the Council of Europe Recommendation 1100 (1989) on the use of human embryos and foetuses in scientific research.

[24] Shannon and Cahill, p. 143.

[25] Shannon and Cahill, p. 125, quoting J. Burtchaell C.S.C. of the University of Notre Dame.

[26] See *IME Bulletin* 49 (February 1989) 'Contemporary lessons from Nazi medicine', pp. 13–20.

[27] M. Banner, 'The medical profession and the corruption of conscience', *Cambridge Gazette* (forthcoming).

[28] H. Oppenheimer, 'Handling life: does God forbid? in G. R. Dunstan and E. A. Shinebourne, *Doctors' Decisions: ethical conflicts in medical practice.* Oxford: Oxford UP, 1989, pp. 205–12, p. 210.

[29] J. Mahoney, 'Religion and Assisted Conception', pp. 94–104 of *Philosophical Ethics* as in note 2 above, p. 91 30 Mahoney, p. 88.

WEALTH IN THE JUDAEO-CHRISTIAN TRADITION

Jack Mahoney

Throughout the centuries many Christians have regularly felt moral disquiet in their lives occasioned by the uncompromising teaching of Jesus about wealth and about the incompatibility between possessing riches and either being his disciple or, indeed, gaining entry into the kingdom of God. In this essay I propose to examine early Christian teaching on the subject of wealth against the background of the Old Testament teaching, and then apply my findings to some contemporary aspects of wealth.

OLD TESTAMENT THEOLOGIES OF WEALTH

If we examine what the Old Testament has to teach on the subject of wealth it quickly becomes apparent that there are several strands to that teaching. In the period of the patriarchs, for example, the attitude to an abundance of possessions of various kinds was a positive one of thanksgiving for the gifts of a generous God. Riches were regarded as earthly blessings and as signs of special favour on the part of God. This is characteristically the attitude to wealth of a pastoral semi-nomadic people composed mostly of small cattle breeders, whose social unit was the family clan. In such a social setting survival was assured by such tribal values as solidarity and equality among its members, and a particular care for its weaker members, who were often the widows and orphans resulting from tribal warfare. In such a culture the accumulation of possessions was valued above all as affording the individual opportunities to extend hospitality and generosity to others. And where such wealth existed it was considered a great blessing from God.

With the entry of the Israelites into the land of Canaan and their encounter with the indigenous culture, however, we find the beginnings of a new stratification in their social composition. As Léon Epsztein describes the transition, 'whereas among the nomads, pastures and

169

springs belonged in an indivisible way to the whole community, when the Israelites became farmers and settled down, the more skilful, as a result of the growing security, were able to consolidate their gains and increase their lands. These economic changes were accompanied by social changes: the principle of equality among the members of the clan disappeared and the differences began to be more marked'.[1]

It was in this increasingly urban culture that there developed the abuses of wealth and power against which the prophets of Israel were to mount such sustained and vehement opposition, and it was within this context that the contrasting attitude of deep suspicion towards wealth developed in Jewish thought. The preaching of the prophets from Amos to Jeremiah and Ezekiel was clear and uncompromising on the subject of social morality. Continually recalling Israel to the Covenant which a generous Jahweh had struck with his new people in the desert, they not only preached single-minded fidelity to the God of Abraham, Isaac and Jacob; they also tirelessly called for brotherly love and social justice under God as inherent to the demands of the covenant. Deuteronomy 8:17–18 sums up the role of riches in Israel. 'Beware lest you say in your heart, "My power and the might of my hand have gotten me this wealth." You shall remember the Lord your God, for it is he who gives you power to get wealth, that he may confirm his covenant which he swore to your fathers, to this day.' As Thomas E. Schmidt explains, 'the wealthy man who keeps God's commandments must give God the credit for his wealth. Wealthy men who do not attend to the conditions of God's covenant – either by neglecting the justice imperative or by refusing to recognise God's sovereignty over wealth – invoke the criticism common to the prophetic and wisdom literature'.[2]

It is interesting to note an element of nostalgia in much of the prophetic writing in recalling and commending the nomadic ideal, and in this may be discerned what Raphael called 'a defence, a reaction against the political and social achievements of the time in the name of the covenant made in the desert'.[3] At the same time there was nothing romantic about the social abuses against which they campaigned: oppression and exploitation of the socially vulnerable in terms of unfair working conditions and remuneration, debts, extortion, imprisonment and slavery for inability to pay, confiscations and other forms of exploitation; and all this underpinned and compounded by corruption in the administration of local justice by the rich and powerful. It was not without justification that a modern writer entitled his book on the Jewish prophets *The Conscience of the Nation*.[4] It was not, however, that the prophetic tradition in Israel was hostile to riches as such. The great social problem of their day, on which they fixed with prophetic single-mindedness, was more that of a serious imbalance in the distribution of goods, and the gross abuses which were resorted to by the rich in order to increase their wealth and in their luxurious use of it.

Alongside the prophetic tradition in Israel, and to some extent succeeding to it, can also be identified the wisdom school of writers, who, in this as in other areas of human behaviour, took a more measured approach to the subject.[5] This is well expressed by Robert Koch, who writes of how 'the teachers of wisdom speak from a rich experience of life of the gain, the advantages, and also the dangers of riches'.[6] Thus, numerous passages teach how riches can be gained honestly by diligence, ability and prudent administration; and how they carry great advantages, such as friends, honour, peace, security and the possibility for helping the needy. But these are balanced by other regular warnings of the serious moral dangers which can be incurred by the pursuit or the possession of wealth, including pride, false security, restlessness, and various forms of injustice. In this way the earlier idea of riches as a blessing of God was still retained, but at the same time this raised a theological problem which was to 'cause the teachers of wisdom the greatest difficulty'. If abundance of material possessions was a special sign of divine favour, how was one to reconcile the apparent material success of those who were irreligious; and similarly, and perhaps more poignantly, what sense could be made of the unhappiness and deep poverty suffered by the great many ordinary people in society who were devout?

Various solutions were attempted to explain the apparent disparity between being god-fearing and being materially well-off. One, which was later to assume prominence in part of the New Testament tradition, was that God would redress the balance or turn the tables, and that at least death was the great leveller of all inequalities. Another, which attempted to raise consideration above the material level, was to identify other values which were more important than those which come with riches; values such as health, freedom, happiness, good name, wisdom, and lack of worries. These too were gifts of God and they indicated that poverty was not necessarily a manifestation of God's displeasure. On the contrary, in fact, the equation began to develop that the poor, who could rely only upon God, became identified as the devout of Israel, while the rich, who had their own apparent sources of strength, became identified with the godless. Thus the idea of the 'poor' which had originally had a purely economic connotation began to take on the religious dimension of being specially cherished and protected by God and of being humbly dedicated to his will and his providence. Devotion to God, or 'fear of the Lord', was more precious than all riches could possibly be.

In a parallel development regarding the rich, the rampant perpetration of social injustice is seen as the expression of greed for wealth, and the conclusion is arrived at, not that the wealthy are necessarily unjust, but that detachment from wealth needs to be cultivated in various ways. This comes primarily through the recognition of what Schmidt calls an 'ethical hierarchy which places reliance on God and the justice imperative above acquisition of property and money'. Thus is formed regarding wealth 'a Jewish tradition that forms the primary ideological backdrop to the New Testament material'.[7]

WEALTH IN THE NEW TESTAMENT

The study of Thomas Schmidt to which I have referred already is a doctoral thesis entitled *Hostility to Wealth in the Synoptic Gospels*, published in 1987, in which the author aims to do two things: to understand the hostile attitudes to wealth to be found in the Gospels of Matthew, Mark and Luke; and also to prove that this evangelical attitude has theological roots and is not simply the reflection of socio-economic resentment among the circles from which the Gospels emerged. His conclusion is that in the Synoptic Gospels (there is no reference to wealth in the Fourth Gospel) there are to be found strong elements of hostility to wealth along with some elements of what he calls a more positive 'evaluation of wealth'.

In the course of his research Schmidt scrutinises the celebrated Gospel passages which are critical of riches, including the way in which, in the parable of the Sower, 'delight in riches' are among the thorns which strangle the growing seed of God's word (Mk 4:19); how the rich young ruler was advised to sell his many possessions and give to the poor and follow Jesus (Mk 10:17–31); the injunctions of Jesus in the Sermon on the Mount on not laying up treasures on earth and on the impossibility of serving both God and Mammon (Mt 6:19–24); the parable of the Rich Fool who died just as he was planning to build larger barns for his harvests; and the 'foolish complacency' of the rich man Dives in his luxurious opulence (Lk 16:14–31). The most forthright passage which sums up the attitude to riches ascribed to Jesus is to be found in his reflections following on the crestfallen withdrawal of the rich young ruler. 'How hard it will be for those who have riches to enter the kingdom of God . . . It is easier for a camel to go through the eye of a needle than for a rich man to enter the kingdom of God.' And when his disciples asked in astonishment, who then could be saved, his reply was that 'with men it is impossible, but not with God; for all things are possible with God (Mk 10:23–27). On which Schmidt comments, 'only God is able to overcome the power of possessions'.[8] As, indeed, we may see Jesus himself doing in inviting himself into the house of Zacchaeus. For here we have a divine initiative which resulted in that 'rich' chief tax collector dramatically announcing that he was giving half of his possessions to the poor and in addition making fourfold restitution to anyone whom he might have defrauded (Lk 19:1–8; 18:27).

The fact that Jesus' reaction on that occasion was to proclaim that 'Today salvation has come to this house' (Lk 19:9) seems to indicate that in Luke he settles for something less than total renunciation of riches on the part of those who accept him. Of course, to pursue this line of introducing qualifications and distinctions into what appears to be the clear Gospel message of hostility to riches can incur the charges of attempting, not to explain it, but to explain it away, and of blunting the sharp cutting edge of Jesus' teaching. And yet in the gospels, as elsewhere in the New Testament – and as we have seen also in the Old Testament – there are both explicit and implicit indications of an accompanying realisation of the value of wealth. It must, for instance, have taken considerable resources for the 'many' women who are described as travelling with Jesus and the Twelve on their missionary journeys to provide for them all 'out of their means', as Luke observes (Lk 8:3). And in general it could only be out of one's private means that one could engage in the almsgiving which is commended in the Sermon on the Mount (Mt 6:2–4).

These are the sort of at least *prima facie* qualifications on the Gospel teaching on wealth which lead one to enquire further precisely why it is that there is so strong an apparent hostility towards it in early Christian teaching. In the Old Testament, as we have seen, the hostility to wealth arose from the injustices which appeared to be an almost inevitable accompaniment to it. In the New Testament as a whole, however, this motive of social justice is almost non-existent. It is generally agreed, in fact, that the New Testament is strikingly lacking in any teaching on social issues, and various reasons are proposed to explain the silence. If the early Church believed that the end of the present world was imminent, there was no point in trying to change its structures in the short time remaining to it. Moreover, in its early years this new small sect of 'christians' was hard put to it to survive on the periphery of the Roman Empire, without any ambitious plans to influence or change its institutions, even if it was so minded, as most notoriously in the question of slavery.

Against such a foreshortened and restricted background it is not, then, surprising that the major misgivings expressed about riches in the Gospel were not social but personal. What is perhaps more interesting is that Jesus made no reference in his teaching to the Old Testament theme that riches were to be seen as a sign of special divine favour to individuals. What he did do forcibly, however, was to warn his hearers that riches were perishable and not to be relied upon, and that one should not set one's heart on them (Mt 6:19–21). As Schmidt expresses it, 'For Luke, as for Mark and Matthew, the evil of wealth consists not primarily in lack of care for the poor but in independence from God'.[9] In Luke's listing of the series of congratulations which we know as the beatitudes there is a contrasting list of comminations, which passes the dismissive verdict on the rich that they have received their consolation (Lk 6:24). In other words, they already have in their wealth all the consolation they are going to get, since 'their wealth keeps them from dependence on God: instead of hoping for his kingdom [like the poor], they are mistakenly secure in their earthly reward'.[10] As Koch also concludes, 'The Christ of the synoptic gospels does not reject riches as such, but only the *evil use* to which they are put, because of the immense dangers which they carry with them'.[11] They prevent what he further calls 'interior emancipation' in the cares which they bring in their wake, they lead to injustice, they are ephemeral idols, but above all they dispose their possessor to a sense of self-sufficiency in life which is alien to the Gospel message of total dependence on our heavenly Father and on his loving providence.

This too, of course, is the central message on wealth in the rest of the New Testament writings. Perhaps the most famous sentence on the subject is to be found in the assertion of the *First Letter to Timothy*, that 'the love of money is the root of all evils' (1 Tim 6:10), which the Jerome Biblical Commentary observes was a 'maxim current among non-Christian writers at the time'.[12] The *Letter of James*, with its sustained diatribe against the rich, unusually, for the New Testament (though cf 1 Jn 3:17), castigates them on social grounds for oppressing people and dragging them into court (Jas 2:6–7).[13] But it also makes the point that they are in personal peril when they boast of planning a business trip in order to increase profits without adding 'if the Lord wills' (4:13–16). The teaching of *First Timothy* and *James*, moreover, is not one of inveighing against the possession of riches as such, but against the destructive practices to which they lead. After all, the letter which we know best for singling out the love of money as the root of all evils (which one commentator describes as a most unPauline sentiment)[14] proceeds within a few verses to instruct the rich on how they are properly to make use of their wealth. There are the standard warnings to 'the rich in this world' not to be proud, nor to set their hopes on uncertain riches but on God who richly furnishes us with everything to enjoy. But these references to the religious dangers of wealth are followed by more positive instructions on its social application: 'they are to do good, to be rich in good deeds, liberal and generous, thus laying up for themselves a good foundation for the future, so that they may take hold of the life which is life indeed' (1 Tim 6:17–19).

If this conclusion appears somewhat bland, that there is nothing wrong with being rich but only with abusing one's position or becoming too immersed in one's possessions, it can, however, be sharpened by the question of Schmidt, 'the question is whether one can *possess* mammon without *serving* it'.[15] And perhaps so long as one remains at the level of the personal implications of possessing riches the most desirable programme is to dispense with them as much as possible. If, however, one adverts to the social dimension of the issue, and goes beyond the avoidance of injustice to consider the positive help of the needy, then the possession of wealth, for all its personal risks, might be not just tolerated but considered positively. This appears to have been the central thinking on the subject by the early Christian theologians whom we know as the Church Fathers.

WEALTH IN THE CHURCH FATHERS

In his study of the social teaching of the Fathers of the Church Peter C. Phan provides an impressive list, including the Cappadocian Fathers in the East and Ambrose and Augustine in the West, as united in finding in the possession of wealth the two elements which we have already considered as the social aspect and the religious aspect. As he writes, they 'denounce the love of money, the luxurious lifestyle of the rich, the lack of concern for the poor'.[16] On the religious aspect, for example, John Chrysostom observes, 'You are the captive and slave of your money; you are tied by the chains and bonds of avarice, and you whom Christ has already freed are bound anew'. And others were to preach the need for personal interior detachment from one's possessions, as did Clement of Alexandria in his monograph, *What Rich Man will be Saved?* For him the solution lay in adopting the Matthaen beatitude, 'Blessed are the poor in spirit' (Mt 5:3) not in the sense of embracing literal poverty but of being spiritually detached from what riches one might possess. More positively, however, Clement viewed riches as an instrument for producing human fellowship and sharing, or for the purpose, literally, of philanthropy, that is, love of human beings. But he and others were all too aware of the way in which they could be abused, particularly in commerce and the greedy pursuit of profit, and above all in the charging of interest on loans.

The social function of wealth was one of the reasons which lay behind the positive patristic attitude towards private property, although they did not so much defend this as a social institution, as take it for granted. A number of them viewed it as a result of the Fall and the state of sin into which this plunged the human race, as Gardner explains in his *Biblical Faith and Social Ethics*.[17] And it introduced inequalities into society.

Nevertheless, all of them viewed property as having a social function and not just as personal possessions. Human beings were only stewards of God in their possessions, and as God had created the earth and its fullness for all his human creatures, property owners were to imitate God's own beneficence and generosity in the way in which they administered his property. Hence the constant message of the Church Fathers to the rich to come to the aid of the poor and the needy by sharing one's own, or rather God's, goods with them, and by seeing in them the Christ who identified himself with all those in distress (Mt 25:31–46).

MODERN CHRISTIAN SOCIAL JUSTICE

In his study of social justice in the Bible Epsztein observes of the stress placed on this aspect of wealth by the Hebrew prophets that perhaps with the exception of the church fathers, the thirst for justice does not occupy the same place in Christianity, and does not attain the same degree of intensity, as it does in the prophets.[18] I find this a strange statement in a book written as late as 1983, given what Edward Norman has written about *The Victorian Christian Socialists,* 'and their contribution to what Frederick Denison Maurice, their greatest thinker, called the "humanising" of society'.[19] Not only did that movement for social and class reform influence the American Social Gospel movement; it also stimulated at home the powerful and growing Anglican current of social concern which ran through William Temple to the present flourishing of its regular pronouncements on the state of society. I find Epsztein's comment equally strange in view of the parallel current of regular papal teaching on social issues starting from the ills resulting from the Industrial Revolution in Europe and broadening in recent years to include statements of the Second Vatican Council and also of various hierarchies throughout the Roman Catholic Church.

There is in all such teaching, as in that of other Christian bodies, particularly in the last twenty years, a new and prophetic concern for the state of society, for the moral responsibilities which are ineluctably attached to the possession of wealth, and particularly for those daily increasing millions who suffer the human degradation of poverty and unfulfilled basic human needs. The range and the scale of the challenges which these pose for Christians are unprecedented in their religious history, and are increasing daily. How are professing Christians to make a contribution to solving such challenges? In writing about the attitude of the Church Fathers to social issues, including the old and new questions raised by wealth and poverty, Phan concluded that 'their fidelity to God's word was not a mechanical repetition of formulas but a creative and dynamic reinterpretation of the scriptural message in the experience of new situations and a critical judgement of these in the light of Scripture'.[20] In that spirit I wish now to offer some reflections on three contemporary issues about which Christians are, or ought to be, concerned: the idea of Christian consumer power; the Christian challenge not just to distribute wealth, but actively to create it; and the possibility of economic growth in a society which is becoming increasingly, and rightly, concerned at the exploitation and state of our planet.

The delicate decisions which individuals have from time to time to make with regard to what wealth they may possess cannot, of course, be read off from the Gospel. Perhaps today we might make more of considering how best positively and as a professing Christian to exercise one's responsibilities in the use of one's wealth, in addition to giving a part or a proportion of it to the needy and to charities. The sovereignty of the consumer, for example, which many providers of goods and services consider the key to success in business, can be exercised in the discerning purchases which individuals make. Campaigns which have mobilised purchasing power in this way can have an appreciable effect in improving the ethical behaviour of business firms and companies. On a larger scale the ethical investment movement, strong in the United States and beginning to flex its muscles in this country, witnesses to a socially responsible use of wealth in the choosing of companies in which to invest. Some do so by avoiding putting their savings into companies or products of which they morally disapprove. Others, however, take a more constructive line by investing in companies which they consider stand in need of improvement, with a view to influencing their policy if this is considered practicable. The most positive expression of ethical investment, however, is in the use of capital to support and promote business activities of which one wholeheartedly approves. Today this is increasingly most evident in the growing support for environmentally sound and ecologically sensitive products and services, but it can obviously apply to other goods and services.

A further aspect of the ethics of wealth which this positive approach serves to highlight is the neglected responsibilities of share-ownership in general, especially on the part of large institutional investors. In the national debates surrounding company mergers and takeovers in recent years, for example, the interests and stakes in a company which were held by many more men and women than its share-holders were occasionally to be found expressed. The prevailing view adopted or implied, however, was that business companies are no more than collections of impersonal assets. Little concern was systematically directed in the free market for companies towards their work force and other so called 'human resources', or towards the consequences for the local and regional communities, and the networks of small businesses, which are heavily dependent on any company's fortunes.

WEALTH CREATION

These are various contemporary ways in which the Judaeo-Christian tradition on the social responsibility of wealth can find expression today, whether on the part of individuals or of like-minded groups. And they raise for consideration the second area of application which I have suggested, that of the creation of wealth, and of one's attitude to it. If riches are inherently bad, then the fewer there are in existence the better. We have seen, however, that this is not characteristic of the tradition we are examining. It is poverty which is inherently bad, because it is a diminishment of the human spirit and of the image of God in man. And the Judaeo-Christian mandate, while it is aware of the spiritual interpretation and the religious significance which can be given to poverty, is to eliminate it wherever possible.

For most Christian writers, at least, the preferred modern way of eradicating poverty in modern society is through the proper distribution or redistribution of wealth. And in this they have strong warrant in the Jewish and Christian traditions of almsgiving and of philanthropy. How much society as a whole should ensure an equitable distribution of wealth through taxation and welfare as a matter of social justice rather than by appeals to 'good citizenship' is matter for strong debate. What appears to be lacking in the Christian contribution to a theology of wealth, however, is a theology not just of its distribution but of its creation. The mediaeval maxim put it well when it said *nemo dat quod non habet;* you can't give what you haven't got.

But it appears that we cannot look to the Judaeo-Christian tradition for a theology of wealth creation in any detail. The Old Testament viewed all wealth when it came as coming from God; while the New Testament, as we have seen, was not particularly concerned with such long-range social issues. As a result, I dare to say, it is easier for modern Christians to call on the prophetic traditions to mount attacks on the existing disparities of income and wealth in society than to get down to the more difficult, but more constructive, task of developing an acceptable theology of how to create wealth by adding value to the earth's resources for the benefit of all its inhabitants.

There is a further complication, in that where a theology of wealth creation is proposed in Western society it tends to emanate from right-wing economic and political quarters. As such, it often reads like a defence of economic and political positions which are already espoused for good reasons, but which are perceived as in need of theological defence against radical Christians who are opposed in varying measure to capitalist economic and political structures. Good theology, however, is rarely done from a defensive position, or indeed from any adversarial position. What are at issue here are the fundamental ethical questions about both the motivation and the conditions of business activities in contemporary society; that is, to what degree self-interest is equated with greed, as it need not at all be; and whether human competition is to be viewed as the negation of human equality, as it need not be either.[21]

GREEN ECONOMIC GROWTH

Finally, however, reference to a Christian theology of the creation of wealth in addition to, and as distinct from, the distribution of wealth inevitably today raises questions of whether this can be compatible with the environmental issues and concerns which are daily increasing at local, regional and global levels. In particular, it raises for consideration whether economic growth is compatible with such environmental and ecological concern. In the eyes of some environmentalists Christianity does not fare well in terms of an environmental audit. The Judaeo-Christian tradition persistently refused to ascribe divinity to the natural world and to purely natural forces, and indeed the charge made to Adam by his Creator was to 'fill the earth and subdue it; and have dominion over . . . every living thing that moves upon the earth' (Gen 1:28). Given this, it is not too difficult to see how an attitude of hostility and of imperialism towards nature could find some justification, if such were needed, for the sorry scars which Christians among others in history have inflicted upon God's material creation. If that has been the situation in the past, however, it is now well on the process of change through the growing realisation and recovery of the idea that 'the earth is the Lord's and all its fullness' (Ps 24:1), and that we creatures of a generation or two are at most stewards or leaseholders rather than owners.

The question to be considered, then, is the one put by *The Economist* in a recent survey, 'Can growth be clean and green, or is it inevitably harmful?' (2 Sept 89). One element of an answer is that if growth is not to be environmentally harmful it must be much more considered, rejecting short-term returns and accepting that it is not just standard of living but over all quality of life which is at stake. In other words, green growth, or environmentally 'sustainable' growth, must be slow growth, and must include strategies of conservation and of reparation of the environment. In this connection it will be interesting to note the fate of the 'Valdez Principles' which have been developed recently in the wake of the *Exxon Valdez* oilspill in Alaska as a voluntary code of business conduct for the environment, modelled upon the comparatively successful introduction in the 1970s of the 'Sullivan Principles' governing trade with South Africa.

Perhaps, however, the most intractable factor in developing economic growth which is environmentally friendly is the need to cut back on consumption, especially of energy, both by savings and by developing less wasteful and less waste-producing alternative sources of energy. At the level of consumption in general, more might be made of the conclusion of the American Jesuit theologian, Richard McCormick, that 'the contemporary asceticism must be ecological restraint'.[22] In terms of efficiency, however, if alternative cleaner and safer energy can be achieved by recycling waste products to enlist biomass energy and produce bio-fuels, then disposal and creation are conveniently dealt with simultaneously. If the forces of the winds and the waters can also be harnessed as a substitution for non-renewable fossil fuels and their waste products, then the attendant inconveniences or even visual blemishes or minor eco-disturbances would in principle be more than offset. All human living is, after all, a disturbance of the natural status quo and an attempt to strike environmental balances. And there are even founded hopes of success in developing nuclear fusion sources of energy which would not create the hazardous problems of nuclear waste resulting from the current process of nuclear fission.

In considering the equation between growth and the environment it is useful to note, as *The Times* pointed out recently (8.11.89), that 'some of the worst pollution problems now facing the globe are the product of the inefficient, *non-growth* non-market economies of Communist Eastern Europe'. Likewise, when the present Minister for the Environment was Minister for Overseas Development he was at pains to point out that environmental damage is a result of affluence in the northern hemisphere but by contrast it is the result of poverty in the southern hemisphere *(The Times* 1.3.89). The destruction of rain forests with greenhouse consequences is associated with the desperate attempts of backward peoples to get to the first rung on the growth ladder by selling timber and by draining and clearing land for the production of cash crops *(The Times* 8.11.89). And if the affluent north is to upbraid southern countries for their short-sighted and wasteful inefficiency in attempting to catch up and to provide the north with its products, then the north easily lays itself open to the charge that its environmental conscience is a comparatively recent growth, and that it has plentiful wealth to be in a position now to afford such scruples. In terms of the social use of wealth which we have been considering within the Christian tradition, the conclusion appears clear. Not only is the rich north morally obliged to devote some part of its wealth to enabling undeveloped and Third World countries to attain to a higher level of human dignity for all their inhabitants. In the area of environmentally sustainable growth it is equally obliged to set examples, in terms of research and development, of how this can be done, and to be generous in exporting the technology which will enable the south to do likewise, to its and our mutual benefit.

CONCLUSION

There are no doubt other contemporary issues which raise for Christians urgent or nagging questions about their attitude towards the abundance of possessions. Underlying the Judaeo-Christian tradition as a whole it is clear that wealth is seen as a creature of God and is as such good. It is not at all clear, however, from the New Testament at least, that the possession or acquiring of wealth is a sign of special divine favour. Far less is it the case, however, that by contrast poverty as such is a state which is to be valued for itself and in its own right. What is clear throughout the tradition is that the possession of wealth can lead to an inflated sense of security and of self-sufficiency, which ill accords with our status as creatures and sons and daughters totally dependent on the providence and love of our heavenly Father. Perhaps in this regard the ultimate word may be given to *First Timothy* whom we have seen both castigate the love of money and instruct the rich how to behave: 'everything created by God is good, and nothing is to be rejected if it is received with thanksgiving; for then it is consecrated by the word of God and prayer' (1 Tim 4:4–5).

In addition, however, to humble gratitude to God for what we may receive from his bounty, we have also seen that wealth has a social function. This function, and the power which attends it, can be abused by the inflicting of injustices on one's fellows. The grosser manifestations of such abuse of wealth and power were rightly the target of the prophets of ancient Israel, as they are today of their modern counterparts. But wealth has also a positive social function in God's purpose, and perhaps the stress on this today would prove more suitable to the climate and needs of the times as well as being more socially constructive. It is in this spirit that I have been considering the positive aspects of ethical investing and share-ownership, the need to be concerned not just for the distribution of wealth throughout society but also for the creation of wealth within society, and the ways of harmonising such growth with respect for the world of God's other creatures and of future human generations. And perhaps this positive aspect and these applications of the Judaeo-Christian tradition on wealth can be summed up in the verse of the prophet Micah which is ever ancient, yet ever new. 'He has showed you, O man, what is good; and what does the Lord require of you but to do justice, and to love kindness, and to walk humbly with your God?' (Mic 6:8).

References

[1] Léon Epsztein, *Social Justice in the Ancient Near East and the People of the Bible,* SCM 1986, 60.

[2] Thomas E. Schmidt, *Hostility to Wealth in the Synoptic Gospels,* Journal for the Study of the New Testament, Supplement 15, Sheffield 1987, 54.

[3] Quoted Epsztein, 59.

[4] R. E. Clements, *The Conscience of the Nation,* Oxford 1967.

[5] Cf. J. Mahoney, *The Ways of Wisdom,* Inaugural Lecture, King's College, London 1987.

[6] R. Koch, 'Riches', in J. B. Bauer, ed., *Encyclopaedia of Biblical Theology,* Sheed & Ward 1970, 776.

[7] Schmidt, 60.

[8] Schmidt, 114.

[9] Schmidt, 136.

[10] Schmidt, 142.

[11] Koch, 777.

[12] *The Jerome Biblical Commentary,* Chapman 1968, 356.

[13] Cf. P. U. Maynard-Reid, *Poverty and Wealth in James,* Orbis 1987.

[14] A. T. Hanson, *The Pastoral Letters,* Cambridge 1966, 68.

[15] Schmidt, 126.

[16] Peter C. Phan, *Social Thought, Message of the Fathers of the Church,* vol. 20, Glazier, Wilmington, Del. 1984, 37.

[17] E. C. Gardner, *Biblical Faith and Social Ethics,* Harper & Row 1960, 286–7.

[18] Epsztein, 103.

[19] Edward Norman, *The Victorian Christian Socialists,* Cambridge 1987, 1.

[20] Phan, 43.

[21] Cf. J. Mahoney, *Business and Ethics: Oil and Water?* Gresham College London 1988.

[22] R. McCormick, 'Towards an Ethics of Ecology', *Theological Studies* 32 (1971), 102.

CHURCH AND MINISTRY

AN INTEGRATING
THEOLOGY IN
THEOLOGICAL EDUCATION

William Jacob

The 1980's saw some very important developments in theological education in the English churches. After a period of twenty years or so during which all the English churches had pursued a policy of linking their colleges and seminaries more closely with university theology faculties and departments and other degree awarding bodies, questions were raised about the nature of the relation between theology taught at a university and theology taught in a theological college or seminary or on a theological course.[1] Whilst recognising that the resources of university theology faculties and departments will continue to be vitally important for the life of the Church, it was also suggested that there were good reasons why the Church should strengthen its own centres of theological education. Not merely the reduction in funds for publicly financed educational institutions but also the increasing tendency for Christian theology to be seen as only one aspect of the study of the Christian religion and the Christian religion to be seen as only one aspect of the study of the religious experience and practice of human beings must raise questions about whether departments of theology and religious studies can provide what is needed by someone preparing for a specifically Christian ministry.

Peter Baelz saw the essential difference in approach to the study of theology in a university as compared to a theological college in the following terms. Whereas in a university the study of theology should be critical and detached, the student approaching his subject sympathetically but, as it were from the outside, as something to be examined, weighed and assessed in a quasi judicial manner and without direct involvement, in a theological college, or seminary or course the student's approach, while still critical and to that extent detached, should also be self motivating and engaged. In ordination training the theology which is being studied should be a theology which becomes the student's own. He goes on to describe such theology as one which a student must learn to inhabit, rather than to remain outside of. It must become a student's own, 'worn' like comfortable clothes rather than left to hang up unused in the student's intellectual wardrobe. The difference between the study of theology in a theological college, seminary or theological course is thus the difference between critical awareness and understanding which is an end in itself and a critical awareness and understanding which is the servant of Christian discipleship and ministry in the Church.

Having established the goal of theological education as education for Christian ministry, Peter Baelz went on to develop the idea of an integrating theology appropriate to the context. He sees this as a theology that both affirms a unified and unifying activity of God in both creation and redemption and focuses on the representative function of the ordained ministry within the ministry of the whole Church, symbolising the ministry of Christ in his Church. It should be a theology earthed and contextualised in the world as it is and not a set of formulae learned by rote at some purely abstract and formal level. He goes on to suggest that one of the functions of theology is, through the articulation of the vision of God's presence in the world, to enable the minister to illuminate the diverse facts of life. To do this, he points out, the minister needs a sense of the wholeness of the Christian tradition, whereas conventionally the study of theology is divided into separate disciplines and appears to have little relevance to the practical work of the minister in the church. It is in response to this that the idea of an integrating theology is developed. It is intended not only to hold together the different disciplines into which the study of theology is divided, but also to draw together into a certain creative unity understanding and response.

From this it was suggested that the function of an 'integrating theology' is not only to give unity to the syllabus of theological studies but it must also provide criteria for determining priorities in that syllabus. It must give it a coherent and manageable shape.

Subsequently the Advisory Council for the Church's Ministry through its Committee for Theological Education, which Peter Baelz then chaired, published a report advocating that ministerial training must attempt to integrate the intellectual, spiritual, moral and practical in a way that is appropriate for the different types of people who offer themselves for the Church's ministry.[2] This report developed the concept of 'an integratory theology appropriate to the context' in terms of ministerial education and emphasised the need to develop an explicit rationale for such education. This was seen as involving three issues: what ordained ministry does the Church of England require; what is the shape of the educational programme best suited for equipping people to exercise this ministry; and what are the appropriate means of assessing suitability for ordination to exercise this ministry? The answers to these questions would provide an integrating frame of reference for the study of theology and preparation for ordination in the Church. Such an integrating approach to the study of theology, it was argued, would be formative for students, enabling them to inquire for the truth, seeking thereby to know the God who presents himself in truth and to learn to maintain the truth with critical rigour and appropriate freedom. The acceptance of this approach to education for ministry by the Church of England's House of Bishops is profoundly changing the nature of that Church's institutions of ministerial education. No longer are they able to rely on the models of university theology faculties and department's syllabuses; they now have the freedom and responsibility, under the supervision of ACCM, to develop their own syllabuses, and processes of assessment. The effect of this is to generate a new enthusiasm and responsibility amongst the theological educators.

The implications of an integrating theology however, raise further and more complex issues. For example, thought must be given to integration between educational methods and the nature and content of the subject being explored[3] and to methods of relating theological study to human experience and the experience of ministry in the Church.[4] This is necessary to ensure that there is not incongruity between the subject matter and the way in which it is taught and the subject matter and the student's own experience or the nature of the task upon which he or she will subsequently be engaged.[4] A further area which requires integration with the study of theology in preparation for ordination is the nature of the institution in which the study takes place, and where theological formation develops. The remainder of this essay will be primarily concerned with a consideration of these institutions as a matrix for developing an integrating theology.

Since the early 1960's almost parallel with the churches' policy of linking their colleges and courses more closely with the universities, in most of the Church of England's theological colleges there seems to have been a tendency to pay less attention to the context of study and more attention to the content and especially the academic level and quality of study. This is in marked contrast to the classic formulation of the rationales for Church of England theological colleges.

At least since the 1870's the element of 'residence' has been seen to be an essential ingredient in ministerial formation by all the English churches. Even when part-time courses for training candidates for ordination began to be established in the 1960's considerable emphasis was placed on periods of residence at weekends and summer schools during which a common life of prayer, study and socialising was emphasised. Both the Evangelical and the high church traditions in the

Church of England have placed high value on this element of residence. The high church rationale was most influentially stated by H. P. Liddon when he was vice principal of Cuddesdon. He argued that the work of a theological college should be as much concerned with moulding character as with teaching truth. He saw the college's duty to be to set a student seriously on thinking about 'the great questions of life and death' but before this could be done a student must dedicate himself to cultivate the 'great features of moral character' beginning with 'practical self discipline'. In addition, he believed that a college must attempt the systematic cultivation of piety. He insisted that devotion must be taught and 'recommended upon system'. At a theological college as he saw it men made preparation for two indispensable features of every real ministerial life, first some kind of systematic meditating upon Christian faith, second by daily use of morning and evening prayer.

Liddon believed that the whole ministerial life needed to be ordered by rule and that time spent at a theological college was the ideal time for establishing a 'system' for life. Not merely study but prayer, meditation, exercise, sleep, recreation, should, as far as possible, be ordered by rule. He saw Christian life as a 'matter of rule, of rule that is the expression of love, of rule which sets us free . . . a house which has a religious purpose should be a house of rule, it should be governed by system', so that men would come to understand that life is given to them to 'be disposed of and laid out from first to last under the eye of Christ our Lord'. The method was to enable clergy to live in the world without being part of it, by taking them out of the world to develop a spiritual, religious and moral consciousness so that they could influence and improve it.[5]

In the Evangelical tradition the rationale for residence during training was based on the idea of family life. The model of life at Ridley Hall in Cambridge was the family. Evening prayer at 9.45 p.m. each day was attended by the Principal's household and by the servants who lived on the premises. The aim was to make the occasion a model for simple and reverent family worship.[6] In 1952 at St. John's College, Durham, the Bishops' Inspectors commented on the sense of a large family created by the Principal and the 'family approach to problems.' This was seen as a way for the College to get 'the best out of a man that was in him' and as a healthy corrective in an ordinands training to any tendency to 'conceive a parish in organizational instead of family terms'.[7]

Although the rationale and the models were different, in all the Church of England's theological colleges during the first two thirds of this century the context of training was seen to be as important, or probably more important than the content. Community life was seen as important for testing and stretching men under pressure. If they were broken by this there would be time and scope for treatment or for withdrawal, to avoid least damage to the individual and the Church.[8] For this to be successfully achieved, it was thought that colleges needed to be detached and isolated, especially from the universities. There was general agreement that 'The best theological college is one in which the Chapel, the lecture room and the common room are all working together to make a fellowship of Christian life both natural and supernatural, the power of which shall remain in the memory of the ordinand as a pattern and inspiration for his future work in a congregation'.[9]

Residence was seen as of the essence of ministerial formation in the Church of England. Emphasis was placed on withdrawal into small-scale religious communities in which habits of self discipline, prayer and study were to be inculcated by means of an ordered, disciplined life under the direction and supervision of a senior clergyman assisted usually by recent and exemplary products of the institution. The discipline, order and close-knit common life would mould and shape people for ministry.

From the early 1960's this approach to training came under increasing pressure from a number of causes. From 1963 there was a dramatic and sudden decline in the number of ordination candidates. This provoked a review of the provision of training places available in the college and resulted in the adoption by the Bishops of a policy requiring closure and amalgamation of colleges which both tried to associate them with universities and to increase the numbers of students in those surviving to between seventy and 100 students. This, by both reducing the isolation of colleges and increasing their size, reduced the traditional close personal supervision by a principal.

The decline in the number of candidates has been greatest in the 21–25 age range with the result that an increasing proportion of people training were aged 25 and over and likely to be married. When married students were the exception rather than the majority, it was customary to require them to live apart from their wives in colleges. The numbers of married candidates, the pressure on colleges to compete for students, and changing attitudes to marriage made this no longer acceptable, with the result that, in many colleges, men were encouraged to move their families to the vicinity and to be 'day boys'. This contributed very largely to the collapse of the former 'common life' which had been regarded as such an important matrix for the formation and testing and stretching of people in preparation for ordination and which reflected a very clearly integrated theological rationale of ministry to which the study of theology was itself subservient.

Changing social attitudes since the 1960's have reduced the general acceptability of semi-monastic discipline even for candidates in the 21 to 25 age range. Social life and church life have became more relaxed and people are less willing unquestioningly to accept the authority and direction which was a pre-requisite of the traditional system.

At the same time there has also been pressure to improve the academic and educational standards of theological colleges and to widen the curriculum to include some element of social studies and practical work. This has reduced further the isolation of the colleges and has introduced a more critical element into studies and, by implication, into the attitude to the institution, as well as giving the impression that the main concern of a college is academic study. It has also introduced more academically able teaching staff, laity as well as clergy, who have not accepted the traditional roles of tutors in relation to the principal. The colleges have become more complex institutions.

The policy since the early 1970's of training women for diaconal ministry in theological colleges has also significantly contributed to changes in the nature of the colleges.

Perhaps, most important, since the early 1960's an alternative pattern of part-time training has been developed, which, superficially at least, has created an impression that the traditional emphasis on withdrawal into an isolated common life was not essential to ministerial formation. This, as has been suggested above, would be a deceptive impression.

The much greater variety of students, the adoption of more challenging and critical approaches to study both of theology and of society as well as changing styles of leadership and patterns of authority in the Church as well as in colleges contributed to the demise in most theological colleges of the former attempt at integration of life style, ministerial formation and theological study which originated with Liddon, on the one hand, and the emphasis in a paternalistic family life, on the other hand.

However, in spite of these very significant changes during the past twenty-five years, the concept of 'residence' itself has remained a very powerful idea in the training of ordination candidates in the Church of England and, in spite of much criticism of the practice, there has been a powerful and widespread conviction that it should not be allowed to wither away by default. But the experience of part-time training, as well as a small number of initiatives in theological colleges, suggest that it may still be a powerful force for managing ministerial formation.

In at least five areas of learning, it is suggested, the context of learning can be a potent integral component in training for ordination. First there is considerable potential in the traditional concept of 'a community of learning' especially if courses are only of two or three years duration. An integrating approach to theological study in preparation for ordination requires that a student should be able to do more than write essays and pass examinations. As has been noted students need to engage with the

Church's traditions so that these traditions become their own so that, in due course, they can preach and minister words of pastoral care with conviction and authority. For this to happen, for students to begin to assimilate and internalise new ideas which may seem at variance with previously held convictions, as well as begin to grasp the integration and interrelationship of the various theological disciplines and their relationship to the life and community of faith, time is required. There needs to be opportunity for informal discussion between students and with lecturers. Research evidence has shown that students believe they have learned most from those informal discussions.[10]

Second, an integrated context of training has the potential to help people to learn tolerance of each other, using a model of learning and change from psychodynamic psychology that suggests that if people are to learn how to live and work with others who are perceived as different, and perhaps therefore difficult, they need to gain insight into themselves, and try to discover what it is in themselves that makes the other so difficult to accept. Such a task requires sharp concentration on inner processes and may lead to something much deeper than 'tolerance'. It may lead to personal change, as well as to more positive attitudes to those who carry their negative projections. This process of learning however, requires more expertise than the traditional approach of simply living together and the more recent introduction in most colleges of working in groups.

Third, a context of training integrated with the content and method of study offers opportunity to explore spiritually both individually and corporately in order to give people the benefit of a sustained and ongoing engagement with God through the Spirit, which has traditionally been found necessary for the nurturing of a sturdy spirituality, a maturing in the inner life. This is especially true of the need to prepare people to pray for the world and the Church in the corporate prayer of the Church, the daily office.

Fourth, the context of training and especially a residential component gives opportunities for experiencing being the Church, of common life in Christ. Living together in close quarters with people one has not chosen, especially for periods of sufficient duration to expose the darker side of the interaction of human personalities, offers valuable raw material for reflecting on the nature of the Church and 'community' and for discovering the need for grace to sustain the common life in Christ when the ease of fellowship wears thin. The capacity to learn to live constructively within the tensions and pluralism of human interaction and to attempt to work with these is essential for a Christian minister.

Fifth, the context of training needs to provide a space and time for people, perhaps especially for mature students, to reflect on the role of minister of the Church and the implications of the role for his or her personal life or family life and their interaction with other people. People need time and space and perhaps rituals to help them to understand the nature of what they are taking on and how to live within it, and with it, and with other people, as well as to enable them to understand this experience of transition from one context or role to another, which is a key feature of human and specifically Christian experience.

A close examination of the issues surrounding the context and especially a significant residential element in theological education seems to take us closer than anything else to the heart of what it is to prepare a Christian for the exercise of ministry. In residence and in the processes involved in entering it, sustaining it, and then leaving it, there is an educational instrument for the formation of the minister and a powerful model of what it is to be a congregation, to be the Church. A fully integrating approach to theological education and ministerial formation must take this element of training as seriously as the content of study and the methods of learning. The traditional expectation has been that if people are put together in a college for ten or eleven week periods over two or three years these things would be experienced and consequently learned. This has clearly not been the case. Such learning requires very skilled design and management. In fact in very few of the colleges has there been much attempt to develop the experience of the context of learning as an educational instrument except as a means of acquiring through practice a discipline of prayer and study.

Welcome though the renewed emphasis on lay ministry is, whatever theologies of the Church and ministry are held, the role of ordained ministers, bishops, priests and deacons is crucial in the institutional life of the Church. If their role is crucial so must be their preparation for that role in terms of pre-ordination training and their continuing education. For this training to be a satisfactory preparation it must not only develop people educationally and theologically so that they have a grasp of the interactions of various strands of the theological and Christian tradition which they inhabit and begin to glimpse some of the ways in which these interact with and may help or not help to interpret the context in which the Church exists and witnesses, it must also help to form people to be able to undertake this task.

The integration of the context of the study of theology, of the development of spirituality, it is suggested, is an essential element in ministerial formation. Properly designed, managed and interpreted the context of study whether it is in a full time theological college, or a part-time theological course offers opportunities for not merely learning about theology but for learning how to take responsibility for one's own learning as well as sharing responsibility with other people for developing their learning through leading seminars, developing group projects, and planning sermons and study courses for use in practical work and placements. The context of learning further offers opportunities for exploring being the Church and for theological reflection about the variety of roles and expectations that exist within the Church. Undoubtedly, the residential elements of theological colleges and courses offer very important opportunities for reflecting on the tensions within the Church and any congregation, on the ways in which the concept of 'Christian community' may be understood and about authority and organisational structures in the life of the Church. The social context offers essential opportunities for the individual preparing for ministry to discover him or herself in relation to other people and to God, to discover her or his potential for working with other people and for a deepening relationship with God and other Christians through prayer and corporate worship.

The concept of an integrating theology offers a framework for continuing development and re-interpretation and re-evaluation of the tradition of English theological education. It will continue to have important repercussions on the life of the Church through the work of those who are now being trained and will train in the future in the institutions which are being influenced by it.

References

[1] Notably by Peter Baelz in *An Integrating Theology: ACCM Occasional Paper No. 15*, 1983, also published in *Insight*, Vol. No. 1, March 1984.

[2] *Education for the Church's Ministry: ACCM Occasional Paper No. 22*, 1987.

[3] There has been some preliminary discussion of this by Anthony Dyson in Theology and the Educational Principles in Ministerial Training: Problems of Collections Codes and Integrated Codes, *Kairos*, No. 6, 1982, pp. 4–16, and in *Experience and Authority: Issues Underlying Theology*, ACCM and the Church of England Board of Education, 1984.

[4] *Theology in Practice*, ACCM Occasional Paper No. 29, 1988.

[5] H. P. Liddon, *Clerical Life and Work*, London 1895, pp. 57–90, which use two sermons, The Life and Prospects of a Theological College, and The Moral Groundwork of Clerical Training preached at Cuddesden Festivals in 1868 and 1873 respectively.

[6] F. W. R. Bullock, *The History of Ridley Hall Cambridge Vol. 1*, Cambridge 1941, pp. 179–180.

[7] T. E. Yates, *A College Remembered: St. John's College Durham, 1909–1979*, Durham 1981, p. 45.

[8] For detailed descriptions of such patterns of training see J. R. H. Moorman, *B. K. Cunningham: A Memoir*, London 1947, Robert T. Holtby, *Eric Graham 1888–1964*, Oxford 1967, and *A History of Lincoln Theological College*, Lincoln 1974.

[9] *The Purpose and Scope of Clergy Training: An Outline of Current Practice*, Central Advisory Council for the Ministry, London 1949.

[10] Mark Hodge, *Patterns of Ministerial Training*, Advisory Council for the Church's Ministry, pp. 38–42.

THE EDUCATION OF THE CLERGY

Hugh Melinsky

From 1974 to 1985 Peter Baelz was chairman of the Committee for Theological Education, a little-known committee of the Church of England's Advisory Council for the Church's Ministry. It has the task of supervising and accrediting all ministerial training, and through its Council, of advising the House of Bishops (where final responsibility lies) and the General Synod (which has to find the means). The task is far from easy because all the theological colleges are private bodies (like the missionary societies) founded mostly in the nineteenth century either by dioceses or by party interests, or even by anti-party interests, and have never taken kindly to central control. They are self-governing and rely for capital expenditure on a 'constituency' of supporters. They, or their students, receive from central church funds only grants for fees. Since in 1988 these amounted to £4.2 million the General Synod is keen to receive value for its money. From 1921 the Bishops required every candidate to pass the General Ordination Examination or its equivalent, but that was a fairly haphazard collection of written papers, and it commanded little respect. It strains belief that from 1959 to 1964 the subject of Ethics was dropped because no examiners could be found to set and mark the papers.

The colleges have always been at the mercy of market forces somewhat alleviated by party loyalties, and a decline in the number of ordinands spelt death for several of them. In 1968 there were twenty-five colleges with 1060 ordinands (an average of forty-two students each) and also the Southwark Ordination Course; in 1974 the number had been reduced to sixteen with two part-residential courses; by 1985 there were fourteen colleges and fourteen courses with 824 ordinands in the colleges and 383 in the courses. In 1968 an Advisory Council Working Party chaired by Sir Bernard de Bunsen produced a report *Theological Colleges for Tomorrow* recommending the closure of small cathedral and suburban colleges and the amalgamation of the rest to form nine colleges in university centres for 950 students and two or three self-contained colleges like Colleges of Education for 300. The proposals met with fierce opposition and were quietly dropped, leaving a good deal of resentment behind.

A more radical attempt was undertaken by the Advisory Council in 1972 to look at alternative patterns of training. It questioned the value of residential training in relation to its length and cost, and rated educational needs more highly than financial considerations. It recommended ten regional centres throughout the country to provide full-time and part-time training with more flexibility, for lay students as well as ordinands, with a common theological foundation course for those without degrees in theology, leading on to the integration of theology with ministerial skills and knowledge. Each college would be encouraged to specialise in particular subjects or aspects of subjects and different kinds of placement, and more importance was to be given to continuing training after education. The report, published in 1975, gained wide approval both in Synod and in the House of Bishops, but it was allowed to die because the bishops had neither the heart nor the muscle for such major reorganisation.

In discussion with his Council in 1974 Peter Baelz commended the report for its realism and flexibility, and looked forward to ministers being trained for a 'comprehensive' rather than a 'grammar'-type church. He welcomed the integration of theology with professional skills, with the provisio that theology is not simply a utilitarian technique, but is concerned with questions of truth. An underlying issue is whether that truth is objective or self-involving (and to that issue he returned). He warned that academic theology might not survive in universities, and that new types of training would need a high degree of maturity in both teachers and learners. An awful warning was contained in a comment of an examiner in doctrine on one candidate's 'complete inability to expound central doctrine in terms which might be meaningful to an intelligent and educated layman'.

The Committee addressed itself, then, to fundamental questions: what should be taught?; how should it be taught?; to whom should it be taught? In 1976 it listened to an expert on modern methods of adult education, and agreed that knowledge is not merely information and that learning is not merely cerebral but affective as well as cognitive. Educators can communicate only by codes with a wide range of verbal and non-verbal symbols, and the codes must be clear.

The issue of non-stipendiary ministry was becoming more important with well over a hundred men a year being recommended in the late 1970s, and several new training courses coming to the Committee for validation. In 1975 the Council asked Mr W. H. Saumarez Smith to review the progress of this experiment since it was first authorised in 1970, and his report *An Honorary Ministry* appeared in 1977. (The name for this new kind of ministry is a thorny question, but in 1977 the Advisory Council dropped 'Auxiliary Pastoral Ministry' in favour of 'Non-stipendiary Ministry'). The first two part-time and part-residential courses set up, the Southwark Ordination Course in 1960 and the North West (later Northern) Ordination Course in 1970 were authorised for the training of stipendiary and non-stipendiary candidates side by side, specifically to avoid any implication that the latter were in some way inferior to the former. Subsequent courses, however, were authorised only for non-stipendiary candidates. The Council having debated the implications of the new report at length, recommended in 1979 that the new-style ministry should continue, that all existing and future courses should be recognised for both styles, and that the Bishops' inspectors should apply equally stringent criteria of the appropriate kind to the new courses as to the old colleges.

In order to keep its view ecumenical and worldwide the Committee invited Bishop Lesslie Newbigin to come and share his wide experience. He spoke of the third world's radical criticism of theological education, that it trained ordinands for an alien type of ministry as a professional élite in a Church allied with privilege. Our own theology, he said, is encapsulated in our culture, and more emphasis needs to be given to case-study and more weight to the social context. He saw the future pattern of ministry as local elders ordained to preside at the eucharist with professional ministers to provide support and continuing training. (This is in fact being worked out in the 'auxiliary ministry' of the United Reformed Church, but the concept is substantially different from Anglican non-stipendiary ministry). Theological education, he maintained must not be handed over to the universities because it is the basic responsibility of the Church, but it is important to create a fruitful relationship between the two.

By 1978 the word 'spirituality' was enjoying wide circulation, partly in reaction to the shallow secularism of the previous twenty years, and partly under the influence of the widespread quest for spiritual satisfaction in eastern religions. The Committee proposed a seminar, and in 1980 some sixty staff and students from colleges and courses met to consider the matter, assisted by nine papers circulated beforehand. These were published the next year as ACCM Occasional Paper No. 9, *Spirituality in Ordination Training.*

Peter Baelz wrote a lengthy introduction, 'What is spirituality?' He referred to the desire to integrate theological and practical, individual and social, of which the new examinable subject of Pastoral Studies was symptomatic. Self-knowledge and an understanding of relationships are vital for ministry, and human relationships with God are the fundamental context. That is spirituality. But is it proper for a Church committee to pry into so private an area? Yes, because though private, there is a rich communal tradition in the Church. At a time when many are looking eastwards it is appropriate for us to look at our own tradition, and the fact that it contains diverse strands is a strength: we need to think in terms of polarities rather than opposites.

All men, he says, are spiritual beings, whether believers or no. They have an area where they are free for transcendence with new possibilities at the centre of their being where they can make a total response with will, intellect, and feelings. Life in the spirit involves love of self (a proper love), love of God, and love of neighbour, producing a growth into wholeness. Since God's nature is love and his gift the world of becoming, he is himself involved in the process of becoming: in some sense he needs us. He is at the centre of the Christian's spiritual life, and we search for him only because he has searched for us first. He has put an ultimate restlessness into our hearts, and he keeps us in being even when he seems absent.

Self-love is important because life in the spirit is a redirecting of the will and all other human elements in a total response where good desires may have to be sacrificed for better. Sin is not to be ignored but grace precedes sin and is not its consequence. The Christian gospel is not simply a remedy for sin; it is good news of God's continuing creative and redemptive work in his world. Christian spirituality requires a detachment from self so that we may be centred on God in order to have a healthy relationship to the world which God loves.

Imagination is important because life in the spirit is nourished through the great images of faith, visual and verbal. It may be that imagination is prior to intellect. Intellect is certainly needed to assess and order images.

In short, we need to look for a spirituality which is natural rather than contrived, gift rather than achievement; the task of becoming what through faith and baptism we are.

Here Peter Baelz draws freely on a long and rich tradition firmly Nicene in basis, from the Cappadocian fathers and Augustine, through Martin Luther and Joseph Butler to F. D. Maurice and the Process theologians, as well as Herbert Farmer, John Oman and Charles Raven. It is a notable piece of integration.

It is not surprising that during 1981 and 1982 discussion in the Committee circled around the theme of integration, how to hold together diverse understandings of priesthood and ministry, diverse patterns of belief and practice in the New Testament and early Church, the diversity of the ecumenical scene and of world faiths. This led, by necessity, to theological reflection of a fundamental and far-reaching kind. In particular it was concerned with the development of 'an approach to theological education which would hold together in a creative relationship the formation of a person's own ministerial formation and character, the acquisition of an appropriate and serviceable knowledge of the living Christian tradition, and an understanding of the forces operating in contemporary culture at the individual and at the social level'. The quotation comes from ACCM Occasional Paper No. 15 of 1983 *An Integrating Theology*, written by Peter Baelz to set out the direction of the Committee's thinking.

The old pattern of training, he comments, was for an academically able candidate to read for a theological degree at university and then to proceed to a theological college to 'complete' his preparation in vocational subjects like the study of Church and Sacraments, Worship and Prayer, Preaching and Pastoralia. There were complications. Not all candidates were graduates and so theological colleges had to teach the whole range of theology, and some critics of 'academic theology' maintained that candidates at university would do better to widen their horizons by reading another subject. At a time when university departments of theology are being cut back or widened in scope to include 'religious studies', the church's own resources in its colleges and courses need strengthening. What, then, is the relationship between the 'academic' approach of a university and the 'practical' approach of a theological college?

It might be claimed that a university is concerned with truth, a college with orthodoxy, the former impartial, the latter committed, the former objective, the latter subjective. In fact there can be no hard and fast disjunction between pure objectivity and pure subjectivity. The difference is, rather, that a university student has to be critical and detached whereas the college student should be critical but engaged: the latter has to 'inhabit' or 'wear' his theology in his ministry whereas the former can remain outside it.

Ministry is inevitably concerned with communication, but the methods of communication reflect different understandings of the way in which God has communicated with man. If God has given humanity a set of propositional truths and moral laws, then the minister becomes a teacher of divine truth. If, however, God has given man a vision and spirit of divine life, then the truths and the laws are the outcome of human attempts to appropriate this living truth: thus the process of communication becomes a mutual conversation through which the living spirit of truth may flow.

What of the context in which an 'integrating theology' must be set? Our contemporary Western culture has three salient features. First, it is pluralistic, that is to say, there are a number of optional ideologies of belief and action and there is, it is claimed, no rational way of choosing between them. Christians must remember that their claim to truth is only one of several, and so simple proclamation is not enough: any attempt to make more sense of things cannot proceed by knock-down argument. Second, contemporary culture has a growing 'ecological' sense. Any theology must do justice to the findings of the natural sciences and to the traditional doctrine of God as creator. It must see nature as the matrix and instrument of the spirit rather than its enemy. Third, in the ecclesiastical context, greater importance is being given to the role of the laity, and all ministry is now being seen as shared ministry in which the clergy have a representative function, acting on behalf of the people of God, not in place of them.

So ministerial theology needs to be earthed and contextualised in the world as it is and cannot be learned by rote at some abstract level. If one function of theology is to articulate the vision of God's presence in the world, the minister needs to be familiar with the Christian tradition in its wholeness, and the study of theology under separate subjects has not always helped. An 'integrating theology' must not only give unity to the syllabus but it must also provide criteria for priorities. Each subject needs both a general view and detailed analysis of parts; and an overall framework of the whole course is necessary towards which different subjects will make their appropriate contributions. There will never be enough time for everything, and ministerial education must be seen as continuing beyond ordination.

A further aspect of integration is the need to hold together the insights of evangelical, catholic, and liberal within the Anglican tradition as complementary rather than exclusive.

In conclusion Peter Baelz referred to the debate about the comparative virtues of residential and non-residential training, and to recent training schemes for local ordained ministry to show how the whole business of theological education is on the move. If it is not to fragment it urgently needs a theological understanding which will hold it together while allowing it to take different forms in different contexts.

An important piece of integrating had been in progress since 1981 between working groups from the Advisory Council and the Church's Board of Education. A first report was published as *Learning and Teaching in Theological Education* (ACCM Occasional Paper No. 11), and a second followed in 1984, *Experience and Authority, Issues Underlying Doing Theology* (ACCM Occasional Paper No. 19). Since the mid-1960s adult education and laity training in the dioceses had been dominated by the concept of experiential learning and the Board of Education had put most of its resources into arranging encounter groups where the dynamics of the group formed the main item of learning: little time was allotted to reflection (including theological reflection) on what had been learned. It was widely believed that theological colleges were mainly concerned with passing on a theological tradition, and considerable tension resulted between traditionally trained clergy and the new approaches in dioceses. The two reports were aimed at clarifying the issues involved and encouraging discussion between the two parties.

In his introduction to the second paper Peter Baelz contrasts tradition (*traditio*), the process of communicating the faith with the crystallised contents of belief and practice (*tradita*). He writes, 'In a *living* tradition, as contrasted with a fossilised tradition, no polarisation is possible between past and present, intuition and understanding, dogma and experience, individual and community, authority and freedom. A *living* tradition with its roots in the past, is one which sets people free to explore the unrealised potentiality of the future. A true obedience to the gift of God is itself creative and responsive rather than repetitive and unreflecting'.

The report maintains that ideologies underlie all types of education. Differences concern not just content and method; the context is as important as the curriculum. Experiential learning is not without authority because any system of interpretation is a theory about how authority is exercised by the handling of symbols. Clergy and laity are different, and the general education of the laity may be prejudiced by too much emphasis on 'ministry', since learning to do may inhibit learning to be. The priest is not an expert in education but is a leader who can liberate and coordinate the powers of those with whom he works. The report concludes that theological education is never wholly intellectual, nor emotional, nor individual. The context is significant and should be made explicit for teacher and learner. All assumptions should be carefully examined.

Between 1975 and 1985 nearly a quarter of all candidates recommended for training intended non-stipendiary ministry, and new training Courses were forming fast (from two in 1975 to fourteen in 1985). This presented the Church with major problems. Bishops' selectors had to make their recommendations although many had never seen a non-stipendiary before and were not at all sure what sort of ministry this could amount to. What sort of training was appropriate for those who had to pursue it in their spare time in evenings, at weekends and at summer-schools? In particular, what was the theological justification for such a radical innovation?

By way of casting some light on to these dark areas Peter Baelz, in consultation with William Jacob who was secretary of the Committee, invited a number of authorities to contribute to a small volume, published in 1985 under the title *Ministers of the Kingdom; Exploration in Non-Stipendiary Ministry*. The chairman himself contributed one essay, *Ministers of the Kingdom* which is both a profound theological justification of this kind of ministry and also a clear illustration of his own manner of 'doing theology'.

It starts with the kingdom of God and not with the Church of God because the Church is not the kingdom, but a sign and instrument of the kingdom. He quotes John Robinson (from *The Historic Episcopate*, p. 17):

> Just as the New Testament bids us have as high a doctrine of the ministry as we like, as long as our doctrine of the Church is higher, so it commands us have as high a doctrine of the Church as we may, provided our doctrine of the kingdom is higher.

Such a doctrine sees the whole created order as the object of God's continuing creative and redemptive love, and it has to be admitted that this cosmic emphasis is stronger in eastern than in western Christian theology. Insofar as people respond to the true, the beautiful and the good, they cooperate with the will of God because these things are signs and expressions of God's will, though the people may not recognise this nor even believe in God. The Church is that part of God's creation where the reality of God's love is recognised, celebrated and proclaimed: there can be no thoroughgoing dualism, though there is a temptation to fail to do justice to the sinfulness of sin and the evil of evil. The kingdom is transcendent in origin and destiny, continually creating and restoring, though it has its shadow side. The kingdom is a reality of being: to be an inheritor of the kingdom of God is to receive a new centre to one's being. In creating the world God lets it be by giving it a relative autonomy. The processes of creation are hazardous; there is no universal law of progress or decline; and the process of history are ambiguous. One function of the Church is to witness to this ambiguity, to confess and contain it, as it does, for example, by special services for secular bodies where it gives neither blanket blessing nor condemnation, but rather a deepening of insight directed toward reconciliation and renewal.

The Church's concern, therefore, cannot be limited to the ecclesiastical or religious sphere: it must respond to a God who is both transcendent and immanent in so far as the ordained minister is an authorised representative of the ministry of the whole Church (which itself derives from the ministry of Christ), he is called to the celebration of God's presence in creation, redemption, and fulfilment as well as to patient service of the needs of the world. So he prepares the way for the coming of the kingdom.

The minister in secular employment is not exercising some different kind of ministry. His presence there is a sign of God's promise and judgment, a witness to the fact that the world is God's with all its ambiguity. In his work secular criteria apply. But he is also an interpreter, either from above, bringing into play the tradition into which he has entered, or from below, by digging deep into the secular situation until its ultimate implications become visible, thus providing stepping-stones between world and kingdom. His sacramental ministry at work will be similarly indirect when symbolic actions (other than baptism and holy communion) may become occasions of celebration, forgiveness and renewal – secular sacraments of the kingdom where some ordinary event in life can be revealed as possessing more than ordinary depth and significance.

Likewise his ministry of prayer, probably largely hidden, will keep open the boundaries between kingdom, Church and world, a binding and holding operation in the face of scattering forces.

The climax of eleven years work with the Committee came in 1987 (after his departure) with a radically new system for the formal assessment of theological education (set out in ACCM Occasional Paper No. 22, *Education for the Church's Ministry*). Each college and course is required to submit answers to three questions: 'What ordained ministry does the Church of England require?'; 'What is the shape of the educational programme best suited for equipping people to exercise this ministry?'; and 'What are the appropriate means for assessing suitability for the exercise of this ministry?'. By their own criteria will they be judged. They cannot claim that they have not been helped by the Advisory Council and its Committee for Theological Education.

Peter Baelz inherited a state of antagonism between Council and colleges and has left a new spirit of partnership. He has done this by a perceptive discernment of the main features of a complex landscape and a recalling of church educators to basic theological postulates. He has listened to experts in current educational theory and learned from them. He has taken research seriously, and encouraged more to be done. Above all, he has been concerned for integration, of theory and practice, of heart and mind, of academic rigour and personal development, of theological insights ancient and modern, eastern and western, but only after critical examination. He enjoys calling himself 'an old-fashioned nineteenth-century liberal', about which readers may judge for themselves. If this is what liberalism is, the Church could do with a great deal more of it.

References

The ACCM Occasional Papers mentioned in the text may be obtained from:

The Publications Secretary,
Advisory Council for the Church's Ministry,
Church House,
London SW1P 3NZ.

They are:

No. 9	*Spirituality in Ordination Training*	1981	50p
No. 11	*Learning and Teaching in Theological Education*	1982	50p
No. 15	*An Integrating Theology*	1983	50p
No. 19	*Experience and Authority: Issues Underlying Doing Theology*	1984	£1
No. 22	*Education for the Church's Ministry; the Report of the Working Party on Assessment*	1987	£1
Also,	*Ministers of the Kingdom: Exploration in Non-Stipendiary Ministry*, C.I.O. Publishing	1985	£3.95

CATHEDRALS AND CHANGE

Alan Webster

Peter Baelz had experience of a catena of cathedrals. Deaconed at Birmingham, priested at Salisbury, he served as a Canon of Christ Church Oxford for seven years, was Dean of Durham for nine, and was Chairman of the Deans and Provosts Conference. A tribute was paid to him in the General Synod in 1988 during the debate on the Care of Cathedrals Measures for formulating the Deans and Provosts attitude to this essential legislation. The Measure requires accountability for major alterations to the fabric, and for the first time gives shared control to Deans, Provosts and national and local planning authorities. It is appropriate that the last tribute to Peter Baelz in the Synod should be for his skill in leading to a new partnership. He could be impatient with the ecclesiastical world, like his friend and mentor the theologian Charles Raven, for a time Ely Professor as well as Master of Peter's own college, Christ College Cambridge. Raven was wont to remark 'Ely Cathedral, Ely Cathedral is a great white elephant which feeds on the souls of men'. Those who have worked at cathedrals may have some sympathy with that, but Peter was an effective worker for gradual and gentle change.

Since 1972, when he arrived at Christ Church Oxford, all cathedrals have been changing more rapidly than in the previous hundred years. They were already far from being embattled Barchesters, but tended to emphasise the obvious fact that every cathedral differs from every other without much concern for the complementary truth that they have much in common – especially the problems of mounting inflation and greatly increased use.

Assessing changes in a house of prayer must always be elusive, tentative and problematic. Peter liked to quote Pascal's remark about prayer. 'Dieu a établi la pière pour communiquer à ses créatures la dignité de la causalité'.[1] At the 1988 Durham Conference of the International Society of Christian Artists he affirmed that the imagination plays an essential part in coming to believe – without it there is no 'disclosure' or revelation. Images are needed, so is the destruction of images, so is the silence of the Cross. The artist, the art appreciator, the person praying in a cathedral, are all called to a certain suspension of egoism, 'not for a distanced objectivity, but for a responsive subjectivity'.

He sympathised with Mary Warnock, 'If, below the level of consciousness, our imagination is at work tidying up the chaos of sense experience, at a different level it may, as it were, untidy it again'. Perhaps it was his own reflections on his severe early illness which made him so appreciate negative capability. Not everything we experience is explicable nor are all hopes achievable. Human character and intricate human institutions may mediate absoluteness and the eternal without being totally rational or explicable. We are right to attend to the philosophical attacks on religion as elusion (Feuerbach, Marx, Freud), and to Karl Barth' criticisms of religion, in some of his earlier writings, as a construction of human pride, but still find God interwoven with our experience.

The Cathedral of Durham is the 'incomparable masterpiece of Romanesque architecture, not only in England but anywhere. The moment of entering provides an architectural experience never to be forgotten: one of the greatest that England has to offer'.[2] For vision, technical skill and daring, Durham and the other major cathedrals of Europe have no rivals, not even among government buildings or fortresses or palaces or great country houses. They were part of a tradition of ability to change and to challenge and to venture on a huge scale.

A modern writer has imagined the thoughts of those who responded to disaster when the Norman tower over the crossing at Ely collapsed in 1322. The Sacrist, Alan of Walsingham, sent for an architect and for one of the most notable craftsmen of England: the King's carpenter. Their problem was the gaping hole where the tower had been. William Anderson[3] suggests that they might have said to themselves 'Let us respond to disaster by founding our design upon the number eight which signifies regeneration, the new life, and the just balance between the powers of the spirit and the powers of nature ... Let us create something new that will be stronger than the tower it replaces and yet will seem more daring, more dangerous, more thrilling than anything ever built before. Let us astound the future'.

Cathedrals, large or small, have the same mission: to proclaim in deed and word, through music and all the arts, through simply being there, by being places of prayer and prophecy and imagination, that at the heart of human concern is the assertion of divine love. Peter's writings in theology, ethics and contemporary affairs – the nuclear threat, apartheid, the new problems of medical ethics, taught and preached with a consistent aim – how the church may respond to the immense changes in politics, economics, psychology, philosophy, and religion.

Bishop Paul Moore, in his final address on 11 June 1989, in the Cathedral of St. John the Divine, New York, summed up the contemporary task of cathedrals in these words:

'Become a Catholic Church in love with freedom . . . exercise your freedom by having courage; this is not a time to be timid. You stand here today because Abraham set forth to an unknown land. Jesus risked all and died on the cross. Paul was shipwrecked . . . Be universal. To be Catholic is to be open to all people. This too, takes courage, because as the poor and powerless become your brothers and sisters you will suffer their discomfort, even feel their wounds as you surrender to them your comfort and security. You will be asked to take on their dangerous struggle for survival. Be free in your mind, explore the outer limits of faith, push forward the boundaries of theology to a new dynamic of the gospel, so that the vigour of its love penetrates the issues of the day – poverty, pollution, pathology. Whatever it is, do it at the behest of Christ. One act of courageous love, however small, leads to another. You are fed not just for your own nourishment but so that you are empowered to go forth with courage . . . do not lose hope.'

Changes in cathedrals in the last twenty years have been encouraged by much greater co-operation. The informal Deans' Conference, once limited to cathedrals with Deans, now always includes Provosts, wives as well as husbands, ecumenical representatives, such as the Minister of St. Giles Edinburgh, Roman Catholic administrators from Westminster and Liverpool, and some clergy from Anglican Cathedrals in Wales, Scotland and Ireland, and occasionally in the USA, where the Conference has met once in New York and once in Washington. The crucial work of other cathedral officials is recognised by the annual meetings of architects, organists, librarians, precentors, vergers, shop managers and finance officials – and this is not an exhaustive list. The Pilgrims Association draws together Secretaries of Friends, Visitors and Education Officers, Chaplains, and the many lay volunteers and members of the congregations who form the human communities who worship and serve in cathedrals. The Cathedral Camps for young volunteers do invaluable voluntary work at about twenty-five cathedrals each year. So professional understanding, friendship, and mutual sympathy grow, so that cathedrals may become more people-orientated despite their great responsibilities for fabric.

'Religion is a plural thing' (John Donne). As they minister to such an immense variety of worshippers and visitors, each with their own perceptions of the truth, this pluralism requires wide sympathy in those who staff them. 'We want a tidy cathedral with no notices to impair the transcendent eternal splendour of the Divine expressed in our architecture and music.' This view is sincere enough, but ignores the fact that through the Samaritans or Christian Aid or Crisis at Christmas, the

Divine speaks to others. If notices are banned for theological reasons, the theology needs re-examination. God is both intimate and other. The homeliness of the Divine as well as God's transcendence needs expression in the way cathedrals welcome and inform visitors. Amongst the changes of the last twenty years has been a recognition of pluralism, not least in Durham where an artist in residence joined the staff, and Archbishop Tutu was enabled to appeal for freedom for black people, both in the cathedral and in the city hall.

Every year Peter addressed the Friends of Durham Cathedral (see Annual Reports 1980–89). The effect of these careful and responsible accounts of what had been achieved and ought to be achieved, surveying all aspects of the life of the cathedral, the people involved, worship, music, education, fabric, welcome to visitors, interpretation and future plans, give a clue to the change which needs further development at all cathedrals from hierarchy to shared life and responsibility. Lay workers at cathedrals, both volunteers and paid, find the remnants of hierarchy one of the greatest barriers to the future developments of cathedrals as centres of prayer and spiritual life. 'We can't change a light bulb without an order from the Dean and Chapter.'

Though there are one or two honorary women Canons, all Deans, Provosts and Residentiary Canons are men. When visual imagery through television is crucial to convey the message, it is alienating for many to see all authority limited to men only, and frequently to ordained men only. The Reports to the Friends with the sense that the Dean was accountable to the men and women who supported Durham Cathedral, had the effect of symbolising the need for the 'Family of the Cathedral' to be open to women and men and to provide occasions when the entire enterprise of prayer and charity could be discussed and considered together.

Perhaps the final fling of the old attitude that the Dean and Chapter know best was exemplified by the Mappa Mundi controversy in 1988, when five clergymen meeting in Hereford, were encouraged by city advisers, to sell the most priceless possession of the cathedral. The Lord Lieutenant, the High Steward, the Chairman of the County Council, the mayors of the city as well as members of the 'Cathedral Family', the Council of the Friends, and the women and men who form the congregation, have all been heard on similar occasions at other cathedrals but were not consulted on this occasion. Not to trust and consult the laity is tragic, for as the Roman Catholic historian, Professor Adrian Hastings, has said the worship of cathedrals on great occasions is 'probably the Church of England's most valuable surviving asset'. The Durham Friends Reports reveal in detail how much time and trouble was taken to consult widely and to explain carefully. No doubt, as changes are made in Cathedral Statutes in the decades ahead, this type of approach will become normal.

At Durham the city, the county, the diocese and the university – in fact the whole community of the north-east – feel that the cathedral belongs to them and should be maintained, and open to them free of charge. Cathedrals have always been community buildings. Jean Gimpel[4] has described how in France alone more stone was quarried by communities for their cathedrals than was quarried in the thousands of years of Egyptian civilisation. In building cathedrals everyone was involved. So amongst contemporary changes is a growth in the sense that cathedrals are community responsibilities. The Cathedral of St. Magnus at Kirkwall in the Orkneys, which, since the last Middle Ages, has belonged to the people, is an example of how it is possible for community and church to co-operate and maintain a cathedral, so that it can be fully used by the Church of Scotland (and even recently for a period by the Roman Catholic Church when they were without their own building). This superb rose-pink cathedral was built by masons from Durham from 1130 onwards, and has much to teach English cathedrals about community co-operation.

Wakefield Cathedral is another example of how a city can combine to support a House of Prayer. On the cathedral wall is a finely illuminated inscription:

> At a special meeting of the City of Wakefield Metropolitan District Council held in the Town Hall, Wakefield, on the eighth day of June 1988, the Lord Worshipful the Mayor, Councillor George Henry Parkinson in the chair, it was resolved that in pursuance of Section 249(5) of the Local Government Act 1972, that this Council do hereby confer the honorary freedom of the City of Wakefield upon the Cathedral Chapter of the Cathedral Church of All Saints, Wakefield, in recognition and acknowledgement of the eminent services rendered to Wakefield and its citizens by the Cathedral and those who have served here over the past century. This is to certify that on the 11th day of July 1988 the Cathedral Chapter was admitted to the Role of Honorary Freedom of the City.
>
> George Parkinson, Mayor
> John Stanbury, Chief Executive

The inscription is surrounded by a flowering vine with symbols of the Sacraments, the City Hall, the Cathedral, and the City Seal.

Relations between cities and cathedrals take time, courage, sensitivity and humour. City councils can be jealous of cathedrals. The cathedral and as many of its workers as possible need to be known to those responsible for the city: the political parties, the officers, the workers. Cathedrals and town halls are the possession of the whole city and not simply of the political party which is in charge of the town hall or the worshipping congregation or, in the case of the cathedral, members of the Church of England. One mayor, arguing in favour of a rate to help the restoration of the cathedral, said that, 'the citizens of Lincoln must remember that the cathedral is as much a part of our city as the drains beneath our feet'.

There are many mayors who may not be churchgoers but have real respect for the religious traditions within their community. A mayor of Norwich, who had belonged to the communist party, read the scriptures with sincerity on Mayor's Sunday, only requesting that a reading from the Old Testament denouncing the rich should be chosen – easy enough if one looks through Amos or Isaiah. The lord mayors of London from the time of Sir Kenneth Cork to Sir Greville Spratt, who stop at St. Paul's on the way to the Law Courts where they take an oath, each requested some personal religious ceremony which built up over the years to a pause where the lord mayor got out of his or her carriage, knelt at a kneeling desk, received a blessing and a Bible or Prayer Book and listened to an anthem of his or her own choosing. Efforts by cathedrals for the deprived, such as the night shelter at Norwich or 'Faith in the City' at St. Paul's, require close co-operation at every level with the community around – at one time three heads of cathedrals were serving on inner cities race relations committees.

The Statutes of most cathedrals were revised in 1963 under the chairmanship of the Bishop of Leicester before the major changes outlined in this chapter began. The revision of the Statutes was conservative, and took no account of the need to create a team to serve such complex and costly activities as those now characteristic of all the English cathedrals. Some cathedrals, such as Coventry and Liverpool, have revised their Statutes. There is need for a general revision in view of the changes in Cathedrals Statutes which make decisions about the day-to-day life, and even the repair of the fabric extraordinarily difficult.

The difficulties start with the appointment of the staff. All Deans, and many Canons, are appointed by the Crown. In practice this involves the Prime Minister's Patronage Secretary carrying our various consultations, always including the Diocesan Bishop, other Canons and local worthies, but the appointment is actually made by No. 10. There is no Appointments Committee with representatives working together and carrying corporate responsibility, analogous to the Crown Appointments Commission for Bishops, or the Committees which make university or school appointments. At the present time, when there is intense interest in the patronage system at the disposal of the ruling political party, the method of appointment of cathedral clergy should come under review. The General Synod is considering this but there is likely to be political resistance to any change. Provosts are usually appointed through various forms of local patronage.[5]

Political influence in church appointments has been criticised. In a leading article entitled 'Dean and Downing Street', a recent appointment in 1988 was analysed in detail in *The Times:*

It will be said in the Church that there has been political bias in the appointment . . . that may be the case. It is not necessarily grounds for criticising Mrs Thatcher. She is a politician; the office she holds is a political office; the powers of patronage attached to it are surely there to be used . . . Nonetheless, the continuance of the patronage system in those cases where it still applies is an anomaly. If it was right to put the nomination of Archbishops and Diocesan Bishops largely into the Church's own hands when the Crown Appointments Commission system started in 1977, it can hardly be wrong to go at least as far as that in the case of lesser dignitaries. Mrs Thatcher would find it difficult to resist a demand for such a reform.

A working party has now been set up by the Synod.

Oliver Fiennes, in his farewell lecture to the Greater Chapter of Lincoln Cathedral after twenty years as Dean ('Bad Dreams and Bright Visions'), delivered on St. Hugh's Day 1988, described the Chapter as:

A fellowship held together with enormous effort against all the odds . . . They stem primarily from the method of appointment and the freehold of the Dean, the Canons Residentiary, and the Canons non-residentiary . . . It is an exciting time for cathedrals, but the organisational structure as set up by the Statutes and by custom, is almost unworkable. It is deadening. It leads inevitably to stress and overwork . . . I plead for escape from the confines of irresponsible and unplanned appointments to senior positions and from life-long freedom of tenure for those who have achieved such positions.

Dean Fiennes' plea is so powerful that special attention will be paid to this well-considered assessment in the reforms which lie ahead.

The difficulty at Lincoln and at other cathedrals to create a group who will work together is damaging. The Dean of a Cathedral is not only, as the Dean of Winchester has said in half-humour, a Curate with four Vicars, but placed in a position where 'major disagreements are inevitable'. No modern enterprise dealing with such intense activities, so large a staff, and such considerable finances, could succeed with such an adversarial system enshrined in Statutes.

Changes are essential. In the view of the Dean of Lincoln, the freehold for Residentiary Canons must be abandoned; an appointment board for all cathedral clergy should be set up; the leading lay staff, women and men, should attend some of the Chapter meetings. Cathedrals are now important in the life of the Church and the nation, employing a staff (in the case of Lincoln of 145, and in the case of other cathedrals of between 200 and 300) so the wholly inadequate system of appointment with life tenure must be reviewed. At the same time the need for the integration of the lay staff, both paid and voluntary, needs to be carried further. The position under most Statutes that absolute authority for decisions lies in the hands of four or five clergy – the Administrative Chapter – is unrealistic. Consultation on all aspects of cathedral life is needed in the future.

A survey of the finances of many cathedral appeals reveals a surprising variety of approach. As the forty-three cathedrals are self-governing, there is no one source for surveying cathedral finances. It is not that all cathedrals are secretive about finance (though some are); it is the absence of an effective office which can collect, analyse and advise. However, the survey carried out in 1988 paints a reasonably accurate picture of initiative, goodwill and hard work.

Taking examples at random: Wells raised and spent £2,300,000 between 1975 and 1986 to restore the West Front and the High Vaults of the Nave. Bristol created a Trust for long-term development. Canterbury's major appeal in 1979, along with endowments, has maintained its very elaborate structure in good condition. Carlisle has recently raised £1,000,000. Chichester has a successful Development Trust with a strong claim on the loyalty of the county of Sussex. Coventry has just raised £600,000. Durham is well endowed and has had no appeals but raises considerable sums from fees for climbing the tower. Ely has raised £4,000,000 for a major restoration. Exeter raised £1,000,000 to endow the music and another million to carry out restoration work, each under an independent and different body to Trustees. Gloucester is appealing for £4,000,000 for major restoration. Lichfield has raised £1,250,000 by a low-key appeal to public authorities and industry, and has recently received a grant of £1,000,000 from European funds in recognition of its work for tourism and education.

Lincoln has a permanent appeal for its fabric fund 'to prevent panic appeals'. St. Paul's has raised £1,000,000 from the City as endowment, and in addition has endowed much of its music. Manchester is financed mainly from endowments but is considering a major appeal. Newcastle has raised £500,000 by appeal (1982–87) and sold its Tintoretto in 1986 for £765,000. Norwich relies on property, endowments and a continuous fabric appeal, a shop, a visitors' centre and its 4,000 Friends. Christ Church Oxford is part of the Foundation of Henry VIII and is independent financially. Portsmouth, which has no endowments, is starting to appeal for £3,000,000. Ripon is appealing for £1,500,000. Salisbury is appealing for £6,500,000 for the Spire, Tower and West Front. Southwark has raised £900,000 for a new Chapter House. Truro has a Fabric Endowment Fund. Wakefield had launched an appeal in 1987 'but it was not a success'. However, a Bishop Treacy Memorial Hall has been built. Worcester is appealing for £4,000,000. York has an on-going appeal and has raised and spent very large sums in the past twenty-five years over major restorations and reconstruction after the fire.

Unlike continental cathedrals which are either maintained by the State, as in France, or supported by a Church Tax, as in Germany, English cathedrals are responsible for their own finances, hence the appeals which have just been listed. Most cathedrals receive some finance from the Church Commissioners, and almost all, with the exception of a few northern cathedrals off the tourist route, are dependent upon the offerings and the takings at shops. Sometimes (as at St. Paul's), large sums come from the tourist gift trade. A few cathedrals charge for admission. Some, like St. Paul's, have an arrangement with commercial tourist companies to receive fees from conducted parties. All receive legacies, sometimes substantial. Most have Friends whose support is valuable as voluntary workers. One cathedral quantifies the value of voluntary service from its Friends as £60,000 a year. A number of appeals have been assisted by local authority rates. In total (though there is no fully reliable figures) it seems that the forty-three cathedrals are appealing for £50 million, all with reasonable hope of success. Despite escalating costs, especially of salaries, the fabric inside and out of English cathedrals is as expertly conserved as that of any cathedrals in the world and probably than ever in their history.

To the sympathetic visitor this determined financial ingenuity is admirable. A more critical view would assess the time, energy and occasionally openness to patronage which the continual task of raising money inflicts upon the staff. Encouragement rather than cash comes from several recent initiatives. Cathedral Camps, a youth movement created and led by Robert Aagaard, arranges each year for 500 students to spend part of their summer holidays at their own expense under expert guidance repairing fabric and maintaining grounds. This fusion of Barchester and Outward Bound is winning a number of the younger generation to realise that privilege and responsibility of cathedrals.

Many volunteers at cathedrals feel that a crucial change is improved communications. The continual noise of moving chairs, organ recitals, arguments among members of the staff, putting up and taking down staging, can repell. People dazed with tragedy enter cathedrals – at St. Paul's relations of those being tried at the Old Bailey. Is there anyone quietly to be alongside them?

Someone committed suicide recently in an English cathedral. Perhaps he was beyond help anyway. But there may be others we do not know about who have been deprived of what they hope to find. A girl who died in the Pan Am Lockerbie disaster spent some of her last hours in a cathedral. Fortunately there was a sister on duty with whom she talked and who was afterwards in touch with her relatives. At Norwich a foreign pair were walking around. The chance that they could be listened to revealed the extraordinary fact that the man was one of the twelve young Czech students who shared the decision to offer his life for Czech freedom in 1968. They drew lots, all twelve of them, and one of the pieces of paper carried a cross. That cross was drawn by Jan Pallach, the student who burnt himself to death for freedom in Wencelas Square. Naturally we prayed together, and Norwich felt a holier place.

The remarkable musical version of the death of Jan Pallach involving 500 people one Lent evening had been produced in the cathedral not long before by Allan Wicks, the doyen of cathedral organists. It seemed more than a coincidence.

We need better communications to strengthen spiritual understanding among Friends, paid staff, clergy, musicians, all who actually care for cathedrals. It is a two-way process. Of course we shall try to convey the knowledge and faith and concern which have brought us to work in a cathedral. So often what we need is the evidence of courage and imagination, love and sometimes even martyrdom, which comes to our cathedrals from the world community of faith.

Communication always requires a sacrifice of time. We save time in the end if communications are good. The former Dean of Lincoln, Oliver Fiennes, in his lecture after nearly twenty years at the same cathedral,

> It is an exciting time for cathedrals, but the organisational structure as set out by the Statutes and by custom is almost unworkable. It is deadening. It leads inevitably to stress and overwork ... I plead for escape from the confines of irresponsible and unplanned appointments to senior positions and from life-long freehold of tenure for those who have achieved such positions.

At cathedrals themselves there is growing concern for better communications. Chapter meetings often now include leading lay assistants in addition to the Chapter Clerk. Organists, architects, lay administrators, Secretaries of Friends, High Stewards and others are occasionally invited to attend. This is an important development. There are also in many cathedrals weekly staff meetings with representatives. Cathedrals with Friends have quarterly or more frequent meetings to discuss their affairs. The new Cathedrals Measure is giving a statutory place to those concerned with the fabric, regularising what many cathedrals already possess. There are weaknesses in this internal consultation system. Many of the meetings are short on lay people and many of these meetings have no women present. The equal opportunities spirit now at work in other institutions in our country, can be weak within cathedrals. A member of a religious order attending the installation of a Dean noticed that 200 men were needed to carry out the institution, but the only woman officially robed and in the procession was one woman verger. This failure in communication with women is in notable contrast to occasions at universities and other educational establishments.

Keys to changing communications are varied: new technology, the computerisation of much of the work, and the circulation to everyone of monthly, if not weekly, information sheets. But we need the human way of holding things together. One of the great cathedral canons of this generation, Canon Peter Bradshaw, a superb town and village pastor before he became Canon of Norwich, made it his business, whether he was in residence or not, at a fixed time every morning to wander around, have time to listen, drink half a cup of black coffee in the Visitors' Centre, and without intruding on anyone else's duties and responsibilities, to be a centre of the mind and heart of his cathedral. Perhaps all members of the staff, lay or ordained, voluntary or paid, should do more listening and laughing.

I was intrigued at one cathedral, where the daily offices circulate from chapel to chapel, to be told that you found out where Matins was by listening for the sound of laughter when rather absurd lessons had to be read in accordance with the lectionary. Perhaps it was in that cathedral that a canon indicated the nonsense which is occasionally read and concluded, not with the phrase 'This is the Word of the Lord' but by substituting his own response '*find* the Word of the Lord'. Laughter communicates so much more than some lectures, just as we might well write up on our notice boards 'Please first use your common sense. Next remember that charity is above rubrics, and last, why not ask him or her yourself instead of making that telephone call, writing that letter, or having that grump about failure in communications'.

The contrast between contemporary cathedrals and their role in 1800 could hardly be sharper. In that year St. Paul's had less than a dozen communicants. Now, like all English cathedrals, worshippers at Christmas are counted in thousands. The atmosphere of every cathedral has been totally changed. When George Eliot visited Exeter Cathedral he found it barred, dark and forbidding. Even when Barchester was benign, cathedrals were not serving their church and the community as they are today. A critical and sympathetic visitor, however, might well contrast the vitality of the crowded streets with the atmosphere, detached and perhaps rather Third Programme which is often encountered in cathedrals. The contrast between the vitality, courage and integration with the people found in a cathedral in Poland or parts of rural Africa, or Hispanic America, is still too great. Perhaps much lies in the hands of the musicians who must not only preserve an incomparable tradition, but find styles of music appreciated and valued by the thronging visitors. To reflect the Mystery of the Divine will continue to tax all those concerned with the witness, way of life and worship of English cathedrals.

A professional man brought up Church of England giving much time to church affairs, described recently why he had left the Church. He described cathedrals as places essentially ceremonial rather than effective. He felt, he said, that cathedrals were like an army which gave all its attention to practising for and preparing for the Trooping of Colour – its ceremonial duties – but never prepared for the primary task of defending the country and going into action. His criticism needs attention but so does the value of cathedrals for simply being there.

It is unwise to discount the value of the repetitive and the ceremonial. The orderly routine of musical worship – how hard it is to maintain the highest standards – and the shining, safe, clean maintenance of great buildings open for long hours every day of the year, often under enormous pressure from visitors and worshippers and the pollution of traffic and noise in the centre of great cities. We must admire those who rebuilt Grace Cathedral, San Francisco, after the 1906 earthquake. The magnificent building survived the 1989 earthquake. The Bishop and the Dean, the musicians, the congregation, the Friends, were all available on the days following the disaster and spoke on radio to the U.K. Dean Alan Jones said that the cathedral was open because people need space and quiet, time to think, time to speak and be listened to. The cathedral was alive and not ceremonial but effective.

The permanence of cathedrals is costly in times of danger. During the London blitz, especially in the fire bomb raid in December 1940, that fatal weekend when the deserted city buildings burned, St. Paul's Cathedral stood firm as an inspiration. The Cathedral Watch, composed of young postmen, civil servants, members of the congregation, young doctors, men and women, were on the roof and tossed the incendiaries away. It was natural that after the war the Cathedral Watch should become the Friends, now numbering close on 4,000 members.

Cathedrals have unique resources in many cities. Cathedrals are laboratories by providing space and often with invaluable day or residential centres open to good causes and educational tasks, Edward King House at Lincoln and the houses at Lichfield, John Kennedy House, Coventry, and elsewhere. Visitors' Centres, cafes, restaurants, all give the opportunity for hospitality and pause in the centre of cities, especially if they are staffed by those who realise that hospitality is a religious duty and the time to listen and laugh and refresh each other can add so much to life.

Services need not be repetitive or routine. In this interim period when women are joining men in the service of the church, it is specially important that planning groups should be both women and men. So much of the worship pattern is still male and monastic.

Janet Morley's prayers 'All Desires Known, M.O.W. 1988', are finding their way into cathedrals, and there is change by osmosis. The great service attended by Bishop Donald Coggan to welcome the Chinese woman priest, the Revd. Florence Lee Tim Moi in Westminster Abbey with its music, Julian of Norwich readings and imaginative ceremonial, was felt by many to be a leap forward. The same was felt at the Canterbury and Coventry services in thanksgiving for creation and at the Canterbury service of thanksgiving for the ministry of women in the Anglican Communion. The enthronement service for the new Bishop of Lincoln, with its emphasis on the role of the clown in human life, the Coventry Cathedral 1988 televised Midnight Mass, the Durham Cathedral celebrations of St. Cuthbert, all showed the power of imaginative liturgical writing. There are few cathedrals today without any use of the new prayer book. The process of change might be helped if three or four times a year the main Sunday morning service was entirely written round some major gift of God.

Just as the earthquake shook Grace Cathedral and gave it that role which the evangelists saw in the passion and resurrection when the rocks were rent, so the crises of modern life, if we see God at work within them both in judgement and in blessing, can give our cathedrals the task of enabling the Spirit so that they are truly laboratories of the Spirit. Children again and again write poetry which they would like to share. The Thousand Norfolk Poets exhibition mounted by education authorities with the aid of Norwich Cathedral, was especially significant. In discussing Faith in the City and the Church Urban Fund, time with the economic correspondents of the newspapers from the *Financial Times* to local radio and correspondence is not wasted. Often the journalists are those who see most clearly the dangers of materialism. When the *Financial Times* was briefed by Sir Richard O'Brien and others about the forthcoming publication of Faith in the City, the editorial staff said it was the first time that this world newspaper had ever been approached by the Church of England despite the fact that it was just across the road from St. Paul's. Laboratories again and again carry out experiments because of changes in human life; it is for cathedrals to be alert to what God is saying in the providential ordering of the world today and tomorrow.

Cathedrals are 'a significant space . . . with generosity of Spirit . . . where anyone may come in faith or unfaith . . . saints and sinners have jostled and will jostle . . . Here God can touch us and heal us'.[6] Here there is space to take to heart John Donne's plea for sensitive toleration of the religious points of view of other people. As he said, 'Religion is a plural thing'. Here the arts of mankind and the worship of God can be welded into one harmonious and eloquent whole.[7]

Cathedrals today and tomorrow meet the challenge to 'combine a warmth of welcome and an induction into the glory and beauty of the Christian tradition with the sense of awe and quietness that every church, large or small, should have to bring us to our knees'.[8] Change comes to cathedrals so that each successive generation may feel both at home and in awe, meeting God who is both intimate and other. Changes happen so that we and our children and grandchildren may continue to say with sincerity and faith

> I was glad when they said unto me:
> Let us go to the house of the Lord.

References

[1] Baelz, 'Prayer and Providence' Preface, S.C.M., 1968.

[2] Alec Clifton Taylor 'The Cathedrals of England', p. 42, Thames & Hudson, 1967.

[3] 'The Rise of the Gothic', Hutchinson, 1985, p. 162.

[4] The Cathedral Builders, The Cresset Library, 1988.

[5] See G. Hewitt, 'Strategist for the Spirit' for the incisive views of Bishop Leslie Hunter of Sheffield, Becket Press 1985.

[6] Archbishop of York in 'The Reality of God', Essays in honour of Tom Baker, Dean of Worcester, Severn House, 1986.

[7] Dean A. C. Bridge of Guildford in 'The Reality of God'.

[8] Archbishop of Canterbury, St. Paul's Cathedral, 30 November 1987.

WORSHIP AND THE
NATURE OF GRACE

BLESSING

Helen Oppenheimer

Peter Baelz has explored and illuminated the intellectual and moral questions about what Christians mean by grace. It seems fitting in his honour to try to apply the kind of approach which he has encouraged, positive and questioning, to a particular aspect of the problem of grace. What bearing can the ancient religious notion of 'blessing' have upon late twentieth century Christian life?

Except in a few expressions like 'with a good grace' or 'she did have the grace to look ashamed', grace is a technical term, not plainly rooted in everyday living. But blessing, in Christian usage, means something like 'grace made perceptible'. To take blessing seriously ought to force us to be less vague about what the words we use mean in practice.

In a letter published in *Theology* some years ago[1] Dr Murdoch Dahl asked about the precept that only people can be blessed, not things: so that there is 'something wrong' about blessing a new vicarage, or the posies at a Mothering Sunday Eucharist. 'I feel,' he wrote, 'that the unacknowledged theological assumptions behind all this are highly dubious.' In reply it was suggested,[2] somewhat encouragingly, that the Church of England does not take an unvarying stand in this matter; but little correspondence ensued and a feeling remained that there may be a Gnostic heresy thriving among us, that matter is beyond redemption; and, more interestingly, that there is a muddle among us which needs sorting out.

The way the idea of 'a blessing' is being used in practice confirms this uncertainty. It seems to hover confusingly between vagueness and superstition. Sometimes it is brought in to allow rigorists not to be rigid: for instance about baptismal policy or remarriage after divorce. Where they feel obliged to uphold Christian standards by refusing easy compliance, they try not to rebuff people altogether and offer them ministrations which seem more honest: often something called a 'blessing' instead of a sacrament. So blessing is treated as a second best, a substitute for something else seen as the 'real thing'. A sort of taming

221

process goes on, domesticating blessing as no more than an innocuous way of affirming goodwill, at the risk of losing the vigorous and perhaps embarrassing notion that blessing is something definite to gain or lose.[3]

I

A useful place to start asking questions is a definition in Pedersen's book *Israel*.[4] 'Blessing,' he says, 'is the inner strength of the soul and the happiness it creates.' The point is not whether this definition is or is not a useful introduction to Old Testament study. There is a vivid notion here. In this primitive but not childish way of thinking the spiritual and the physical are not distinct; and moral values do not seem to have been separated out from other kinds of value. Is it a primitive category mistake or is it ancient inspiration that joins these ideas together, body and soul, is and ought, moral values and human happiness, instead of keeping them austerely apart?

The notion of 'the blessing' in our ancient holy documents is powerful enough to be awkward. It is so closely connected with the idea of straightforward human prosperity as to be bound to worry philosophers and moralists: philosophers who are determined to separate 'is' and 'ought', and moralists who believe that disinterestedness is all-important. These people have a point. 'Blessing' can easily degenerate into the unsubtle notion of a reward, worldly or other-worldly, dealt out for good behaviour; or a boon handed out to a favourite without even being earned. But that ought not to be, and is not, the whole story. If we pay some unscornful attention to the maybe naive notions of blessing which we find in our tradition, they may suggest an enrichment of meaning which could be salutary for Christian thought now. In ordinary speech 'blessing' still finds a use which suggests a deeper meaning, a kind of double emphasis both practical and pious. To bless someone is not just a matter of providing advantages: some notion of relationship comes in. Yet on the other hand relationship is not the whole story either: a blessing is meant to be something more solid and tangible than an inward assurance of being loved and held in goodwill.

We can make some statements which do not depend upon detailed Old Testament scholarship. Christians believe their faith to be recognisably continuous with the faith of God's ancient people. Whatever we are able to say about Abraham, Isaac and Jacob and all their struggling, obedient and disobedient descendants from whom eventually Christ came, there is this notion of 'the blessing' which it seems that our long-ago religious ancestors persistently wanted. It is too easy to leave it out of today's religion as crude, so that the sophisticated becomes the impoverished.

In the Old Testament stories blessing has a paradoxical quality. It is found and lost, enjoyed but not appropriated once for all, given unmerited in order to be communicated to succeeding generations. The younger brother may be chosen, but the one who is not chosen is depicted with a certain tragic grandeur. A sort of purposeful pattern recurs, not simply moral nor out of relation to morality, and certainly not coolly neutral.[5] Jacob outrageously wins the birthright and is granted the vision, and goes limping when God touches him; Joseph welcomes with real joy his murderous but beloved brothers; Moses sees the promised land but is not allowed to reach it because of the sins of the people of whom he is in charge; Samuel, Saul and then David are solemnly appointed, partly succeed and partly fail, and take their honoured places in the history of the people of God; Solomon is the wise king and yet his decadence is superimposed upon his wisdom without cancelling it. Commonsense moral ideas are given some strenuous exercise. We find ourselves invited to use 'blessing' as a bridge word: a bridge between the bodily and the spiritual; between the religious and the secular; between ought and is; between morality and the kind of satisfying appropriateness one finds in a work of art. To deny any possibility of such linkages seems to deny a certain depth to human life.

A way to start putting these ideas together is to root them in the most fundamental notion of blessedness. It is God Himself who is the Blessed One; and in the blessedness of God it seems to make sense to say, without solecism, that happiness can be included in holiness: in other words, that the notorious gap between fact and value is not unbridgeable. Within blessedness, goodness and well-being need not belong to different worlds. Are these unsubstantiated assertions? They are offered as clarifications of what is meant by 'blessing' in the light of Christian belief in God, with which of course they must stand or fall.

Browning's Paracelsus[6] affirms that

> God tastes an infinite joy
> In infinite ways . . . where dwells enjoyment there is he'.

He revels in His creation:

> . . . strange groups
> Of young volcanoes come up, cyclops-like,
> Staring together with their eyes on flame -
> God tastes a pleasure in their uncouth pride . . .
> . . . savage creatures seek
> Their loves in wood and plain – and God renews
> His ancient rapture. Thus he dwells in all,
> From life's minute beginnings, up at last
> To man . . .

If we warm to this description of God's pleasure but have to admit that it is splendid fiction, we have the assurance of Julian of Norwich that God showed her that 'We are his bliss, we are his reward, we are his honour, we are his crown'.[7] Or we may be convinced by Thomas Traherne[8] that 'The LORD GOD of Israel the living and true GOD, was from all Eternity, and from all Eternity Wanted like a GOD. He wanted the Communication of His Divine Essence, and Persons to Enjoy it. He wanted Worlds, He wanted Spectators, He wanted Joys, He wanted Treasures. He wanted, yet he wanted not, for he had them'. If God's holiness can be envisaged as comprehending delight, there is less need to suppose anxiously that maturity and rationality must keep these categories severely quarantined in human life.

Philosophically-inclined Christians need not be nervous of affirming that God's purpose is to impart the whole range of His blessedness to His creation. It may be thankfulness not muddle that persuades us to talk with such mysterious comprehensiveness about God's blessing, and even the blessings we offer one another. A little Wittgensteinian exercise of asking about use rather than meaning suggests itself. In the characteristic, we might say all-purpose, Hebrew prayer 'Blessed be Thou O Lord our God, King of the universe, who. . .' God's people call upon their God who is Himself blessed, and name the mighty acts by which He has imparted His blessedness, in the faith that this is the proper way to invoke like blessings in the present: '. . .who brought Israel out of Egypt'; '. . .who bringest forth bread from the earth'; 'who makest bridegroom and bride to rejoice'. In this recital thanking and asking are combined; and the desired and the desirable are all of a piece. 'Blessing', as our forebears used it and as we still naturally tend to use it, is shown in action as a bridge between different categories of experience.

II

The idea of blessing may be illuminating because of its very oddness. Certainly we use it in odd ways. So we come to Dr Dahl's question, and begin to ask about the verb 'to bless' and what we think it means to pronounce a blessing. The curious and deep-rooted idea of human beings blessing God is stranger than blessing either people or things. When religious people in mentioning the Lord find it natural to add a prayer such as 'blessed be His Name', the subjunctive is not a pointless archaism.[9] The indicative 'He is blessed' would not serve the same purpose. God's people bless God, in the same way as they magnify Him, as a way of worshipping: not of course conferring blessing or greatness upon Him, but ascribing them to Him with gratitude, hoping to come into the orbit of the blessedness or the power that they ascribe.

Blessing and magnifying are forms of praise. Anglicans have been more in the habit of magnifying the Lord, ascribing to Him 'all might, majesty, power, dominion and glory', than of adding the pious little prayer 'Blessed be He' on mentioning His Name; but whether we magnify or bless, we are not just making an indicative statement but, as the philosopher John Austin put it,[10] 'doing things with words'.

When we bless one another the *performative* character of what we utter is all the clearer. From the superstitious or friendly 'Bless you!' when someone sneezes, to the profound solemnity of 'The Lord bless you and keep you', a blessing sets about imparting some good. More than that, in so far as 'Bless you' is sincerely meant even in a small way, the good it sets about imparting has a foot in two worlds, the spiritual and the natural. The verb 'to bless' is at least as much a bridging notion as the noun. If the state of blessedness includes fact and value, the activity of blessing offers the promise of bridging another famous gap, the dualist gap between body and soul. Blessing characteristically treats people as wholes. For some people who had a simple Christian upbringing, 'God bless . . .' assorted relatives and friends is still the most basic prayer, never fully outgrown, though capable of enlargement. It asks for what a child understands that the Heavenly Father will be pleased to give; so unselfconsciously it uses blessing as a bridge between earthly and spiritual, without needing to take these apart.

What answer does all this suggest to the question about blessing things? It is facile to answer the question by definition, oversimplifying Buber's distinction between Thou and It, warning us off the plain mistake or superstitious error of saying 'Bless you' to inanimate objects. There is more to be said about the wholeness of the person, and indeed about the wholeness of Creation, and a discussion of blessing is a good place to say some of it.

There are living bodies as well as bodies that are merely things. A comprehensive blessing of a person must include a blessing of the 'thing' which is the person's body. Can we take this further? There are all sorts of ways in which we appropriate matter for our use: and sometimes we say that we consecrate it for our use. If my hand is not simply a thing, is the wedding ring on it simply a thing? Of course it is: if I unluckily lost it, it would be superstitious to make too much fuss. Common-sense likewise knows that it is macabre to cherish the cut-off fingernails of a saint. But common-sense is capable of missing opportunities: in this case, the opportunity to enrich the idea of the bodily by understanding that physical things can be endowed with meaning.

If we decide to talk, with care, about blessing things, we may say that to bless a physical object is to set about making it part of somebody's personal reality. It is not just high-falutin' pious talk to say that matter can be blessed in the sense of consecrated: primarily our own bodies, which are 'temples of the Holy Spirit',[11] but by extension from this way of thinking any of the raw material for the activities of our lives. This indeed is the sacramental principle; and the sacramental principle cannot be an optional extra for anyone who takes to heart the doctrine of God the Creator, whose world is a physical world and whose people are physical beings.[12]

For those Christians who put the Eucharist, *the* Sacrament, at the centre, the bread and wine have human meaning before they have theological meaning. Their continuity with ordinary nourishment is the basis of their becoming heavenly nourishment. Just as the Eucharist is continuous with ordinary life, so ordinary life is full of sacramental activities, great and small. Things can be blessed for our use by being taken and as it were adopted, whether or not with the words, 'This is my body'.[13] Human beings by working upon 'raw material' bring it within the scope of human life and human energy. If they pause first to pronounce a blessing there is no point in trying to keep this blessing strictly 'spiritual'. The prayer in Psalm 90, as we may use it in Coverdale's translation, 'Prosper thou the work of our hands upon us', asks for a blessing in a way which can include both our hands and their work. This is the kind of comprehensiveness which spreads from embodied persons out into the physical world, and makes the blessing of things intelligible not magical. So it may be gracious, not superstitious, to bless wedding rings, or the houses in which people start new lives. Posies on Mothering Sunday can become the 'elements' of a kind of mini-sacrament.

III

If even material things can be candidates for blessing, what can be wrong with offering to bless people with a 'service of blessing' when this seems pastorally appropriate? If we are afraid of profaning the great sacrament of Baptism by using it for babies who do not seem likely to get a Christian upbringing, why not make available a 'mini-sacrament' of thanksgiving and naming? If we want to witness against divorce by refusing to allow people who are remarrying to make their paradoxical new vows in church, why not show the Christian concern we still truly feel by offering them a blessing after a civil wedding?

For all the thought and care which is being put into these alternatives, there is a question mark against them. They seem to be defined by what they not. The difficulty can best be explained by contrast. A little girl at Heathrow was nearly separated from her father in the crowd. A white-haired man who checked his trolley and smiled at her received her father's good-humoured benediction in the words, 'Have a nice day'. An old lady struggling with a roll of carpet said 'God bless you' to a girl who came to her rescue. We may hope that God will in some way honour such little blessings. Is a high-principled but kindly incumbent contributing anything as performative when he offers a blessing as an alternative to Baptism or Matrimony, or lays his hands upon unconfirmed people at the altar rail rather than give them bread and wine? Could a second-best blessing answer the poignancy of Esau's plea 'Bless me, even me also, O my father'?[14]

Once upon a time there could be no substitute for baptism: it was the only gateway to heaven except for very special dispensations. Having come to believe that the Father of our Lord Jesus Christ would not reject anyone for other people's fault, we still want to maintain the importance of baptism; so we emphasize that it makes someone a member of the church. The corollary is that many clergy have become reluctant instead of eager to baptize, when they have no confidence that the membership will be more than nominal.

There is of course a lot to be said for the Baptist principle of believers' baptism;[15] but since the comprehensive abolition of infant baptism is hardly a live option, and some babies are anyway going to be made members of Christ and children of God, we are obliged to ask, what is this distinction we are trying to make between babies? What does a 'blessing', offered instead of baptism, ask God to do; and more particularly, what does it not ask God to do? Its point seems to be that it shall refrain from being the sacrament which makes someone a Christian. It cannot be a rite making someone a catechumen, since the expected absence of Christian instruction is the very reason for discouraging baptism. So is the child who has been blessed in church to count as a Christian, or not?

Whatever we think about the pastoral advantages or disadvantages of 'indiscriminate baptism', undiscriminating blessing is hardly an improvement. Is 'blessing' supposed simply to serve as an assurance of the loving care of God? It is all very well to remind people that the Lord took the young children up in his arms and blessed them: when baptism, of course, was not the point.[16] We are not in a position to imitate what the Lord did: he blessed the children because their parents came asking him to touch them. When twentieth century English parents come asking for their children to be 'done', they are asking for 'christening'. What the church is in a position to offer, or effectively to refuse, is a rite of belonging. To make conditions for proper belonging and offer 'blessing' as an alternative may look realistic; but folk religion here seems more in touch with the spirit of Christ, who restricted neither his giving nor his demanding to the religiously well-organised. Can we not symbolize his generosity? To make a baby a member of Christ is a real gift, indeed a real blessing. It is more like marking a lamb in a flock than enrolling a subscriber in a club: is this theology so wrong? Belonging is something a child can appropriate as time goes on and grow into in ways which cannot necessarily be predicted. If the harvest seems scanty, at least we have not nipped it in the bud.

Similar but slightly different considerations apply to the blessing of people who are remarrying after divorce. For the sake of witness, the service in church is to be something other than the wedding service: so again a 'blessing' comes in as a second best, an alternative to the real thing. If the blessing we can offer to a bride and bridegroom is not the nuptial blessing, what do we, and they, suppose it to be? If there is doubt in our minds whether they really are a bride and bridegroom, it is no answer to make 'blessing' equivocal as well as remarriage. A service of blessing may be a way of not facing the question whether the church can properly encourage this particular man and woman to be united now for life. If their enterprise is invalid or sinful, how can it be blessed? If they really are getting married, can blessing not be applied where it is most needed, to the new promises which we are not forbidding them to make?

It remains appropriate to insist that in fairness to everyone the second-best character of the situation should be indicated. Remarriages need to be differentiated from first marriages, and maybe the way forward does lie in special services.[17] The present argument is a plea for the church to think out and explain the meaning of what it does. Clarity, witness and generosity might not be so divergent after all.

IV

It matters that 'blessing' should not be used as a hold-all, because it could be more useful than that. It could shed light on other practical problems, for instance about abortion and about what we may or may not do with 'pre-embryos': problems made urgent by medical technology and exacerbated by being inappropriately subsumed under one heading, principle versus expediency.

What have embryos to do with blessing? The answer to this rhetorical question might well be, everything. Parenthood is one of the clearest illustrations of what it means for one human being to bless another: it is not just an analogy but an example. Not all blessing is a matter of words. To carry, protect, nourish and cherish is to bless. We can look for the characteristic way in which blessing links fact and value, and is concerned with human beings as embodied wholes. It is hardly a metaphor to recognise parenthood as a natural sacrament, endowing matter with spiritual meaning. Procreation is pro-creation, blessing creatures into life.

There is practical point in this theologizing. It can rescue Christian attitudes towards embryonic human beings from legalistic dualism. If the making of a human being is the blessing of matter into spiritual life, we can be allowed to give weight to the empirical evidence that this is not done in one instant. It is convincing not just convenient that 'the soul' develops gradually, and that a cluster of cleaving cells before the beginnings of the nervous system has not so far become someone.[18]

Does there remain a feeling that some sleight of hand is going on here for the sake of unprincipled permissiveness? Unless we affirm an immortal soul with inviolable rights from 'the moment of conception' do we encourage too easy abortions? There is more to be said about blessing. The language of blessing is meant to be part of the language of grace, which does not repudiate rights but transcends them. When rights have to come into play between parent and child, as between husband and wife, something is amiss. The true role of a spouse or a parent is to bless.

Ideally the conception of a child is a mini-annunciation. If so, the heart of what is wrong with non-therapeutic abortion may not be child murder, to be bluntly forbidden, but a kind of rejection of vocation more difficult to judge: the parent's vocation to nurture not reject, and maybe the doctor's vocation to heal not destroy. Not every conception can be anything like an annunciation; but abortion, not always wicked, remains tragic. To allow a woman to refuse to bear this child, to cut off this potential life at its source, is to have the courage of the conviction that what parents have to give their children is grace; and to recognise that grace cannot be compelled. What is acceptance unless refusal is a possibility? Far from trivializing parenthood, such choice brings out its proper character of free blessing. The ancient comparison with the grace of God is not denied but reinforced.

At least it is worth keeping the notion of 'blessing' in good working order. If its sacramental meaning evaporates, whether in superstition or sophistication, there will be one bridge the less between the earthly and the heavenly. At present we seem to be at risk of getting the worst of two worlds, pushed by sophistication away from sacramental ideas, towards assumptions not free from superstition.

References

[1] September 1981, p. 367.

[2] Peter May, January 1982, p. 47.

[3] I have touched on some of these matters before in various places; especially in 'Making God findable' in *The Parish Church* ed. Giles Ecclestone, pp. 76–7 (The Grubb Institute), Mowbray 1988.

[4] Johs Pedersen, *Israel* O.U.P. 1926 [p. 182].

[5] I tried to explain this in *The hope of happiness* S.C.M. 1983, especially p. 181.

[6] 'Paracelsus' V.

[7] *Showings* 22.

[8] *Centuries* 41.

[9] e.g. Julian of Norwich, *Showings* Chapter 77 '. . . for that is his own delight and his glory, blessed may he be'.

[10] John Austin, *How to do things with words* O.U.P. 1962.

[11] See Anne Primavesi and Jennifer Henderson *Our God has no favourites* Burns & Oates 1989, p. 68 on the Epiclesis and the hallowing of bodiliness.

[12] Christians such as Quakers who dispense with the sacraments of the church may do this because they affirm the more strongly the sacramental character of the whole creation.

[13] I discussed this further in *Looking before and after* Collins 1988, pp. 64–5.

[14] Gen. 27 : 34.

[15] Though Mark Dalby in *Open Baptism* S.P.C.K. 1989 has persuasively urged that infant baptism *is* the norm, except where the Gospel is preached for the first time.

[16] See Mark Dalby, ibid., Chapter 4.

[17] Peter Baelz in an article in *Crucible* (January-March 1981) argued for 'services of prayer and dedication', as 'a pastoral and provisional expedient' just because the church is still 'unable to reach an agreed mind'.

[18] I have argued this in 'Handling life: does God forbid?' in *Doctors' decisions* ed. G. R. Dunstan and E. A. Shinebourne O.U.P. 1989. This way of thinking is not so contrary to our tradition as may be supposed. See e.g. G. R. Dunstan *The Artifice of ethics* SCM 1974 pp. 82–3; and 'The human embryo in the western moral tradition' in *The status of the human embryo* ed G. R. Dunstan and Mary J. Sellar. See also Norman M. Ford, S.D.B., *When did I begin?* Cambridge 1988.

OLD WINE IN OLD BOTTLES

John Sweet

In June 1972 Peter Baelz led a group of Cambridge lecturers to Leicester Cathedral to speak to a gathering of clergy on 'The use of the Bible today'. We had a hilarious time trying to think of a title for the course, and he finally came up with 'Old Wine in New Bottles', drawing on a saying of Rabbi Jose ben Judah, 'Look not on the jar but what is in it; there may be a new jar that is full of old wine, and an old jar in which is not even new wine'.[1] His own paper addressed the problem of the old and the new: the scriptures are fixed, given, central, fundamental in the life of the church; we cannot do without them. But interpreting them raises daunting problems. Critical study has revealed the variety and diversity of the scriptures; the Jesus of history retreats behind the text of the four gospels. We become aware of the pastness of the bible: we cannot hear it speak to us direct, or if we do we may mishear it, for the 'plain sense', or what to us is the plain sense, has no guarantee of being the right sense: 'although the scriptures continue to speak to us today, they do so in a form which is often distant or strange. They move within a horizon which is not the horizon within which we ourselves move'. We must allow a dialogue to develop between their horizons and ours, and out of this dialogue, out of this interaction between the old and new, a contemporary expression of the gospel may emerge. We need to write, so to say, a 'fifth gospel'. We have to learn to speak, and do, the old truth in new ways. Old Wine in New Bottles.

However true this may be of preaching and teaching, it will hardly do for the use of the Bible in worship. Certainly we have new translations, and some of them do have a (sometimes disastrous) modernity, but this is hardly more than a new label on the old bottle. The content of the Bible, its horizon, stays the same, and if there is to be 'common prayer' it has to be so. In practical terms there is no escaping old wine in old bottles. In the eyes of some this is open to radical objections, but I shall argue that it is not only unavoidable but may also be salutary.

T. G. A. Baker put the issues sharply in an essay on 'New Testament Scholarship and Liturgical Revision' in 1975.[2] He agrees that liturgy has to be conservative in its use of biblical material, while the church in general searches for a fresh approach to biblical interpretation, but changes in theological perspective cannot be ignored: the Bible is no longer regarded as an encyclopedia, or as an infallible oracle, directly applicable to all situations, and we recognise the variety of thought and action it contains, with no pristine unifying principle; revelation is seen to lie not in propositions but in 'disclosure situations', but the pastness of the Bible means there is no direct line from exegesis to exposition and application. The religious experience of the writers is too closely bound up with first century thought-forms to be easily detached and translated (and by the same token, twentieth-century readers are too bound up in their own thought forms easily to step out); and the first-century mythology and imagery are at their highest in passages which had great influence on liturgy: the sending of the Son, his descent from heaven, his birth from a virgin, the resurrection, the ascension, the heavenly session, the coming again in glory at the Last Day (p. 184). The problem of 'translation' is particularly teasing, and Baker thinks current Anglican liturgies 'invite a hard and wooden interpretation of the words that are used' (p. 195). In fact there is too much Bible altogether; this encourages a doctrine of *sola scriptura* at the expense of Christian hymns and readings (from the Acts of the Martyrs, for example), and weakens our understanding of the Holy Spirit. The present, and the nearer past, deserve a larger place, especially when there is 'some evidence to suggest that, as human history develops, the past, and especially the distant past, is losing its hold upon the minds and imaginations of men' (p. 192).

All these factors affect use of the Bible for doctrine and ethics and in the classroom, but in worship the Bible is (or should be) taken out of these instructional or legislative contexts into what is (or should be) a dramatic, participatory context, where stories can be heard as stories not historical information, and symbols responded to as symbols, not coded doctrinal or ethical statements, a situation where a disclosure may take place – all within a controlling context which, whether the service is specifically euchrastic or not, is centred on the life and death of Jesus Christ for the salvation of the world. This could soften the worry about those key passages 'where first-century mythology and imagery are at their highest', and bypass the need for demythologisation. After all people can still respond in the theatre to Shakespeare and Greek Tragedy without any 'irritable reaching after fact and reason'.[3] It is sadly true that worship does not always work like this. It can become a forum for controversy, for anathemas and exclusions, or for moral or political exhortation. The stories can evoke pugnacious assertion of their literal truth. Or the worship can be dull and uninvolving. But *abusus non tollit usum:* abuse of a good thing does not (or should not) take away its proper use.

We must admit that, as things are, the Bible is often administered neat, in small doses – no context, no explanation. Yet if we put the wine into new bottles, if we translate the antiquated thoughtforms, say, into terms of modern existentialist philosophy, then we may lose more than we gain: we stand to lose our continuity with the Christian past, which of course stretches back far beyond Christ, and lose our unity with other Christians across the world. We need the wine in old bottles so that liturgy can unite us with previous generations and with our separated brothers and sisters. How valuable it would be if we had a common Bible, like the Septuagint for the early church, even if it were antiquated and unintelligible in places, like the Septuagint, so that we could all pick up the same echoes and allusions.

Even without a common translation the use of the Bible in the liturgy can serve to bind us into our Christian past, and this is the more urgent precisely because 'the past, and especially the distant past, is losing its hold on the minds and imagination of men'. The past is vital for the present health of any society (and any individual). It has often been remarked that there is no hope of peace in Northern Ireland till Catholic and Protestant children sit down and study history together. H. Richard Niebuhr explored the theme in *The Meaning of Revelation.*[4] In the chapter called 'the Story of our Life' he distinguished between the external history of the objective historian, and internal history which belongs to a community of selves, and which speaks not in arithmetic but in poetry, as when Abraham Lincoln said at Gettysburg 'four score and seven years ago' meaning not eighty-seven but our remembered past. 'When we became members of such a community of selves we adopt its past as our own and thereby are changed in our present existence. So immigrants and their children do, for whom Pilgrims become true fathers and the men of the Revolution their own liberators; so we do in the Christian Community when the prophets of the Hebrews become our prophets and the Lord of the early disciples is acknowledged as our Lord' (p. 71).

In the next chapter he explored the obstacles to church reunion in our partial memories: 'the groups use their separate histories as means of defending themselves against the criticism of others and as weapons for warfare upon rival parties' (p. 119). There can be no integration until we each remember our whole past and appropriate each other's pasts. This is equally true of the even more urgent problem of human reunion: 'to remember the human past as our past is to achieve community with mankind' (p. 117). I conclude that the past we need, the story we need, is not external scientific history, but the internal poetic history of 'a wandering Aramean was my father' (Deut. 26 : 5) or the promise to Abraham that 'in thee shall all the nations of the earth be blessed' (Gen. 18:18, 12:3; Gal. 3:8). Indeed in appropriating the Christian past we need to go back not just to Abraham with Matthew, but with Luke to Adam.

Fitting in with Niebuhr's theme is the flowering of recent interest in 'narrative theology', and the encouragement for greater use of stories in worship, given for example in *Patterns for Worship*, recently produced by the Liturgical Commission of the General Synod.[5] The characteristic biblical way of doing theology, or making theological statements, is through stories, whether the myths of Genesis or the narratives of Samuel and Kings or St Mark, where the theological point is not explicitly stated, but emerges from the stories read as a whole. For example von Rad in his commentary on Genesis saw a theme through the 'Primeval History': 'where sin abounded, grace did yet more abound' – ever widening circles of sin and punishment, yet always the hidden work of grace: the clothing of Adam and Eve, Cain's mark, the rainbow, and after the scattering of the nations at Babel, the call of Abraham, to be a blessing to all families and nations.

This family history is followed through in the stories of the patriarchs, the twelve sons of Jacob-Israel, the settlement, the monarchy, the dispersion of the twelve tribes – through to John the Baptist, and Jesus calling twelve disciples, with a mission to regather the lost sheep of the house of Israel, so that Israel might take up on its vocation to be a light to the nations, and the promise of Abraham be fulfilled. This family history could become a shared past for all Christians, especially those like the Dutch Reformed Churches in South Africa who place great value on the Old Testament, and modern lectionary planning has already given us a widely used scheme, running from the ninth Sunday before Christmas to the second Sunday in Advent, in which the Old Testament is the 'controlling lesson', beginning with the Creation story. The family history beginning with Abraham could provide a shared past not only for Christians but also for Jews and Muslims, for whom also Abraham is 'our father'.

But even Abraham is too late and exclusive a starting point for what Niebuhr recognised as the even more urgent problem of human reunion. In John Taylor's study of African religion, *The Primal Vision*,[6] there is a chapter entitled 'the Second Adam'. On an African view we are human not as individuals but by virtue of involvement in mankind, members one of another by virtue of the history that binds us to a particular past and future. The African shares with the Bible the sense of belonging to a people, in which he is incorporated and maintained by stories, rituals, laws and customs, in a covenant of mutual responsibility and obligation. But Christ comes into this world, as he came into the Jewish world, with a revolutionary challenge. He points men further back and further forward, to the Beginning and to the End. In most African myths the first ancestor is the equivalent of Abraham; responsibility and obligation do not extend to the outsider. Africans are still building their security on the old narrow claim 'we have Abraham to our father'. But 'As in Adam all die, so in Christ shall all be made alive' gives a charter for human solidarity when tribal ties break down, in a common destiny as well as in a common ancestor.

For if we are to find not just a Christian but human unity and peace, we need as well as a shared past a shared future, a shared goal and hope. For this too, the Bible provides a story, but one even more problematical for biblical scholarship than the stories of the past: I mean the visions of the End in Revelation. If we were to have a common core lectionary, controlled by the Old Testament stories of the Beginning, we should need to weave in the pictures of Revelation which so powerfully balance the opening chapters of Genesis.

But here too as with narrative, there may be not a blind alley for theology but a way ahead. Tom Baker remarked that first-century mythology and imagery are at their highest in things like the heavenly sessions, and the coming again in glory at the Last Day, and the problems of translation are at their most acute. 'The hope of the Lord's parousia was something of an embarrassment even to some of the New Testament writers (let alone to us moderns)' (p. 195). It requires mental contortions to join in the acclamation in the Rite A Eucharistic Prayers of the *Alternative Service Book*, 'Christ has died, Christ is risen, Christ will come again'. Taken on its own, as a bald factual statement, 'Christ will come again' certainly does raise problems. But what if it is an *acclamation*, linked for all who make it with a tapestry of imagery, embodying the Christian hope in colour and music rather than factual description? However embarrassed New Testament writers like the author of the Fourth gospel may have been by misunderstandings of Christian eschatology in doctrine and ethics, in worship their enjoyment of these images would have been uninhibited by mental reservations such as we suffer. There may be other reasons for doubting that the John of the Gospel was the John of Revelation, but as Austin Farrer[7] claimed, eschatology is not one of them: having made his meditation on the Last Things to-day John could well sit down and meditate on the incarnation to-morrow; the difference of idiom would spring from the difference of genre.

We can go further and say not only that the images of Christian eschatology may have a proper place in worship, but also that there may be here a way ahead for Christian theology. It is not just that *Lex orandi lex credendi* is a vital perspective in building a systematic theology. Rather it is that the characteristic biblical way of doing theology through telling stories is bound up with the use of symbols and images rather than direct statements; and this is not something to regret and try to extricate ourselves from by mental contortions, but to embrace, as Robert Murray argues in his study of early Syriac tradition, *Symbols of Church and Kingdom*.[8]

Studying a theology which is mainly symbolic, he says makes one ponder on what theology is and what it ought to do. The Bible does not go far beyond symbolic or figurative expression of theological truths, but the church in its move out of the semitic world began to seek language to formulate its reflections. 'There is a moment of optimum equilibrium when, without violating the veils of divine mystery, religious symbols are intelligently presented in such a way as to evoke a heuristic response leading to valid conviction and action – valid, even though the believer could not give a full rational account of what he understands. When that equilibrium is lost the way is open to 'iconoclasm, demythologisation, rationalism and the other mental troubles more characteristic of the west than the east'. The demand for greater clarity has too often led to a narrowing of vision, disputes, anathemas and separations. The Syriac churches faithful to the old, ambiguous pictorial formulas 'kept their consciences from the scandal of irritation against other Christians who had developed other ways of expressing their belief'. G. B. Caird suggested the value of Revelation for a generation starved of imagery.[9] My modest proposal is for a common core lectionary, consisting of the stories of Genesis balanced by the visions of Revelation, to be used for a small part of the year by all Christians everywhere. To be regularly baptized into such a shared past and shared future might be a tiny move towards not only Christian reunion but also human reunion.

But as Richard Niebuhr suggested, a shared past is not enough: we need also a true past – true not in the sense of historically verifiable, though we do need external history as a basis for self-criticism, but true internally – unbiased, generous not defensive, true to the nature and destiny of mankind as defined by the Second Adam, which means we need a true future also.

It is not hard to see the damage that has been done by biased and partial memories. The sharpest objection to the Bible is the one articulated by Marcion against the Old Testament: the picture of a capricious and vengeful deity, who not only desires the death of a sinner but also the extermination of most of his own creation. Very near the beginning we have the story of the Flood, and right at the end the vision of the Lake of Fire, reserved for all who are not written from the foundation of the world in the Lamb's book of life. The Bible has bequeathed a lethal heritage of chauvinism and genocide: Joshua commanded to exterminate the Canaanites, Saul punished for not exterminating the Amalekites, and so the story goes on. All this is part of Christian internal history, but it can be tracked in external history too, for example settlers in North America reading Joshua as a command to exterminate the Indians *(Dei facta sunt praecepta nostra)*,[10] and the chauvinism if not genocide read off from the O.T. story in S. Africa; it is a tendency aggravated by the Western demand for clarity which leads to anathemas and separations, and burnings at the stake. There is a line from the Flood to the gas chambers, a line given clearer definition by images like the Lake of Fire.

Such stories and images are the more dangerous in worship, insofar as it is a dramatic and participatory context, in which attitudes may be shaped beyond the reach of reason. It is vital, then, that the alpha and omega of this lethal Christian memory should not be bowdlerised out of the Churches' lectionaries, as is largely the case (the 9th Sunday before Christmas sequence jumps from the Fall to Abraham, and Revelation barely appears on Sundays and Festivals except in harmless snippets).

The nettle should be firmly grasped: the story of the Flood should have a major slot, and the lections should include both Noah's taking unclean as well as clean animals into the ark (balanced by Peter's vision in Acts 10 when God cancels the Levitical apartheid), and God's promise, guaranteed by the rainbow, never again to destroy all flesh with a flood (balanced by the vision of rainbow and sea in Rev. 4 and the new heaven and earth with no more sea, in Rev. 21). The call of Abraham should be linked with the story of Babel (Gen. 11:1–9 plus 12:1–3) and balanced by Galatians (eg. 3:23–4:7). Controlling the whole series would be the story of Adam, taken up by Paul in the figure of the Second Adam. And at the centre, whether actually celebrated or not, would the Eucharist, the story of the slain Lamb, his blood shed not for the few but for the many – the story which, if rescued from Western demands for clarity and definition, can unite not only Christians but all mankind. All other stories and images would take their place within this controlling pattern, the 'unifying principle' which Tom Baker saw as missing.

But would such a universalistic reading of these key passages be what people *heard?* It would need to be determinedly put across, by lesson introductions, expository sermons, teaching in church and study at home – and there are obvious objections: the Bible should be allowed to speak without clergy or others trying to impose interpretations, and stories and images, like jokes, are spoilt by explanation. More seriously, such a reading is controversial, as the word "universalistic" betrays. But what I am suggesting is not dogmatic universalism (a statement of what will be the case, which would lead to anathemas and separations), but on the one hand recognition that universalism and particularism, salvation and extermination stand side by side in our shared biblical past, for example in the Psalms, and in our shared biblical hope, for example in Rev. 21:1–22:5; and on the other hand, recognition that universalism has a certain priority, in God's intention, over human sin and its results.[11] Universal salvation, for the whole of nature, is the goal, the hope, towards which we move (Rom. 8:21), even though its stories and images stand side by side with those which reflect God's radical intolerance of evil and the self-destructiveness of sin. This is no plea for a formula to resolve the two stories – which would lead to anathemas and separation – only for the 'negative capability' to let the two stand side by side, within the controlling frame of Genesis and Revelation, as outlined, with the Eucharist at the centre.

The precise spelling out of my proposed lectionary chunk would not be easy: a normal service could not accommodate long enough lections to achieve the aim. Patterns cannot be grasped from snippets. But we could meet this difficulty, and at the same time Tom Baker's complaint that there is too much Bible in the liturgy already, by having at a certain time of year, say before Advent, a splurge of Bible reading, which might justify a smaller dose at the other times of year, allowing room for post-biblical things. Just as we have extended readings of the Passion story in Holy Week, so on Sundays before Advent we might have extended readings of Beginning and End – a celebration of the biblical frame analogous to the celebration of the centre.

The Bible is so fundamental as our family history, giving a past and a hope all can share, that we should devote as much energy to getting it right as to getting the Eucharist right. That would mean deploying, as for the Eucharist, all the resources of teaching, preaching and presentation that we can muster – particularly presentation. The standard of Bible reading, and the care taken in choosing and preparing readers, is generally patchy, to put it mildly. Should not readers be selected, trained and authorised for this ministry as carefully as those who are to celebrate the Eucharist? Should not the hearers be as carefully instructed and prepared as for the Eucharist? Should not the Bible be handled as carefully as the eucharistic elements? If the Bible is to be heard as revelation rather than as doctrine or law, it must, like Shakespeare or Greek Tragedy, be so presented as to draw in the hearers; and if it is to capture them for good and not ill they must come to it with a Christian pre-understanding of origin and goal, drawn from the Bible itself.

Such a shared lectionary core could contribute towards the interaction of old and new Peter Baelz wanted. Using the Bible in worship we are committed to old bottles for the sake of continuity, but worship can and should illumine the hearts and minds of those who are properly devising new bottles for the good old wine.

References

[1] Mishnah, *Aboth* 4:20 The course was published in *Theology* LXXVI (March, 1973), pp. 115ff.

[2] *In What about the New Testament?* Essays in honour of Christopher Evans (S.C.M., 1975).

[3] Quoting Keats' 'Negative Capability, that is when man is capable of being in uncertainties, mysteries, doubts, without any irritable reaching after fact and reason' (Letter 32).

[4] The Macmillan Company, 1941.

[5] G S 898 (Church House Publishing, 1989), p. 8–11

[6] S.C.M., 1963.

[7] *The Revelation of St John the Divine* (Oxford, 1964), pp. 42ff

[8] Cambridge, 1975, pp. 346–7.

[9] *The Revelation of St John the Divine* (A. & C. Black, 1966), p. 13.

[10] See H. C. Porter, *The Inconstant Savage, England and the North American Indian* 1500–1660 (Duckworth, 1979), pp. 106–115.

[11] The translators of the Septuagint, the first Christian Bible, took a universalistic view wherever they could: for example in the promise to Abraham, where modern translations render the verb, no doubt correctly, as a reflexive: 'by you all families of the earth will bless themselves' (Gen. 12:3; 18:18), that is, Abraham will be an example of blessedness. Paul followed the LXX. Should not we?

SPIRITUALITY FOR SURVIVAL

Monica Furlong

To read the advertisements at the back of religious papers nowadays is to receive an impression of Christians fleeing like lemmings to retreat houses, and taking courses by the dozen, avidly in search of prayer and contemplative wisdom. You might imagine that we were on the verge of a spiritual revolution, a second Thebaid. Study the ads. more carefully, however, and you discover that a lot of it seems to be about something else, a *professionalisation* of spirituality, as elaborate academic structures are set up to provide diplomas in spiritual direction, or master's degrees in pastoral care, lining the pockets, naturally, of those who provide them. Before this growth industry entirely takes us over, it might be worth having some public discussion about what spirituality consists of, and what kind of help would heal us.

What troubles me most about the professionalisation of spirituality is the tendency to complicate something that is simple, and to mystify that which is straightforward. Spirituality has always suffered from an élitism that made 'ordinary people' feel that their own experiences and insights were useless, and that gurus, clergy, monks, must *really* know what it is all about. I suspect that if there is to be a spiritual revolution for our time it cannot be by way of a further professionalisation of the arts of direction, nor of yet another gathering of power into the hands of an élite, but on the contrary, by means of a vast dissemination of confidence, knowledge, wisdom and awareness amongst a much larger group of people. Everyone has a curiosity about meaning, a sense of wonder, a memory of unity, inklings of God, a capacity for prayer, however much they have learned to be embarrassed about it and to hide it, in an age which, in R. D. Laing's phrase 'represses transcendence.' Everyone has a unique experience that has given them unique, and precious, perceptions. What is needed is more curiosity about, and respect for, others' spiritual experience – (Christians often just seem to be waiting for other people to stop talking so that they can tell them what life is *really* about) – an ability to take our teaching from an old woman in a slum, an illiterate mother of six, a young man dying of AIDS, the homeless person on the street who begs our help, as well as from more orthodox founts of wisdom. Rather as doctors cornered the whole field of health to the point where we all became helpless and ceased to feel responsible for our own physical wellbeing, so in the matter of spiritual health we have too easily handed over our souls to 'experts' who, often enough, knew little of lives unlike their own. The first step to spiritual health is to 'call our souls our own.'

So if we in the churches think spiritual discipline is a desirable good, and we seem to do so, what is it that we are talking about? Something, I believe, devastating in its simplicity and ordinariness, something which every person in a primitive community might know about naturally, which is taking the space to stay in relationship with ourselves and the natural world, thus opening ourselves to God.

In order to achieve this we need both to borrow ideas from the past, yet also to find ways perfectly tailored to our own twentieth century wisdom. At different stages of human development consciousness operates in different ways. Many ways of approaching God which seemed relevant to the saints are no longer relevant to us; they feed into neuroses that we need to discard. Is there a spirituality relevant to us, and to our problems? Perhaps one that does away with the self-punishing exercises of the past and concentrates instead upon getting all of our life into the right sort of harmony – rest, exercise, work, warm relationship with others, aesthetic pleasure, closeness to nature and a consequent respect for it – a gentle and 'natural' form of spirituality.

If a spiritual director has a usefulness (and I suggest that the 'guru' relationship should be regarded more as an exceptional 'one-off' event than as a universal necessity; even then it should be treated with some wariness) it is thoughtfully and gradually to wean us away from our self-destructive and masochistic tendencies, our cluttered and overworked lives, with our guilts and exaggerated sense of responsibility, in the direction of simplicity, harmony and cheerfulness. The better the director, in my view, the keener she will be to hand the power back to us, to encourage us to learn how to care for ourselves. For the only way in which any sort of spiritual change of heart can take place is by cultivating and enriching the soil in which new insights can grow.

Many years ago, when I was a Confirmation candidate, we were taught to prepare ourselves for Communion, I remember, by a process of self-examination – 'How many lies have I told?', 'Have I been unkind to anyone?' etc. Over the years I have discovered what I believe to be a much more useful questionnaire for myself, which goes something like 'Do I feel well? Have I got a stiff neck, headache, indigestion, rash, constipation, insomnia? Do I get constant colds? Am I eating or drinking unwisely? Can I sit still? Am I able to listen properly when other people talk to me? Do I take time to listen to music, to read books, to look at pictures? Am I overworking? Or spending too much? Losing things? Forgetting things? Are money, or success, or possessions, or sex, obsessions? Do I live close enough to the natural world? When did I last look properly at an animal, a tree, a bird, the sky? Can I bear to be alone? Do I take enough time out to let uncomfortable thoughts rise to the surface? Do I use holidays to deepen my awareness, perhaps to challenge my assumptions by living in the wild, or by learning new skills, or by enjoying great art? Am I opening myself to the awareness of people who frighten me – people of other races and religions, homeless people, prisoners, tramps, sick people, old people, mad people?'

To care for oneself in this way is immensely difficult in a society preoccupied with money, possessions, consumerism, haste, and largely indifferent to the natural world. It is sacrificial. It makes one an oddity in the way that the early Christians were oddities, and it challenges the presuppositions of Thatcherite Britain in a way that is inevitably costly. It is also immensely interesting and exciting, a gradual erosion of fears and defences that have kept us imprisoned for years.

I find it helpful to see it in terms of perceiving oneself as an eco-system in which it is important to keep the parts working in harmony with one another, not out of selfishness – nature knows nothing of selfishness – but in order to maintain the delicate and essential equilibrium with other eco-systems. If I am sick, exhausted, depressed, violent, addicted, terrified or mad then, inevitably, my condition will react negatively on others. If I am well, cheerful, peaceable and sane then others who have to live alongside me are going to feel better too.

Needless to say, any spirituality worth its salt is going to be profoundly taken up with ecological concerns in the more usual sense of the term. One of the things which makes me doubt the genuineness of the present Christian spirituality craze is how little it seems concerned with the environment – this makes me wonder whether it is being used as a defensive system rather than for the real demand of growth and change.

It is, of course, immensely tempting to defend ourselves against many of the feelings aroused by the destruction of the environment. I used to think that fear was what we were defending ourselves against – the fear that our planet is inevitably doomed. No doubt that plays a big part, but what I notice repeatedly in myself now is something even stronger – a powerful sense of grief. I believe that we may need to recognise a process of mourning going on within us for so much that is lost and destroyed – for people dying of starvation, for the death of creatures, forests, oceans, for the heartbreaking loss of what is innocent, beautiful, helpless. Yet Christianity knows in its very bones about the resurrection that follows crucifixion, about the life that follows death, and if we do not bring this knowledge to the crisis of humanity we have betrayed our own insights.

Our spirituality, our growth, our prayer, begin with a loving and gentle ordering of ourselves, and then work outwards to a loving and gentle care for the Other, whether the neighbour with Aids, the seals dying of a virus, or the air poisoned by our car exhaust. The most difficult, worrying, yet hopeful, spiritual task is one of *connection* – of seeing how what we do, as individuals, and as groups, brings life or death to our world.

Perhaps the most chilling aspect of organised Christianity – one which non churchgoers unerringly pick up on – is our inability to make life-giving connections, our tendency to lock ourselves into a dogma, a prejudice, a habit, an administrative detail, and not to move. To sit in on Synod discussions, or to read the Church Times correspondence columns, is to be reminded of the massive irrelevance of medieval debate – what would happen if an elephant swallowed the host, how many angels could dance on a pin? It is not so much that any form of speculation is entirely inappropriate as that all our religious thinking needs to be related back to a centre of meaning that maintains perspective, commonsense, sanity. If we sever our link with that centre then we are lost in a monstrous and trivial egoism.

There is a fascinating way in which what happens to us, either as individuals, or as societies, is itself a kind of comment, or critique, of our lives, one which invites us to learn and to change. You do not have to believe in God to experience life in this way though because I do (in that difficult and question-begging phrase) 'believe in God', I read God in the book of my life in a thousand echoes and reflections. More and more I see how I shape my own disasters and disappointments as well as my own joys and happinesses.

Reading in the collective book of humankind what leaps from the page at the moment is a tragedy, the tragedy of our contempt for Nature. Our very real fears of being overcome by Nature – and an earthquake, an avalanche, a hurricane, a drought, reminds us of how right we are to fear her – hardened our attitude over the millenia, into abuse, exploitation and rape. It was easy to forget how gently and wisely she also sustained us, and only now when, on all sides, we perceive that Nature is dying, do we begin to have regrets.

Christianity, following that fateful passage in Genesis about the 'domination' of the earth, not only did not demur, but positively encouraged the degradation of Nature. Nature was, tragically, seen as the enemy of spirituality, as sexuality was seen as a regrettable diversion from the life of the spirit. Celibacy was the ideal, and marriage a regrettable necessity for the weak – it was better to marry than to burn.

It is not only in the field of ecology that the huge implications of this sort of spiritual teaching have become apparent. The women's ordination issue has forced the Churches, with almost paralytic unwillingness, to examine the way in which attitudes to women are entangled in attitudes to Nature.

As questions began to be asked about why women might not be priests, a whole hinterland of fear was gradually revealed. Women might become pregnant and wouldn't it be dreadful to see a pregnant woman in the sanctuary? At certain times of the month women bleed. Suppose a bleeding woman was to handle the wine and bread? Shock, horror!

Women in the sanctuary would have to wear vestments. Everyone knows women are a 'funny' shape, so they would look ridiculous, wouldn't they? Women arouse erotic feelings in men. If a man saw a woman standing at the altar, isn't there a danger that instead of thinking of God he would think about sex? The banality of such discussion conceals a neurosis that goes to the heart of Christianity, the split between sensuality and spirituality. A woman celebrating the Mass evidently brings with her a reminder of sexuality – in the case of a pregnant woman, particularly, evidence of having made love in the not too distant past. Inevitable she brings together what is sensual, bodily, with what is divine. You might think that that is precisely what Incarnation is all about, what the act of Holy Communion itself is all about, yet the rigorous taboo on women touching the holy objects suggests that maintaining the split is of cardinal importance to churches with sacramental concerns. Once you permit women to celebrate Mass it becomes impossible to hold to a spirituality that is divorced from our physical nature.

Often, when speaking of 'mankind' dominating the earth, there has been the entail of man dominating woman. So powerful has the need been to dominate and control women that although, in the early church, women seem to have been prominent as nourishers of the Christian faith, as speakers, and hostesses to the young communities, quite soon their voice faded from the councils, and for nearly two thousand years they were virtually silent, unable to speak up for the Nature that had been so rigorously repressed.

Although many of the writings of the Fathers spoke disparagingly of women, it seems doubtful that they really believed women were contemptible any more than that believed Nature was negligible. They denigrated women, perhaps, for much the same reason that they denigrated 'Mother' Nature, because her power seemed so inexplicable and alarming, and they felt safer if it was rigidly controlled. Yet in both cases their denial – of love, sexual attraction, and fear – was deeply destructive. Women were, and are, silenced, exploited, abused, battered, raped. Nature was, and is, silenced, exploited, abused, battered, raped. And Christianity, however little it may like to think and talk about it, is deeply implicated in both of these disasters.

If we in the churches can bear to look steadily at the world around us, at alienated nature, alienated women, alienated races, and people alienated in the sense that they rarely expect the churches to have anything to say that is relevant to their lives, we are looking at a scene of devastation so great, so little flattering to our self-esteem, that it behoves us to observe and think much more than we act, and when we do act to do it modestly, tentatively, exploratively. Large gestures – Decades of Evangelism and the like – simply ignore that we are as lost and uncertain as the people next door, that we exist in a spiritual poverty that keeps us no more than one lesson ahead of the class, and not always that. I believe that we should be eschewing the 'know-all' arrogance that takes in nobody, and initiating a Decade of small gestures, of simple initiatives carefully applied to very specific situations, any one of which could be jettisoned quickly if it was shown to be useless.

The most important thing we can do is to relate our love for God to a love for the environment, and set up innumerable Christian initiatives designed both to change the damaging habits of living, but also to reach out towards alienated Nature with a love that has too long evaded us. This, like the matter of women priests, opens up the most lamentable gaps within us, gaps of which, in the past, Christians have been quite proud. For to love Nature, we have to be able to feel – terror, weakness, insignificance, awe, ecstasy, as well as love – emotions so disturbing that we have done our best to banish them from the comfortable suburbs of our religion. We have to open up our senses – those same senses that the Fathers taught us to regard with such fierce suspicion. We have to learn again how to look, to listen, to smell, to touch, to empathise in the life of wild creatures in the knowledge that we share our consciousness with them. We have, to know how to set on one side our overweening intellects which have made us the swots of the universe, pale, bespectacled humans as divorced from natural processes as we can manage, and put ourselves back into our natural context, the way women are forced to do in childbirth. We have by studying plants, animals, birds, trees, peoples who live by Nature, to learn the lost language of our ancestors until at least we can stammer a few words of it.

I do not know whether parish churches, so set into the concrete of tradition, can take us into the places where we now need to be. It already looks as if courses, workshop, day conferences, evening classes, feel a more natural environment for the necessary explorations. Small groups and communities, many of them extra-mural, can offer opportunities for new kinds of worship. I have been involved for three years in such a group, the St. Hilda Community, which began in order to invite visiting woman priests to celebrate Communion for a small congregation of women and men, an act forbidden in parish churches. It has met weekly in East London. It has had a mixed history, depending on how much energy any of us felt able to put into it at any one time. I have glimpsed extraordinary moments of religious insight at St. Hilda's, and gone through dark periods, as the very real difficulties of holding a community together have surfaced. But the prayers, the Biblical discussions, the jokes, the care for one another, the ability for people to be open about themselves and their problems, the extraordinary financial generosity, particularly when we have given money to women's refuges or Third World women, has been remarkable

Not surprisingly, we have had no kind of official support – indeed we were thrown out of our first venue, a university chapel, by the intervention of the Bishop of London – but enormous kindness and generosity from innumerable clergy and others. Most of the people who come to St. Hilda's either cannot stomach 'regular church' or feel that they need St. Hilda's to help them survive the disappointment of parish life. Perhaps it might be a sort of model for many other communities with special concerns to set themselves up on the margins of the Church – communities majoring in the environment, peace, racism, homelessness, poverty, addiction, mental illness, and other matters of desperate urgency. Some of these issues – peace for example – are hot potatoes in the Church, political dynamite, so that Synodical discussion always ends in a fruitless cul-de-sac. But the need to look steadily and inclusively at our world, and not to ignore its wounds, is the only thing that can make our spirituality even approximately real, and if it cannot be done properly in the central councils of the churches, then it must be done extra-murally.

What I am talking about is flexibility, and the building of confidence in 'ordinary people' so that they can try to change the world and themselves, instead of being obliged to harden themselves into indifference as they watch one more famine cross their television screens, or pass one more beggar in the streets. Women in particular need their self-esteem strengthened, yet at the moment the institutional Church shows no awareness of this, no knowledge or repentance at how women have been, and are, put down and ignored, in almost every aspect of Church life.

Part of our spiritual flexibility must be to do with breaking down the provincialism of which Christianity, and perhaps particularly English Christianity is so often a victim, and working much more vigorousy with ideas drawn from other disciplines besides theology. Novels, plays, poetry, history, anthropology, biology, physics, astronomy, psychology all nourish us creatively, making it possible to move nimbly between ideas, to find fruitful metaphors, to understand our predicament from many different angles. It seems important too to be able to listen to people with different experience from our own – people who are unlike us sexually or racially – and to try to move through the fear that this so often throws up. Or people who work differently from us – writers, actors, painters, dancers, craftspeople, therapists, teachers. Everyone and everything can help orientate us, can give us clues as to who we are and where we are going.

Again, there are rich seams to be mined in other religions, and if we never read a book by a Buddhist, a Hindu, a Muslim or a Jew describing their religion, still less seek out the opportunity to get to know people of other religions, then we are keeping ourselves unnecessarily poor. If we refuse to learn other spiritual languages, we are choosing a very partial literacy, often with a contempt that masks fear.

I guess there is a real question whether the Christian churches can free themselves sufficiently from past preoccupations to offer any useful leadership in the environmental (which is also the human) crisis, to do more than utter unexceptional platitudes about poverty or race. In areas where real courage and leadership has been required of them – homosexuality, for instance, attitudes to women, the rethinking of marriage or family life – they have showed themselves either chickenhearted, narrowminded, or too concerned at keeping the institution going to offer any prophetic witness. Yet happily within the arthritic structures there are individuals of energy and courage who *do* see what is going on and try to respond to it, so that even if the churches go down, and it is difficult to see how they can survive, Christian voices will still speak, and perhaps all the more powerfully for being released from stifling and inflexible institutions.

It is too late to prevent major damage to the environment – much is already irreversible, and the next quarter of a century will reveal more and more of the extent of the tragedy. But a wise and courageous spirituality can, I hope, limit the damage, can free us from compulsive consumerism, help better decisions be made in the future, bring comfort and consolation in the suffering that we have glibly compounded in the past, and repentance that frees our own guilty souls from helpless preoccupations with sick fantasies. So, in Blake's phrase, we may 'cleanse the doors of perception.'

BEYOND THE WESTERN HERITAGE

AFTER LIBERALISM

Don Cupitt

Until not very long ago theology and the religious scene generally were dominated by the conflict between conservatives and liberals. It was a dispute with ramifications extending far beyond the English-speaking world, and indeed far beyond Christendom. The question at issue was how far traditional religious ways of thinking could or should change in response to the Enlightenment.

There had of course been a period of Enlightenment previously in the Western tradition, during classical antiquity. In that period Enlightened intellectuals who concerned themselves with religion had already explored many of the options available to them – fideism, allegorism, nature-mysticism, syncretism, introvertive or negative mysticism and so forth. But classical antiquity was not democratic, and the Enlightened mentality was a predominantly literary phenomenon, confined to a smallish minority of the population. At first the modern Enlightenment, beginning in early Renaissance Italy, was also a minority affair. The immense power of a persecuting Church obliged it to be relatively discreet and low-key until the late seventeenth century. But then it began to spread rapidly. Democratic and historicist ideologies developed, claiming that before long everyone was going to go over to the Enlightenment mentality. Laws of historical development made the progressive, and ultimately the complete, secularization of culture unstoppable. To survive, it seemed that religion must change. It must come to terms with Enlightenment.

Accepting all this, and being themselves at least half-Enlightened, the liberals set about reshaping religion to make it more humanistic, democratic, progressive and rational. After Descartes the touchstone of truth tended to be located within the subjectivity of the Enlightened individual. The highest court of appeal was the free individual's reason, conscience and experience. So in liberal religion faith duly became more internalized, with more emphasis upon the human Jesus, upon personal religious experience and upon moral action to reform and improve

251

society. In place of the old passive supernaturalism which saw God as having already fully prescribed the whole framework within which human life must be lived, so that nobody but God could bring about any major change in the human condition, it now came to be held that we human beings are historical agents, called upon ourselves to change our world. The Christian individual was invited to join with others in the great work of building the Kingdom of God on earth. This was a christianized version of the contemporary secular ideologies of historical progress. The liberal God was an inspiring moral ideal, a moral Providence perhaps, a side-of-the-angels for us to be on, and the Goal of the whole historical process; but he was no longer quite the admonitory Voice in one's head, the transcendent cosmic Lord, the dreadful Judge and the loving Heavenly Father of the conservatives. He just wasn't quite so *vivid* as he had been. The liberal view of God was no more than semi-realist, at least so far as divine personality and divine interventions in the world were concerned. Yet in other respects, as many people will have noticed, the liberals are usually found to be determined and tenacious realists. They still stand in the old platonic tradition, and believe both in one-truth-out-there and in moral-standards-out-there. They are almost without exception scientific realists, and also social-historical optimists who believe, like John Robinson, if not quite in a guaranteed final historical triumph of the Good, then at least in a constant Love-out-there at the root of things. And they use a good deal of traditional vocabulary.

The consequence of this has been that throughout the hundred years and more of sharp conservative-versus-liberal controversy, much though the two sides might dislike each other, they were in many ways still talking the same language. They were frenemies, despite the fact that conservative religion has remained so determinedly medieval (or, in the case of orthodox Calvinism, in a very distinctive manner, *post-medieval*) in its vocabulary and ways of thinking. Religious truth was cosmic-political. We human beings, it was thought, are lost unless our life is anchored and held steady within an immovable framework of objective divine authority, divine law and divine truth. The conservative cosmology is an upward extension of social authority, sacred, hierarchized and animistic. Conservatives lack, or claim to lack, the Enlightened type of consciousness and for the sake of the social order take pains to ensure that they shall go on lacking it, and they view the humanism and the 'laxity', or charitableness, of the liberals with abhorrence.

Yet sharp though the conflict between them could be, I am suggesting that old-style conservatives and liberals seem in retrospect to have been on pretty much the same side and talking much the same language. The conservatives were ironical enough to have themselves at least a tincture of the Enlightenment mentality (enough to enable them to direct their attacks against it accurately), and the liberals were only half-Enlightened anyway because there was still so much realism left in their theories of knowledge and morality. So beneath the superficial disagreements it is not difficult to detect areas of continuing agreement. Conservatives tend to operate in terms of binary oppositions, whereas liberals are usually universalists. Conservatives tend to believe both in Heaven and in Hell, whereas liberals hope for universal redemption; but both parties believe in an otherworldly salvation after death. Conservatives tend to take a realistic view of miracles such as the Resurrection, whereas liberals interpret them in more 'spiritual' terms, but both parties believe in 'the myth of the normative Origin.' The liberals may refer back to Jesus' consciousness, his character and the early Christian experience of him, whereas the conservatives refer back to propositions and prodigies, but both continue to appeal to the origins of Christianity as authoritative. Conservatives see sin in more ritual terms, and liberals in more social-moral, but both parties go on using the word. And in general, the conservatives did not by their behaviour seriously threaten the liberals' belief in reason, because the two parties were after all able to reason with each other.

In Britain there are still old-style religious liberals and old-style conservatives, bickering cosily in bed together as they have done for so long. But, I want to suggest, during the 1980s we witnessed their dispute turning into a new and altogether less cosy battle, that between the post-moderns and the fundamentalists. To use Jean Baudrillard's useful term, post-modernism may be seen as the ecstatic form of Enlightenment, and fundamentalism is certainly the ecstatic form of religious conservatism. With the end of realism in our century, the loss of all objective bearings, and the steady erosion of the distinction between the real and the fictional, everything tends to be transformed into an excessive, hyperbolical and superreal version of itself; and both post-modernism and fundamentalism are ecstatic in this sense. As we saw in the Salman Rushdie affair, the two mentalities are still preoccupied with each other – but now, they are locked in mortal conflict. For whereas old-style religious liberals and conservatives had some sort of reciprocal understanding, there can be no accord between post-modern and fundamentalist believers. Those who look in one direction see only blaspheming nihilism, and those who look the other way see only absolutist fanaticism. Each seems like a damned soul to the other. Both have gone over the top.

This total breakdown of communication is fatal to the old liberal belief – today associated especially with Jurgen Habermas – in the possibility through dialogue of achieving universal and complete mutual comprehension. Who today can think that possible? But then, in recent years the liberal creed has been failing article by article. The belief in 'clean' and uncontaminated data of experience by which to check theories, the belief in self-present, self-scanning and undeceived individual consciousness, the belief in universal moral and intellectual standards, the belief in the distinctions between the real and the fictional and between fact and interpretation, the belief in the progressive historical growth of both consciousness and freedom, the belief that language can be used to tell the truth, the whole truth and nothing but the truth . . . And when everything is seen to be invented and the belief in truth is recognised to be only a highly-desirable fiction, then Enlightenment passes completion and begins to turn back upon itself and devour itself. There is no longer anything left, in the name of which we are entitled to set out to deprive other people of their fictions. In any case, do we not often nowadays catch ourselves envying other people the fictions they live by? Why be demythologized? Thus Enlightenment in recent years has seen through even itself, and in becoming hyperbolical has lost all grounds for thinking of its own point of view as being in some sense privileged. So the reflexive difficulties into which it has got itself have transfigured it into its ecstatic form, post-modernism. Nihilistic, self-sceptical, super-enlightenment.

Now, as in the 1840s among the Young Hegelians, the question of religion is the heart and centre of the whole affair. If during these past few years you have watched the difficulties of Enlightenment as from outside and with a certain malicious satisfaction, then you are surely gravitating towards fundamentalism. And indeed, is it not obvious today that in the most advanced countries millions of people are reverting with almost-audible relief to a pre-modern mentality? But if on the other hand you have in recent years experienced the difficulties of Enlightenment as darkness and travail within your own soul and as epochal religious events, then you will be sympathetic to the new post-modern theologies now appearing.

The difference is something like this: post-modern religion is religion that fully accepts that it is just human, being made of human signs, and which after having gone through the fires of nihilism knows that it must now continually remake itself as art. And indeed, post-modern religious faith is very close in spirit to present-day painting and writing. By contrast, fundamentalist religion is religion that has glimpsed but has repressed as intolerable and unendurable the knowledge of its own humanness. It has glimpsed nihilism because, of course, it arose precisely out of and in sharp reaction against Darwinism and the later Victorian crisis of faith. So to that extent it really does know the alternative. Its brief glimpse into the Abyss has given to it its sense of urgency. It clutches at authority, charisma, tradition and certainty. It desperately needs to think of religious ideas and religious truth as divinely-given, fearsome and uncriticizable. As everyone who has ever belonged to a fundamentalist or ultra-conservative religious group will know, the group goes to great lengths to exclude unwelcome questioning. Literature is controlled, members must speak in stock phrases and have stock experiences, religious meanings are insistently assumed to be univocal, critical reflection is implicitly (and therefore doesn't *need* to be explicitly) ruled out, and individual deviance is sensed and dealt with instantly. All this bears painful and eloquent testimony to the intensity of people's fear of the Abyss, and the high price they are ready to pay to be shielded from it.

By contrast, post-modern religion thinks that we need to train ourselves to look steadily at the Abyss. In fact, the message of both Christianity and Buddhism (*Die to the self!* and *There is no self!*) is that to gaze steadfastly into the Void purges us of anxious egoism, and liberates us for love and creativity. There are plenty of hints of this in the religious tradition: the Wholly Other, the Absurd, the Sea without a shore, the Divine Darkness, the Dark Night of the Soul, the Incomprehensibility of God, dying with Christ. You must collide with something Unthinkable that unselfs you, and it is the Nihil. Poetically speaking, the Abyss is merciful and gracious. It puts us to death and raises us to life again.

Old-style liberal religion was reluctant to let go completely. It clung to at least semi-realism about God, the objective world and moral value. Post-modern religion is ecstatic liberalism in that it insists upon letting go. It says: Nothing is sacrosanct, everything is revisable. There's nothing out there or in here, and we should be truly beliefless. It is spiritually liberating to be free-floating, and to regard all religious ideas as being human and therefore open to criticism and revision. To *hold on* is to risk falling into superstition and fanaticism. The peculiar sort of poise, strength and sanity that religion can give is only to be had if the full price is paid; one must embrace the Void.

Here, there is undoubtedly a considerable gap between the older liberals and the newer radicals and post-modernists. In the language of William James, the liberals were once-born types. Their outlook was in general kindly and optimistic, their universe solid, comfortable and well-furnished. But they now seem dated. Liberalism is being squeezed out, in society, in the Church and in the intellectual world. Western thought has been getting more and more sceptical for a long time. The main theme is very simple: it is the realization that our knowledge-systems, our beliefs, our myths, our norms, our meanings, even our values, are as human and local and transient as we are. *That* is the thought that freezes the blood. The older liberalism could not bear it, and turned away. But the post-liberal sort of theology I have been trying to describe will be nihilistic. It will head determinedly into the darkness. It knows that Western religious thought now needs to turn in a somewhat early-Buddhist direction, and it claims that in doing so it will not become any less Christian. Quite the contrary. We are talking about renewal.

THE CHRISTIC COGITO: CHRISTIAN FAITH IN A PLURALIST AGE

Simon Barrington-Ward

In the 1960s, coming back from Nigeria to Cambridge to be Dean of Chapel at Magdalene was a cultural shock. I had been studying other people in deserted shrines and new movements in Africa. Now I was to be plunged into the falling apart of my own culture.

Peter Baelz, coming to give the Lent Addresses in our Chapel, was a reassuring figure. He loomed over us in the candlelight and seemed to proffer a thread to guide us circuitously through the shadows. He hinted at a 'metaphysic of love'.[1] We in the West should have begun not from that lonely and self-dividing 'cogito' of Descartes, 'I think therefore I am', but rather from a fresh laying hold on our true source and theme in Christ, 'I am loved therefore I am'.

At the time we were experiencing a sudden fresh spiral of the enlightenment and of romanticism, like that first devastating encounter with Descartes' great 'turn to the subject' and the slide into sceptical relativism that followed. People were losing their bearings in a flux of possible visions and yet the gulf between the surface of life and any over-arching meaning was increasingly hard to bridge.

Peter's words inspired me to search for resources to bring that essential relatedness in Christ alive in this new context.

Poets and artists seemed to help more than theologians. One voice that suddenly won a dramatic response was that of Gerard Manley Hopkins. Readings of his poems opened up a new perspective. No doubt this was partly because of his own peculiar spiritual pilgrimage, breaking tragically with his family, rebelling against the mechanised materialism of his times, championing the endangered natural world, like so many round me.

But the real reason is more significant. Hopkins, in his famous sprung rhythm as his fellow poet, Geoffrey Hill,[2] points out in one of the finest comments on him, was grappling with the deepest issues of his time. At one level he was going with the new tempo he could sense, the turbulent drift and disintegration of the society. But at another level Hill suggests he was pressing back against it.

Wordsworth,[3] in the Intimations, had used a change of time-signature, breaking with his resigned iambic meter, laden with the burden of his times:

'Heavy as frost, and deep almost as life'

to the sudden movement of

'O joy that in our embers,
Is something that doth live'.

Hopkins himself called this 'a magical change' and Hill sees it as a key point in 'the developing life crisis of the nineteenth century'. 'Wordsworth transfigures a fractured world.' Far from being, as critics suggest, 'an injury sustained' it is 'a resistance proclaimed'. Hopkins himself is engaged in the same redemptive resistance.[4]

He uses brief phrases to mediate between a primal cry of agony and an exclamatory prayer, '(My God) my God' in Carrion Comfort, or the drowning nun calling out in the Wreck of the Deuschland, 'O Christ come quickly' in which cry, like the whole poem itself she 'christens her wild worst – best'.

Nicholas Boyle[5] similarly illuminates the Christian poet's sacrificial task. Hopkins seeks to 'repenetrate the secular subject-matter of the experiencing self' with the grace of Christ. He plunges into the flow and fragmentariness of experience and there discerns the instress of Divine Presence, of flashes or glints which fuse Divinity and the created object and which become 'moments in the life of Christ the God-Man'. To do this Hopkins must be immersed in the pain of the very loss and distance from their true destiny of his family, friends and contemporaries. In loneliness and failure he comes to utter, out of the depths of his weakness, poems that with great power break through to a reintegration, a resurrection until 'this Jack, Joke, poor Potsherd, patch, matchwood, immortal diamond, is immortal diamond!'[6]

This struggle for coherence and integrity in the midst of an unprecedented freedom and diversity becoming both spiritual and social is strangely contemporary all over the world. Werner Kretschel, Superintendent and Pastor in East Berlin, has described the vast crowds of demonstrators at the time of the silent liturgy of their marches, gathering in a congregation larger than he had ever seen and singing refrains that were hymns. Many of them were workers, many young. Few had ever been in a Church before. Looking out over that diverse throng, sensing their hunger for meaning, their hanging on his words as had no other congregation before, he longed for a new word, a new pattern. He longed to reach back to the beginning and start all over again.

When Werner described this I thought of Erich Auerbach's incredible evocation in his 'Mimesis' of the Gospels as a new literary form.[7] Auerbach saw in them an astonishing new phenomenon from which sprang the whole development of Western realism he went on to trace, a previously unknown intermingling of the sublime and the humble. Between Eastern and Semitic religion there came into being here a new 'ground of becoming', in which the sacred seemed to enter and in-dwell the secular, the Spirit penetrates the material. Shepherds, fishermen, prostitutes, tax gatherers and ordinary people enact a response to a tremendous composition of human and divine. Out of this Judaeo-Christian source flows a new revelatory mode, in which the Eternal purpose is embodied, in the seemingly inconsequential and contingent histories and actions of particular human beings. A fragmentary succession of detail, almost incidental encounters, actions, gestures, are clothed with everlasting purpose and significance.

It was in the West that this earthing and historicising of Spirit was to take on the freest and most far-reaching form. Auerbach examines its effect in the birth of Western medieval art and literature.

The climax of his story is Dante's 'Divine Comedy', where, as on the facades of Chartres, allegorical and typological figures take on a new human expressiveness, almost breathing and moving, forever held in the characteristic attitude of a living moment. Through Beatrice herself the most passionate human responses and bodily desires are drawn up into the ascent into divine fulfilment. After this high point of balance and interplay of spiritual and material, Auerbach suggests there is a breaking free of the secular. Out of the tension of the central nexus of divine purpose and the free and varied flow of earthly life, were to arise the natural sciences and the beginnings of Western democracy. Finally, through Renaissance and Reformation comes the Enlightenment, as an almost necessary alienation and estrangement, as if its rational and empirical and individualistic impulse had to break free into a final movement towards relativism and pluralism to secure real human liberty. But although the enlightenment was a vital, critical process, the catastrophic distortions of the central spiritual/material nexus at the heart of Christian history continued. Anti-Semitism, the crusades, the aggressive expansion of Europe, two world wars, the holocaust, nuclear destruction. Corruptio optimi pessima! The corruption of the best is worst. But we still have, at the blocked spring of the genuine Christian tradition, with Werner Kretschel, to reach back to the beginning and to find and be found by the essential movement of Divine love, in a story and a person whose 'hour has come'. At the apparent source of some of the world's greatest problems and conflicts we could then rediscover the real means of their ultimate resolution and cure.

If Dante provided the climax of an earlier phase, I believe that it is Hegel who can give us the clue to a new beginning now. Hegel set out to think through the movement of the Divine Spirit into its opposite, into the material, the temporal, and the relative, its willingness to be identified wholly with it, poured out into it and broken by it, and thus to overcome it and to draw it back into a genuine communion. Hegel set out to think through the unfolding of nature and history 'in Christ'.[8] Trinity, Incarnation and Cross provided his new 'Cogito', developed this time not at the outset but in the by-going. 'Hegel', H. S. Harris declares, 'does for the age of knowledge what Dante did for the age of faith.'[9] Indeed the Phenomenology of the Spirit is a vital re-working of the central mediation in Christ between infinite spirit and finite life which Dante also sought to express. But human society has undergone a sea change. The world now has broken more free and Spirit, following the trajectory of Incarnation and Cross, has to pervade the created order more precariously and vulnerably still, to draw an ever richer and more complex world back into relation with its divine source.

The Enlightenment had seen Descartes' 'turn to the subject'; that moment when the philosopher withdrew into himself, shutting his eyes, closing off his senses, determined to accept as true only what had inner evidence in consciousness. Stephen Houlgate has brilliantly outlined the whole story of what followed and of Hegel's response.[10] Traditional Western metaphysical thinking had always seemed to posit a series of opposites set against each other, such as infinite, finite, God and the soul, spirit and material, but now they appeared severed permanently from one another. Once empiricism had culminated in Hume, the last connections were cut between sense perceptions and those necessary connections between observed events such as causality, which had always been assumed to be contained in experience. If these universal determinations were just assumption and habit, then the last links between our subjective experience and any overall meaning were destroyed. God faded away and even the self was dissolved. Even Kant's great analysis of our processes of thought and perception could not, for sure, restore what had been lost. Kant demonstrated that the world, as we understand it, emerges from a synthesis of the basic categories of our thinking with our sense perceptions which yields a sense of continuity and objectivity. But even he kept the Humeian idea that these categories cannot be said necessarily to apply to reality in itself. Beyond all our knowledge lies a reality we can never know or grasp in the 'noumenon'. Our categories, generated by our minds, remain subjective. Their contradictions could never apply to what must be the perfect consistency of reality, whatever that may be.

Hegel went with the flow of this whole movement of thinking a long way. He accepted the turn to the subject, the emphasis on our own inner consciousness. He accepted Hume's view that sense perceptions cannot yield universal, necessary, causal connections. He took gratefully Kant's description of the basic categories and forms of human thought with which our sensory experience must be synthesised. Indeed, he took the argument further and said that these categories were in themselves one-sided and must needs give rise to a process of continuous contradiction. If the categories are this one sided and contradictory, they cannot be used to produce the abstract notion of reality 'in itself', the mysterious 'noumenon', at all.[11]

But, in fact, all we have to do is to render our own thought more explicit and allow the categories to develop, through a constant dialectical process of thought, through a kind of continual death and resurrection. As each contradiction and opposition is over-reached and taken up into a more comprehensive whole, we realise that the structure of our consciousness *is* the structure of being itself. Thought and Being are one. The process of our thought *is* the process of life. *There cannot be a 'noumenon' beyond our knowledge since we cannot even comprehend at all a reality which is inconceivable.* Rather, as we reflect on our own consciousness and understanding and grasp its continuous cruciform movement we find not even a way to bridge a real gap between thought and being. We simply see that gap 'collapse and disappear'.[12] Our consciousness becomes the point at which Being is conscious of itself.

Hegel sees spirit through the continual flux of human thought and consciousness developing and refining an ever subtler and richer complexity. Nothing is lost. Each thought, each entity in life, as it gives itself over to that which over-reaches it is transfigured by it, into a greater whole and preserved and fulfilled as a part of that whole.

This is the law of human self-consciousness and of human interrelationships and of the emergence of human society itself. 'Human self-consciousness comes to be by negating or dying to partial modes of itself' and by growing into a fuller identity. So, 'what Christians worship in Jesus Christ is the incarnation of man's true character, identity and determination, an identity which brings fulfilment if it is accepted, but, which "damns" man, if it is rejected.'[13]

This is how Hegel sees the Spirit working through the whole disintegrating process of the Industrial Revolution and the emergence of a plural market society of free and autonomous individuals. He lamented that we could not get back to the ideal community of the Greeks. But this led him into a quest for a form of society combining individual freedom and mutual commitment which is strangely appropriate to our universal concern at the present.[14]

Hegel has often been read as the developer of some total rational system in much too literal and shallow a manner. For Hegel, reason yields itself to work its infinitely patient and hidden course through unreason, through the mass of contradiction and chance occurrence. What he is depicting is a movement not of inexorable progress, but, of something nearer to the process in the natural world envisaged by scientists like Prigogine[15] or Paul Davies[16] where order emerges continually through, and out of, chaos into an ever-increasing complexity. The Universe thus has a 'pluralistic, complex character'.[17] Structures appear to break down and are subsumed into richer, more highly elaborated structures in 'a creative act taking place through time'. The unfolding organisation has less the character of a mechanism than of 'a work of art, involving change and growth, . . . rejection and reformulation of the materials at hand, as new potentialities emerge.'[18]

Nietsche, like many of his disciples since, misread Hegel, seeing him only as the author of a 'fixed and discredited system'. In contrast he reverted to the scepticism of Hume and became, with his brilliant and wayward creative imagination, a philosopher of total pluralism and fragmentation without remainder. His great claim was to face the reality of a life stripped of all meaning with either Dionysiac ecstasy or, in another mood, heroic defiance.

But neither he nor his disciples seem to have grasped the fact that Hegel had already faced this reality, and discerned, within the dynamic pulse of thought and life itself, an emergent meaning and unity, a resurrection beyond the death of God.[19]

Thomas Mann saw Nietsche as the source of German irrationalism in which ultimately he found the context of Fascism. Adrian Leverkuhn in Faust is certainly, like many of his Cambridge equivalents in the 1960s, a Nietsche figure. He clearly 'lives in a period pervaded by Nietche's thoughts on culture and society'.[20]

I have always seen the less attractive, more seemingly bourgeois Zeitblom, his faithful friend and companion alongside him, with his dogged devotion to truth and morality, as a kind of Hegel figure. The possibility remains of a far more open reading of Hegel than that of Nietsche and his followers allows, of the fullest possible acceptance of the chaotic flux of thought and life and the continuous dream-like appearance and shifting, collapse, and reintegration of religions and philosophies. But through it all Hegel discerns most subtly a movement of order and purpose and continuous growth into wholeness genuinely symbolised in the death and resurrection of Christ and in the corporate experience of his risen life in the Spirit. Hegel's philosophy becomes itself a 'metaphysic of love'. It is the divine love which pours itself into our creation, which makes itself vulnerable to our self-assertion and self-alienation, and which, at cost, re-penetrates the heart of our existence in order to draw us back, and, with us, the whole created order into an ultimate reunion with itself. As we give ourselves in love and as we yield ourselves to this love, so we discover that it is the truth of everything. 'I am because I am loved.' This is the Christic Cogito which I believe is still to emerge in and through the intermingling of faiths, ideologies and cultures in the melting pot of the coming century.

The enlightenment has been effectively exported along with modern technology to every part of the world. Every faith has now for some time been undergoing the same crisis that first befell Christianity. The Christian task now is to let the Cross of Christ through the action of the Spirit be planted deep within the consciousness of all faiths. But the only way to do this is above all to plant the Cross again in the heart of the consciousness of Christians themselves. We need a more far-reaching repentance and a self-criticism, a deeper humility, a costlier readiness for long-term loving. We need to learn what it means to take up the Cross and follow, to be 'crucified with Christ' as we are 'plunged into the life' of worlds in crisis. To such a witness (martyria) these worlds are open.

Much of Africa, for instance, is a vast, open 'laboratory of the Spirit', where traditional localised spirit worship and reverence for fathers and mothers, and for founders of the community or the family, have increasingly given way to more wide-ranging new cults, offering healing, witchcraft cleansing and the promise of new belonging. Intermingling with these are many varieties of new churches or praying groups, often founded by a visionary healer, woman or man, who may well have begun from some kind of vision of Christ, as Himself either a supernatural healer and intermediary or as some kind of spirit power. But as these leaders have developed their grasp upon Christ and deepened their vision, sometimes they have come nearer and nearer to the Christ of whom the missionary poet Arthur Shirley-Cripps wrote in the 1930s:

'The black Christ with parched lips and empty hands,
A black Christ bowed beneath a heartbreak load'.

Gabriel Setiloane wrote long ago of

'This Jesus of Nazareth with holed hand
And open side like a beast at a sacrifice.
Stripped naked like us,
Browned and sweating water and blood,
That we cannot resist Him,
How like us He is –
Beaten, tortured, put upon, truncheoned,
Denied by His own and chased like a thief in the night . . .'[21]

The fullest expression of this vision comes in African oral tradition, in folk sermons and spirituality and in dreams and visions. The whole story of Simon Kimbangu[22] and the symbolism of his being seen as the black Simon who carries the Cross behind Jesus, and the many liturgies associated with the movements which have converged in Kimbanguism in Zaire are typical. Similarly the deepest and richest fruit of the East African revival in people like Archbishop Luwum show a very profound perception of Jesus's suffering lordship, where His sacrificial blood offers an internal cleansing which restores trust and dedication. Jnani Luwum, hunter,[23] warrior, dancer, who gave his heart and life to Christ and then suffered for his resistance to injustice, is still one of the most powerful icons or reflections of this black Christ, bearing the pain and struggle of the people. As Christ penetrates more and more deeply into the consciousness and imagination of African spiritual creativity, new black theologies and visions have still to unfold.

The crisis in Islam is bound up with the question as to what is the true nature of Islam itself, an issue frequently debated over the years in, for instance, the press in Pakistan. Must its identity depend upon the imposition of Sharia Law and a total Islamic society within an egalitarian theocracy, or will other ways have to open up beyond the present Iranian model or the Wahhabi[24] inheritance of Saudi Arabia? There is the question raised long ago by Dr. Muhammed al Nuwaihy,[25] 'Can Islam find its way to a discovery of transcendence which allows, indeed necessitates, a suffering identity with creation and humanity?' He found this suffering identity in the Qur'an itself. Others, crossing a sufist bridge, have begun to find it in the person of Jesus, sometimes discovered first through the Qur'an and later through a reading of the Gospels. There are little groups and individual pilgrims, often led by dreams and visions as well as by detailed study of the New Testament, coming into being in tiny ways in the very heartlands of Islam. Among them is one such leader whom I met in Pakistan, who has meditated profoundly over the radio on the agapé love of Christ and whose group, meeting and worshipping, chant fragments of the New Testament as they might chant the Qur'an. Many of the scattered Christians in Iran itself have stories of this kind and may well be preparing the way for a future reaction. These, of course, are well outside any Church and are mostly people developing their own movement on the very fringes of Islam itself and in relation to it, though discovering the Cross and Risen Presence of Jesus as transcending and replacing the Islamic Law. One Sufist theologian, Hassan Askari,[26] drawn first by Bach's Matthew Passion when he was in Germany, and, studying the Cross as the heart of Jesus's whole life and teaching, increasingly has seen the relationship of the Cross to Islam itself. For him 'Christ becomes a sign for all of us'. 'There is no Cross but the Cross of Jesus.' And again, 'The Cross is a sign in the realm of relationship between God and humanity for people of all faiths today.' It may yet be that the Person and Cross of Christ will be enabled to penetrate from within to the heart of the Islamic consciousness, just as Christians begin to recognise the Jewish-Christian inspiration which lies behind Muhammad, and his genuine prophetic calling.

In the crisis which Indian religions and Buddhist patterns are also confronting in the face of the modern urban industrialised world, renewed questions arise as to the role of the Sangha, the monastic community, or indeed of sadhus and gurus, in relation to the social and political world.

There is a real sense in Eastern tradition in which it is difficult for the 'renouncer' or the Bodhisattva ever fully to return and grapple realistically with the transformation of this world. It is fascinating to speculate what effect it would have had even on Gandhi's own miraculous mission, if he had come nearer, as Stanley Jones longed for him to do, to the apprehension and acceptance of a fuller and richer Christology.

Certainly, again there is a wide scattering of pilgrims and disciples in the tradition of the famous Narayan Tilak,[27] the poet of Maharashtra, who became a Christian Sannyasi, or Sadhu Sundhar Singh, with his Sikh and Bhakti Hindu[28] background, who became a devotee of Jesus Christ through a vision. There are those who come first to this understanding through perceiving Christ as their Guru or Avatar and growing into a fuller sense that He is the presence in a newly unfolding history of the pleroma, the fullness of the ultimately transcendent in our midst. There are a host of such visionaries within and beyond the Church in India. Stanley Samartha has also pointed out how many Hindu and Muslim artists 'have been inspired by themes in the life of Jesus Christ, particularly his sufferings, death and resurrection'.[29] Christ is beginning to dawn in new ways, and within a Hindu or Sikh or Muslim milieu, He discloses elements of a new relationship with the Divine. He is not just absorbed into another way of thinking, but, within the growing interchange of faiths, begins to modify the sensibility of others.

So much of all this movement points to changes in the deep structure of human consciousness and in the imagination and perception as well as intellectual conceptualisation.

Indeed, the crisis in Christianity itself might well be said to be to do with the loss of capacity for this kind of imaginative thinking which Hegel called 'reason'.[30] A great deal of Western Christian theological writing today is Kant-ian in spirit and starts from the assumption of the relativity and limitation of all our religious perceptions so that beyond there is a kind of Divine 'noumenon'.

Many of the contributors to two recent conferences and anthologies attempting a pluralistic theology of faiths, the one presided over by John Hick and Paul Knitter,[31] and the other by Leonard Swidler, have something of the general tone given by Hick and Swidler in their introductions to the two resulting volumes. Hick's exploration of the cultural relativity of religions, like that of Gordon Kaufman and Cantwell Smith himself, essentially seems to rest on this type of Kantian distinction. Gavin d'Costa[32] in a brilliant critique of John Hick, has drawn attention to his Kant-ian roots.   Kaufman[33] speaks of the various religions as 'products of human imaginative creativity in the face of the great mystery life is to us all!' Leonard Swidler talks of trying to develop some kind of 'Ecumenical Esperanto', and we all know what has happened to that particular linguistic experiment. One of the most penetrating comments in either anthology is that of Stanley Harakas,[34] an Eastern Orthodox theologian in the Swidler volume. Commenting on a long rambling paper of Cantwell Smith on the history of 'religion', he asks whether it is possible that a Western, rationalist and individualistic bias has weakened Cantwell Smith's sense of the inner cohesion and integrity of religions. Is this kind of theology, in fact, seeking the formation of a new world-wide religion 'after the fashion of that described in Isaac Asimov's novel Foundation?' 'Are not the methods of the history of religions somewhat anaemic for the accomplishment of such a goal in the face of the powerful revelatory claims at the source of most organised religions?' A weakened Christology[35] leading to anaemic and abstract concepts in which the proponents of new universal theologies circle round a Kant-ian void is scarcely likely to be productive. Significantly those with a greater intensity of imagination and depth of spiritual consciousness at the conferences, such as Raimundo Panikkar, came nearer in their colourful flamboyance to a Nietschian pluralism, and in the end proved equally incoherent, retaining from their Christian roots only a vague and seemingly groundless optimism. Sadly they were all trying, with some degree of success, to drag Hans Kung across what was regarded as a crucial rubicon as his Christology weakened and his general abstract humanism thickened into the murky waters of their own relativism.[36]

All this conversing was a long way from the real, deep spiritual interaction in the melting pot of religions amongst people of profound prayer and faith at a time when out of the West we need to be able to bring something beyond our Western enlightenment heritage. We need not to lose our corporate hold upon the Living Christ in whom we have indeed been given the supreme disclosure of the Divine Love. The last thing that those of all faiths, who struggle with us at a profound level to find new visions and new social patterns for humanity, need is for us to lose our own testimony to the fullness of Christ. This, after all, is what, in the heart of the disintegrating movement we set in motion throughout the world, we still have to bring. The historical passion through which so many are passing is here comprehended in its central critical moment. The content of the faith in Christ becomes the immanent content of thought itself. The way of love and self-giving, the way of the Cross opens up a way that runs through all ways, a way in which God is finally known to be, in the confusion and through the relativity, absolute.

> Quaerens me sedisti lassus
> Redemisti crucem passus
> Tantus labor non sit cassus
>
> Seeking me you became weary
> Redeeming me you suffered the Cross
> Let not so great a labour be in vain![37]

I recall once Bishop Lakshman Wickremesinghe of Kurunegala presiding at a Communion amongst Buddhists, Hindu Tamils and Christians all working for peace and justice in his strife-torn country. He towered over us tall, refined and austere, as he broke the bread and put forward the cup. I was reminded strangely of Melchisedek, bringing forth gifts from beyond and into the flux. Lakshman's fine face was absorbed, his form trance-like, his hands moved in the characteristic gestures of giving thanks and breaking. He had spoken in a way which drew upon both Buddhist and Hindu stories and legends. His central action was now such as to affirm the reality of the infinite presence and power of God's love released in the midst of our struggles, confusion and pain. Nor, glancing at the faces around was there any doubt anywhere that this essential brokenness of the God-Man on the Cross undergirded and strengthened their own hold upon faith and life and opened up for all of us a way through meaninglessness and death. The same movement which we glimpsed through Manley Hopkins, through African prophets and Indian artists and poets and devotees, through Auerbach and Dante, was there disclosed: 'the love that sways the Universe and the other stars . . .' This is the love that in Hegel, as in Peter Baelz's 'metaphysic of love' bears all things, believes all things, hopes all, endures all, the love that releases life into its infinite outpouring of variegated forms and fusions, to draw all back ultimately into communion and union with itself.

References

[1] In Peter Baelz's lectures, 'Prayer and Providence' and 'Christian Theology and Metaphysics', Epworth, London 1968, he develops allied themes.

[2] Geoffrey Hill, 'The Lords of Limit', Andre Deutsch, London 1984, 'Redeeming the Time'.

[3] ibid., p. 87.

[4] ibid., pp. 98–9; p. 101.

[5] Nicholas Boyle, 'The Idea of Christian Poetry', p. 436, Vol. 67, No. 798, October, 1986 (special issue for Kenelm Foster O. P.). It will be seen that I am heavily indebted to this article and its author. He links Hopkins with a development in which also Erich Auerbach and Hegel figure and he indeed led me to both. I don't want to lay any any blame on him, however, for the use I have made of this linkage.

[6] Gerard Manley Hopkins, 'That Nature is a Heraclitean Fire and of the comfort of the Resurrection Poems', p. 111, Oxford 1948.

[7] Erich Auerbach 'Mimesis: The Representation in Western Literature' tr. Willard Trask, Princeton, 1953, ch. 9, 'Farinata and Cavalcante'. Page 101 of Charles Williams', 'The Figure of Beatrice', Faber. 'A Study in Dante', Faber, London 1953.

[8] Even J. N. Findlay in 'Hegel, A Re-examination', in one of the more 'secular' interpretations of Hegel, acknowledges this: 'In the Christian study of the Incarnation, Passion and Resurrection of Christ', Hegel comes to see a pictorial expression of his central thesis: that what is absolute and spiritual can emerge only in painful triumph over what seems alien and resistant. Hegel may, in fact, be said to have used the notions of Christianity in the very texture of his arguments, and is almost the only philosopher to have done so!' p. 30, 'Hegel a Re-examination', George Allen & Unwin Ltd., London 1958.

[9] 'Hegel's Image of Phenomenology', H.S. Harris, p. 106, in Cho K.K. (Ed.) Martinus Nijhoff, 'Philosophy and Science in Phenomenological Perspective', 1984, Dordracht/Boston/Lancaster.

[10] Stephen Houlgate: unpublished paper presented to the Society for Systematic Philosophy, A.P.A., Washington, December, 1988. Hegel Society of Great Britain, Oxford 1989: 'Thought and Being in Kant and Hegel', pp. 11–12, Houlgate here quotes, 'The Philosophical Writings of Descatres tr. John Cottingham, Robert Stoothoff and Dugald Murdock, 2 vols., Cambridge, Cambridge University Press 1984, II, 24. My argument at this point is taken entirely from this paper and the development by Stephen Houlgate of elements of the same argument in 'Hegel, Nietsche and the Criticism of Metaphysics', Cambridge (Cambridge University Press), pp. 100–18, 1986.

[11] p. 118, 'Hegel, Nietsche and the Criticism of Metaphysics'.

[12] Stephen Houlgate, 'Thought and Being in Kant and Hegel'. For whole argument, see pp. 15–17.

[13] p. 98 Stephen Houlgate, Hegel Nietsche and the Criticism of Metaphysics.

[14] There is much here of relevance to the struggle, in this country and world-wide, for ways of evolving a genuine 'social market', where no-one is marginalised and all are equipped continually to take part and to benefit.Hegel, over and over against Marx, who misread him, is coming into his own as a social philosopher. Compare 'Hegel An Introduction', Raymond Plant, with the development of Plant's own thought in Kenneth Hoover's and Raymond Plant's, 'Conservative Capitalism in Britain and the United States', Routledge, London 1989 (and 'Faith in the City: Theological and Moral Challenges' Diocese of Winchester, S023 9GL, an implicit critique of recent Christian social thought).

[15] Ilya Prigogine and Isabelle Stengers, 'Order out of Chaos', Heinemann, London 1984.

[16] Paul Davies 'The Cosmic Blueprint', Heinemann, London 1987.

[17] Prigogine & Stengers, op. cit., p. 9.

[18] Louise Young, 'The Unfinished Universe'. Simon Schuster, New York, 1986, p. 15 quoted in Paul Davies, op. cit., p. 6.

[19] There is scope here for a careful critique of deconstructivism, and of what seem misreadings of Hegel such as that of Jacques Derrida and of his fascinating and stimulating theological disciple, Mark Taylor (e.g. Erring – A Post Modern A/theology, Chicago, 1981). Don Cupitt less plausibly shares some similar approaches in 'The Long Legged Fly', S.C.M., London, 1987. For a trenchant critique of Nietsche from a Hegelian viewpoint cf. Stephen Houlgate (Hegel, Nietsche and the Criticism of Metaphysics) see Note 10 above.

[20] Thomas Mann: 'the Uses of Tradition', T. J. Read, Oxford 1974, p. 367ff.

[21] 'Theology in Africa' Kwesi A. Dickson, p. 196, Darton Longman & Todd, London, 1984.

[22] 'Simon Kimbangu', Marie-Louise Martin, Blackwell, Oxford 1975.

[23] 'Jnani Luwum: The Making of a Martyr', Margaret Ford, Lakeland, U.K., 1978.

[24] For one exploration of this question see, 'Faith and Power, The Politics of Islam', Faber, London 1982.

[25] In an unpublished lecture given in Cairo Cathedral in May, 1974. This is a theme richly explored by Bishop Kenneth Cragg, more than any other, recently in 'Muhammed and the Christian', D.L.T. London, 1984. 'Jesus and the Muslim', G. Allen & Unwin, London 1985, and, more generally, 'The Christ and the Faiths, Theology in Cross-Reference', London 1986.

[26] Hassan Askari 'Inter-Religion A Collection of Essays', Printwell, Aligarth 1977.

[27] 'The Experimental Response of N. V. Tilak', Plamthodatil S. Jacob, C.I.S.R.S., Madras 1979.

[28] 'Sundar Singh', a biography, A. I. J. Appasmy, London 1958.

[29] pp. 82–3, Stanley J. Samartha 'The Cross and the Rainbow in the Myth of Christian Uniqueness', eds., John Hick and Paul Knitter, S.C.M., London 1987.

[30] Hegel took from Kant the distinction between 'Understanding', ordinary, objective rationalising, and 'Reason', a more far-reaching participatory activity of mind and spirit with power to enter into the real development of the structures of consciousness and being.

[31] John Hick and Paul E. Knitter, ibid. Leonard Swidler, ed., 'Towards a Universal Theology, of Religion', Orbis, New York 1987.

[32] Gavin D'Costa, 'Theology and Religious Pluralism', Basil Blackwell, Oxford 1986, esp. p. 39 Scottish Journal of Theology 39, (1986).

[33] p. 8, Jn. Hick and Paul F. Knitter, op cit.

[34] pp. 77, 78, Leonard Swidler ec., op. cit.

[35] There is usually a sublime assumption in these theologies that New Testament criticism must lead to a reduced and relativised understanding of the significance of the claim that Jesus is the Christ. 'The Myth of God Incarnate' is the necessary foundation for the 'Myth of Christian Uniqueness'. Christian theologians of Pluralism have made so many foolish self-destructive disclaimers about the true nature of Christ and done so much to damage the very treasure they have to bring. Other readings, however, suggest otherwise, e.g. C. F. D. Moule, 'The Origin of Christology', Cambridge 1977, for an earlier response. Nearer to the present argument, Gerd Theissen, 'The Shadow of the Galilean', S.C.M., London 1986, evokes a great sense of the mystery enigma and unclassifiable quality of Jesus transcending shallow judgements. The crucial point is that, even if Jesus's presentation of the Kingdom is that of 'God in Strength' ('God in Strength', Bruce Chilton, Freistadt 1979), that strength in all three synoptic gospels and strikingly in Paul, Hebrews and John, is realised and released in the 'weakness' of the Passion.

[36] For an analysis of Hans Kung's 'progression', see Scott Cowdell, 'Hans Kung and World Religions, The Emergence of a Pluralist in Theology', March 1989. But he is, in fact, still not quite submerged by the end of 'What is True Religion?' at the end of Leonard Swidler, ed. (op. cit., Note 29), although Christianity is now true 'for me' and 'cannot claim to have comprehended God', p. 25, op. cit. The Kant-ian noumenon hovers ahead. Both Gavin d'Costa (op. cit., Note 31) and Michael Barnes's 'Religions in Conversation: Christian Identity and Religious Pluralism', S.P.C.K., 1989, have recently offered lively critiques of current Christian approaches to Pluralism and propounded positive and creative approaches. Both begin to transcend the tired typology of 'exclusive' and 'inclusive' and offer good critical surveys of the main protagonists. Neither seems quite to have grappled adequately with the central Christological issue. Rahner's framework no longer seems adequate on the one hand and a dialectical pneumatology not a sufficient alternative on the other. Keith Ward's stimulating but rather static attempt to draw out an 'essence' from selected representatives of various faiths (Images of Eternity D.L.T., 1987) is also lacking in this vital area.

[37] From 'Dies Irae' Latin Mass of the Dead. See Hymns Ancient and Modern Historical Edition, London 1909.

RELIGIOUS EDUCATION IN A MULTIFAITH WORLD

Jean Holm

'Why should I teach falsehood when I can teach the truth?' This rhetorical question appeared in a letter in the early seventies. It was written by a teacher in charge of religious education in a secondary school, in response to one examination board's suggestions for revising its O level syllabus. The revision was a cautious one, allowing schools to continue with traditional biblical teaching if they wished, but including, for the first time, optional sections on non-Christian religions within two of the papers.

This teacher was expressing, albeit rather forcefully, what many felt; they had been trained to present Christianity as unquestioned 'truth'. It was the natural legacy of the Church of England's contribution to the education system of England and Wales. Elementary schools were founded in the nineteenth century by the National Society – or, to give it its original title, The National Society for the Education of the Children of the Poor in the Principles of the Established Church. The 1944 Education Act, with its religious clauses, was only regularising what had, by tradition, been the practice in many schools, and the spate of Agreed Syllabuses which followed the Act enshrined the confessional aim of the subject: to nurture pupils in the Christian faith. The 1949 Cambridgeshire Agreed Syllabus, *Religious Teaching for Schools*, for example, ends its introduction with these words, 'To teach Christianity to our children is to inspire them with the vision of the glory of God in the face of Jesus Christ, and to send them into the world willing to follow Him who was among us as one that serveth, because they know that in such service alone is perfect freedom'.

The syllabuses consisted mainly of biblical material, plus stories about Christian missionaries and social reformers. They conveyed Christian doctrine, not only by teaching about God and his actions in the world and the divinity of Jesus, but by the syllabus being set within the framework of the Christian year.

The content of the subject and the method by which it was taught were challenged in the sixties. Ronald Goldman's research, published as *Religious Thinking from Childhood to Adolescence*,[1] and Harold Loukes' research, described in *Teenage Religion*,[2] raised serious questions about the effectiveness of the traditional Bible-based approach. The consequent shift of focus from biblical material to the experience of the pupils (life themes in the primary school and the discussion of personal and social issues in the upper forms of the secondary school) was attacked by many Christians who described the 'new RE' as humanist. This was not, however, its intention. The aim was no less confessional than in the traditional Bible-based form of the subject. The life themes Goldman advocated turned out to be ordinary primary school topics with Bible stories added, leading to an explicitly Christian conclusion, for example, an exploration of the topic of light leading up to Jesus the light of the world. And the book Loukes wrote to show how religious education could be experience-based was called *New Ground for Christian Education*.[3]

One interesting development in experience-based education was the setting up of a Schools Council project on the humanities, which included history, geography, English and religious education. Its aim was to provide resource material which fourteen and fifteen year olds could use in coming to their own conclusions on such issues as education, the family, war and race. The project suggested that the teacher should be a 'neutral chairman', so that when the pupils' discussion showed that they could see only one side of the argument he or she should feed in material on the other side.

Many of the religious education teachers who volunteered to take part in the pilot stage of the Humanities project were committed to the 'open-ended' approach to the subject, but they were shocked to discover, when they listened to the taped discussions they had had with their classes, how much they were actually influencing their pupils by the tone of voice in which they responded to pupil contributions and by their use of such comments as 'That's a good point' or 'Well . . .'

Even more problematic was the question of teacher neutrality on ethical issues. This came to a head with the topic on race. If the pupils were developing a positive attitude towards race relations, should the teacher be a 'neutral chairman' and feed in contrary material to try to restore the balance? It raised the question: are there limits to tolerance? In the end the resource pack on race was not published.

In the sixties educationists were becoming aware of the presence in schools of children from Hindu, Muslim and Sikh backgrounds (having had a blind spot about Jewish children). One or two of the new Agreed Syllabuses acknowledged this, but it made no difference to an otherwise completely ethnocentric syllabus. West Riding (1966) was the first of the new 'family' of syllabuses. A one-page article on 'Jewish children and their religion' explained the Jewish calendar, and a one-paragraph article on 'Immigrant children and their religion' acknowledged that 'English children need to be helped to appreciate these different beliefs and ways of worship', but five of the six books listed for 'further information' were from the *Christian Approach to . . .* series,[4] and the only ways in which the actual syllabus acknowledged the existence of other faiths were the suggestion that one of the eleven themes for sixth formers could be 'Comparative study of religion', and that 13–16 year olds might include 'World religions', along with such themes as 'Mass media', 'World hunger', 'Alcohol and drugs' and 'The colour problem' under the general heading 'Facing world problems'.

It is widely assumed that the move to multifaith religious education is the result of immigration to Britain of members of other religions. That certainly helped to speed up the change, but the more fundamental reason was the challenge presented by the philosophers of education at the beginning of the seventies; they asked, How do you justify what you are doing as a good educational experience for *every* pupil? Religious education's response to this challenge was to suggest that the aim of the subject should be to help pupils to understand the nature of religion and what it means to be committed to a religion, and most of the post-1975 Agreed Syllabuses have included some form of this aim.

If pupils were to be helped to understand the nature of religion, there had to be three major changes in the way the subject was taught. First, the approach could no longer be confessional. Teachers would need to describe what 'Christians' do or believe, rather than what 'we' do or believe. Secondly, the syllabus would be broader than before; it would need to include several religions. To study only one religion would lead pupils (or adults for that matter) to assume that, for example, other religions had a similar attitude to doctrine or accorded similar authority to their sacred texts. Thirdly, the focus would shift from the past to the present. Pupils would need to learn about living religions, including, for example, what Jesus means to Christians today, and not only the gospel stories about him.

This new approach to religious education paralleled the development of religious studies in higher education. In fact, A level and O level examinations in the subject were renamed Religious Studies, and many secondary schools now have religious studies departments.[5] It is not really an appropriate name, however, for what is done in the primary school, especially with the five to seven age group. Perhaps the simplest solution would be to call the subject Religion.

Such a name might be a useful reminder of the aim of the subject. Many people have assumed that multifaith religious education means putting the emphasis on teaching pupils about *religions*, rather than on helping them to understand the nature of *religion*. One consequence which follows from adopting the first of these two emphases is that the selection of religions to be studied becomes problematic. Where does one draw the line? In the sixties it had been argued that the religious education teacher's job was to help children to 'find a faith to live by',[6] with the choice being between a religious and a non-religious interpretation of life, in effect between Christianity and Humanism. When the syllabus was broadened to include other religions, many people automatically assumed that the purpose of the subject was still to help pupils to find a faith to live by, and felt, therefore, that all the options available in Britain should be put before them. Such a supermarket approach betrays a lack of understanding of the nature of religion, ignoring the importance and complexity of religions' truth claims, and implying that they are rather like different brands of coffee or baked beans, from which one chooses according to one's preferences.

Of course the faith by which some people live is not religious, so there was a call to change the name of religious education to 'stances for living'. This expression was used in the Birmingham Agreed Syllabus of 1975, which, before the notorious legal action brought against the local authority, had advocated courses in Communism as well as Humanism. The material on Communism had to be withdrawn from the teachers' handbook which accompanied the syllabus, but Humanism remains in the secondary school section. Humanists complained that if children heard only about religious stances for living at primary school, then Humanism as a faith by which to live was being put at a disadvantage. The British Humanist Association made its plea for parity with religions in a pamphlet titled *Objective, Fair and Balanced*.[7]

Another consequence of emphasising religions rather than religion is that teachers have been tempted to 'do' a religion at a stage when children are too young to understand it at more than a simplistic level. When it became obvious that multifaith religious education was gaining in popularity, publishers rushed to produce textbooks, many of them including five or six religions, with a chapter on each. Not surprisingly, youngsters tended to think that when they had learnt about Muhammad and the Five Pillars of Faith they had 'done' Islam. Not surprisingly, also, with such a superficial knowledge they found it difficult not to confuse one religion with another. Ironically, these textbooks tended to treat Islam, Hinduism and Sikhism as living religions but for Judaism and Christianity they reverted to presenting mainly biblical descriptions.

What then does multifaith religious education look like when the emphasis is placed on religion rather than religions? There is, of course, no such thing as 'religion'; it is found only in the form of particular religions. However, if one looks at what makes up the framework of a religious person's life, one finds that there are a number of elements through which the beliefs of a religion are both encountered and expressed: places and forms of worship, festivals, sacred texts, pilgrimage, ethical teachings, symbols (including symbolic actions), rites of passage and the traditions associated with the culture in which the religion is being practised.

It is a study of both the similarities and the differences in the form of these elements and their place within the religions which will help pupils to understand what religion is and what is involved in being a committed adherent of a religion. This is best accomplished by cross-cultural themes, where, for example, nine or ten year olds might spend some weeks on 'sacred places', learning about mosques, synagogues and churches, although in a community which included Hindus or Sikhs, their places of worship should obviously be included. As the children find out about the architecture, art, furnishings, place of the scriptures, holy days, etc., they are being pointed to significant beliefs of the religion. A cross-cultural theme on 'spring festivals' or perhaps 'festivals of light' will involve not only the way in which the festivals are celebrated today – the focus on living religions – but also make possible some understanding of the significance of past events which are re-experienced each year in the life of the religious community.

Where pupils have access to a range of reference materials, particularly primary sources, rather than working from a textbook, they become aware of how much more there is to a religion than the aspect they are learning about, and where they are encouraged to produce a display or a class book to show others by words and pictures what they have learnt, they are much less likely to confuse one religion with another. Such confusion is nearly always the result of superficial teaching.

Diversity exists within religions as well as between them, and pupils must be aware of this if they are to understand the nature of religion. This does not have to involve a study of all the main denominations or sects within a religion; the awareness can come from discovering, for example, that the Russian Orthodox Church celebrates Christmas on 6 January (perhaps in a primary school topic on 'seasons'), or that Orthodox Jews interpret the Torah differently from the way in which Reform Jews do (perhaps in a secondary school scheme of work on 'sacred writings').

A recognition of diversity in Christianity is possibly one of the greatest differences between traditional religious education and the approach now being adopted in many schools. In the former each teacher presented his or her personal understanding of the Christian faith, ranging from the most conservative to the most radical. Pupils became aware of the pluralism of Christianity only as they met different interpretations from different teachers, but as these were seldom acknowledged, let alone explained, pupils tended to discount Christianity altogether as 'contradictory'.

The question of which religions to include in a religious education syllabus can be more easily answered when the emphasis is on religion rather than on religions. Understanding something of the major religions represented in Britain is obviously important for young people growing up in a multifaith society, and where children from faiths other than Christianity are represented in the school those faiths should certainly be included. Beyond that, however, the aim of the subject provides certain criteria for selection. In order to avoid the conclusion that religion is expressed in a similar way in all faiths it will be important to choose religions with some contrasting features, such as Judaism, which subordinates theology to practice, Islam, which gives to the Qur'an the place which in Christianity is given to Christ, and Hinduism, in which epics and myths have a much more fundamental role than scriptures in the religious life of the people.

What then about Christianity? The introduction to Cambridgeshire's 1982 Agreed Syllabus includes these words: 'As the Christian tradition has profoundly influenced our culture, Christianity will be the religion that is studied in greatest detail.'[8] A similar statement can be found in most syllabuses. Surprisingly, this represents an agreement between people with highly divergent views about religious education. On the one hand there are those who are most reluctant to concede that other religions should be taught in this 'Christian' country, and who therefore argue for what they see as the pre-eminence of Christianity in the syllabus. On the other hand there are those who regard a multifaith religious education as essential for the study of religion. They feel that it is appropriate for more time to be spent on Christianity because pupils living in a predominantly Christian culture will find it easier to understand the significance of the elements of religion – places of worship, festivals, rites of passage, the influence of scriptures on the culture, etc. – when they can, quite literally, see them in the society around them. Those who hold this view would argue that in Israel, for example, it is Judaism which should be studied in greatest detail.

So far I have mentioned only major world religions, but pupils would not have an adequate understanding of religion if they had never considered traditional religions. There are thousands of religions practised by tribal peoples, for whom the concept of religion separate from the whole life of their society is inconceivable. This is not, however, an easy topic to handle, and it is best left until the senior years of the secondary school, when pupils are more mature and, on the basis of the study of religion which they have already done, can appreciate the practices and values of traditional religions.

Unfortunately, religious education has not been immune to the British education system's obsession with beginning with origins and working chronologically through historical developments, with its built-in implication of progress. Many teachers consider that the 'origins' of religion provide the ideal starting point for a secondary school religious education syllabus. Eleven year olds are presented with discredited theories from nineteenth century anthropology about 'primitive' forms of religion before moving on to short courses on major world religions. One widely-used textbook was called, significantly, *From Fear to Faith*.

Multifaith religious education has come under attack for a variety of reasons. To some people it represents a threat to the Christian faith, though experience shows that pupils are more willing to take Christianity seriously when it is taught in a wider context. Some people say that pupils should learn about other religions only after they have a solid grounding in their own – an argument which raises interesting questions about what should be done in the multitude of schools which now have at least some children of those 'other religions' in their classes. Others claim that it is not necessary in their area because there are no 'immigrants' there, as if education has no relevance to pupils' future. Yet others argue that pupils find learning about 'world religions' boring and confusing.

This last point is sometimes made by teachers who have tried to teach religions. It is regrettable but understandable when one considers the situation in which they have had to work. The textbooks produced by the educational publishers tended, until very recently, to deal with religions incredibly superficially and not always accurately. Most of the teachers were trained to teach either a Bible-based or experience-based form of religious education, and they merely added 'world religions' to an otherwise unaltered syllabus. In the early eighties it was not uncommon to find twelve year olds doing a rapid gallop through several religions (usually excluding Christianity), after a year on the life of Christ and before moving on to discussing personal and social issues.

During the eighties considerable thought was given to developing a genuinely multifaith religious education, in contrast to merely tacking on a course on world religions. Cambridgeshire's Agreed Syllabus is an example of what such an integrated religious education would be like. Its aim is to 'enable pupils to understand the nature of religion, its beliefs and practices', and it explains that if this aim is to be achieved pupils will need 'a knowledge of religions . . .; an exploration of those aspects of human experience which raise questions about the meaning of life; skills of interpretation to help them to understand the significance of religious beliefs and practices; a sensitive attitude towards other people's deep convictions and towards their own maturing ability to think about

THE WEIGHT OF GLORY

questions of belief and value'.⁹ These four sets of objectives are then
spelled out in some detail; for example, the first of the six skills listed
is to 'understand the nature and use of language in religion'. Then follow
sets of staged objectives, indicating which aspects of the main objectives
are appropriate for the 4–7, 7–11, 11–14, 14–16 and 16–19 age groups.
On this basis a coherent syllabus can be constructed.

Religious education was, like all other subjects, affected by the 1988
Education Reform Act. This involved both gains and losses. The 1944
Act had assumed that Religious Instruction and the collective act of
worship would be Christian, though it nowhere stated that. The 1988
Act states that any new Agreed Syllabus 'shall reflect the fact that the
religious traditions in Britain are in the main Christian whilst taking
account of the teaching and practices of the other principal religions
represented in Great Britain'. So multifaith religious education is now
recognised in British law.

However, in its section on worship the Act takes a step backwards. It
states that in a maintained school 'most' of the acts of worship during
any school term 'shall be wholly or mainly of a broadly Christian
character'. Many schools had developed assemblies which were times
of sharing and reflection – a focus for the school as a community. The
requirements of the Act are potentially divisive. In addition we have the
irony of a multifaith religious education whose purpose is no longer to
teach for religious commitment, alongside the requirement for pupils to
be placed in a position of commitment when they move from the
classroom to the assembly hall.

It is of course possible that schools may continue with their present
practice, though there are signs that some parents will exercise their new
powers as governors to make certain that head teachers observe the letter
of the law. Churches could make a positive contribution to education
by initiating open and informed discussion, not only among their own
members but wherever possible including members of other religions,
about the issues relating to religious education and worship in the
schools which all their children attend.

References

¹ Routledge and Kegan Paul, 1964.
² S.C.M. Press, 1961.
³ S.C.M. Press, 1966.
⁴ Edinburgh House Press, c.1958.
⁵ Peter Baelz was largely responsible for getting the Cambridge A level
Religious Studies syllabus revised at the beginning of the seventies, and it was

his suggestion to Sheldon that they should publish books which could be used in the new style A level Religious Studies courses which eventually bore fruit as the *Issues in Religious Studies* series (edited by Peter Baelz and Jean Holm).

[6] This expression was first used in the 1959 Crowther report on the education of pupils 15–18, referring to education as a whole. However, it was taken up by the religious education world, and eventually canonised by being included in *The Fourth R*, the Durham report on religious education commissioned by the National Society (S.P.C.K. 1970).

[7] 1975.

[8] *A Framework for Religious Education in Cambridgeshire*, p. 5.

[9] ibid., p. 1.

EXPERIENCE IN INTER-RELIGIOUS DIALOGUE

Peter Donovan

In the development of religious understanding we must make room both for the basic structure of religious experience, which provides the point of reference for religious language, and for the whole series of concepts and analogies in which and through which this experience is apprehended and expressed.

Peter R. Baelz, in Christian Theology and Metaphysics.[1]

Inter-religious dialogue has been moving steadily into the centre of Christian debate. More books and scholarly articles than ever before are being written on the subject. Comprehensive ecumenical statements and guidelines have been drawn up and published, church advisory bodies and consultative councils established, international conferences and local workshops and courses held.

As Robert Morgan says, surveying the past decade's developments, the theoretical issues raised by the Christian evaluation of other religions 'are on every theologian's agenda'.[2]

One aspect of the subject, however, deserves more theological attention than it has yet received. It is the part played in inter-faith encounter by religious experience itself. For far from being merely an incidental accompaniment to the process of dialogue, first-hand, up-to-the-moment experience provides, as Peter Baelz puts it, the 'point of reference' for all other religious understanding.

Any theology of religions, any response to 'the challenge of pluralism', which neglects the experiential dimension (particularly that of the layperson and the theologically unselfconscious) will be depriving itself of some highly relevant primary data.

It is one thing to affirm that religious experience must be taken account of, in thinking about dialogue, and another to accept the theological consequences. The report *Towards a Theology for Inter-Faith Dialogue*, for instance (circulated in preparation for the Lambeth Conference of 1988), in almost its opening paragraph, states:

Theological reflection ought not to be undertaken in the abstract. It must engage with the experience of those whose lives are daily caught up in inter-faith situations.[3]

However, the role which the report envisages for experience turns out to be a somewhat limited one:

The insights of Scripture and Tradition have to be related to experience, so that experience may speak to Scripture and Tradition. At the same time it is to be expected that Scripture and Tradition will sometimes confirm and sometimes judge what is perceived in experience.[4]

Experience, on this view, is on a par with scripture and tradition; and consensus among them, not conflict, is what is to be expected.

But for a great many ordinary folk who find themselves engaged in inter-faith dialogue, things are by no means so straight-forward. What they discover through their day-to-day encounters with people of other faiths may seem only remotely related to what theologians or the Church have to say on the subject. Scripture and tradition may, in their eyes, make very little positive contribution to the urgent task of building relationships and healing divisions within today's pluralistic and multi-racial societies. Religion itself, indeed, may be felt to be largely to blame in helping to create and reinforce the divisions and tensions.

This is not simply a situation calling for increased pastoral activity or ecclesiastical leadership. It raises issues beyond the Church's social or missiological concerns, going to the very heart of Christianity's contemporary relevance and indeed the credibility of religious belief in general in the present world.

BEYOND THE CHURCH

The official spokespeople and theologians of mainstream, ecumenical Christianity are in danger of overestimating the significance of the Church's part in the inter-faith debate. Religiously significant contacts between people from different races and cultures will take place whether or not the churches seek to promote them, and whether or not Christian scholars are successful in drawing up satisfactory 'responses' or 'positions' on the subject.

Undoubtedly inter-church and denominational organisations during the past couple of decades have taken the lead again and again in fostering dialogue at local, national and international levels. They have the personnel and commitment to ensure that they will continue to play an important part. But Christian organisations, nonetheless, are by no means always the prime movers or the major participants in today's inter-religious encounters.

There are also composite organizations such as the World Congress of Faiths, the Council of Christians and Jews, the World Conference on Religion and Peace, and the recently formed Inter Faith Network for the United Kingdom; along with other specialized bodies which provide training and opportunities for dialogue (the Multi-Faith Centre, Birmingham, for instance).[5]

Vital participation in inter-religious activity occurs also, of course, in the context of public education. With school, college of education, and university curricula having expanded to embrace world faiths, a wealth of fresh information has become available to the learning public, the effects of which are by no means confined to the cognitive level. The lessons learned and skills acquired may be put into practice well beyond the range of the churches or other traditional religious bodies.[6]

Many other professional and vocational paths also lead into the territory of religious diversity. Those employed in social work, public health, community relations, refugee resettlement, citizens' advice and similar agencies find religion-based cultural differences and sensitivities coming to their notice every day of the week. Likewise, international aid and relief organisations (United Nations agencies, Amnesty International, Red Cross, Save the Children Fund, Oxfam, and the like) provide countless occasions for people of good will to share the common ground of humanitarian action, while seeking ways to understand and to bridge religious and cultural boundaries.

It is far too simple, therefore, to portray the theological challenge of religious diversity as simply 'a dialogue between Christians and those of other faiths'. In fact, the vast majority of the people in modern societies who encounter religious pluralism at first hand do so from positions well outside the normal bounds of organised religion, whether Christian or otherwise. They do so, above all, in the form of personal, non-institutional contacts: as neighbours and work-companions, customers and clients, friends and lovers, sporting rivals and political opponents. Their thinking on the subject of religion is likely to be far more shaped by family background, the news media and the fashions of popular entertainment than by multi-faith religious education or Church-organised efforts at dialogue.

Far wider, then, than is generally recognised in official church thinking on the subject, is the experiential domain emerging and evolving out of contemporary religious diversity and interaction. Here is a vital source of fresh evidence to be taken into account by today's theologians and philosophers of religion, as they frame their proposals for future inter-faith theologies, their theories of religious pluralism.

INTER-RELIGIOUS EXPERIENCES

What is distinctive about the inter-religious experiences of people today, that theology should take particular notice of them? A reference to new or fresh forms of religious experience, brought to the public's attention by 'other religions', might suggest a venture into the exotic or the occult. Indeed in becoming acquainted with other religious traditions and cultures, modern-day Westerners are sometimes intrigued to find mysticism, magic and psychical phenomena still playing a prominent part: astrology, spiritualism, the powers of yoga, the miraculous achievements of monks or 'god-men' like Sri Sathya Sai Baba, and so on.

No doubt there is serious theological thinking to be done about the persistence of traditional supernaturalism and mysticism amongst the world's religions. But the sorts of inter-religious experience to which I wish to draw attention are of a quite different order. They are pre-eminently modern and this-worldly; experiences at the leading edge of contemporary society's value-consciousness. They involve issues and situations which feature in our most penetrating literature and drama, our most perceptive social comment.

One feature especially characterizes inter-religious encounters, whether they are formally organised between official representatives, or impromptu meetings between laypeople. It is a shared sense of standing together on 'holy ground', a recognition that awesome issues are at stake, awesome risks being taken. For almost without exception each participant can be found representing one or more of the great divisive forces of our world – race, culture, power, territory, ideology. All can find, in their national and often their own personal histories, memories of involvement in oppression, persecution, genocide, slavery, terrorism, hatred and enmity – whether as guilty parties or as sufferers at the hands of others.

Such occasions, with their common recognition of portent and peril, evoke a collective awareness of being engaged in a challenge to the *forces of evil*, in the very forms in which that phrase still has some meaning and power. They thus put religion and theology crucially to the test.

Are there, given the record of history to date, any reliable resources at all on which human beings in such situations can draw? Are there any grounds for confidence in the power of goodness, any bases for optimism about love for others and the desire for peace? Is ultimate reality – God, in any theological scheme of things – up to the task of guiding humanity to right resolutions of such issues? And is grace or inspiration available to meet personal and spiritual needs in the meantime?

The testimony of people today experiencing multi-faith encounters at all levels is that, from time to time at least, those questions seem to receive affirmative answers. What their experiences bear witness to, above all, is a tremendous capacity for forgiveness and generosity of spirit – often emanating from those who have suffered the most wrong at the hands of others. This capacity, this power for peace-making and acceptance, is perceived to be more than of mere human origin. It is recognised as a blessing, a gift from God.

Those experiencing such things, especially when not taking part in any official 'inter-faith encounter', may well not choose to use anything like the traditional terminology of religions in seeking to express or record the spiritual meaning they find in the occasion. Even in the case of deliberate inter-religious dialogue, organised as such, there are obvious reasons for the avoidance of pious or confessional language, with its risk of patronising or triumphalist overtones.

That very sensitivity and restraint in the expression of experience and profound insight can easily disguise the fact that thoroughly religious responses are taking place, momentous spiritual discoveries being made. The nature of the situation is often such that those outcomes are understated, perhaps even concealed behind what to an observer may appear to be mere politeness, or excessive caution and diplomacy.

Thus second-hand accounts of what is discovered, valued, or achieved in inter-faith encounters commonly seem somewhat bland or unremarkable, particularly to the ears of traditional believers. Accusations of settling for 'wishy-washy humanitarianism' or 'lowest-common-denominator spirituality' are sometimes levelled by those who feel too much is being made of the virtues of dialogue. 'Sloppy syncretism', 'Esperanto religion', 'theosophical mish-mash', are among the epithets that have been used by more mainstream religionists, in criticism of the seemingly low-level achievements of the inter-religious enterprise.

Yet such criticisms leave unanswered the question: what other common language is there, beyond the range of established doctrinal systems and confessional usage, by which contemporary people (especially lay-people) can grasp and express fresh experiences of transcendent and spiritual reality? And after all, is simple humanitarianism, without overt piety or doctrinal verbalisation, so obviously an unfit mode in which to appropriate and articulate profound theological discoveries?

Situations characteristic of inter-racial, multi-cultural, and inter-religious encounter are undoubtedly occasions of intense spiritual significance for those involved. Regardless of the fact that they may express their experiences not in the well-formed sentences of conventional belief but in modest and stumbling phrases at the very fringes of religious language, for the participants themselves the sense of challenge to inner integrity may be nothing less than terrifying, the ethical and inter-personal sensitivities exquisite.

Mixed feelings, divided loyalties, and conflicts of principle combine with anxieties about understanding and being understood, decisions when to speak and when not. Constantly at hand is the possibility of failure to be true to oneself; the easy way out through avoiding real issues, retreating into dogmatism, or lapsing into stereotyped judgments. The sense of spiritual peril, the existential predicament characteristic of such occasions, may not be consciously before the mind of all participants. But it is there, nonetheless, as an inner struggle or tension with its own peculiar feeling-tone and characteristic emotional qualities, recognisable to all who have any experience of typical dialogue situations.

Because the potential is great both for success and for dismal failure, and because the implications either way are of global significance, inter-faith encounters are occasions of maximum spiritual intensity. When they disappoint, there is a sense of profound human defeat and loss. When genuine insights are gained, modes of resolution and sources of healing discovered, there is an awareness of encountering resources beyond normal human capacity – evidence of transcendence, in a real and immediately relevant sense.

In the inter-faith domain, then, a distinctive and often intense form of religious experience can be identified. Arising as it frequently does beyond the sphere of Church authority and influence, few established doctrinal guidelines may be applied to it, few approved responses or paradigms invoked to evaluate it. Yet it brings into focus some of the most profound human issues of modern times, setting them in actual, living contexts, and creating through them both existential and epistemological possibilities. Any discovery of spiritual truth and moral insight made in such situations must be all the more valuable because of the difficulties involved. Any reassurance about transcendent sources of wisdom, forgiveness or grace must be of genuine theological significance – and indeed, in a sceptical, secular age, of considerable apologetic significance as well.

INTER-FAITH THEOLOGIZING

If the experiences of a broad range of people in the inter-faith domain have anything like the degree of religious or spiritual significance I have suggested, whose task is it to respond theologically to that fact?

The Lambeth Conference report tells us:

> Exploration of the theological aspects of dialogue must not be left only to those who live in multi-faith situations nor to the theologians. The reflection is the responsibility of the whole Christian community open to the guidance of the Spirit.[7]

But even when conducting its deliberations in the light of the 'wider ecumenism' reflected by the World Council of Churches Dialogue Sub-unit or the Vatican Secretariat for Non-Christians, the Christian community will inevitably tend to view religious diversity primarily as a crux for traditional Christian theology' or as a challenge for the Church's social and evangelical mission. Such a view, while perfectly proper as far as it goes, may still not do justice to the theological importance of multi-faith experience as a general religious phenomenon in its own right.

While Christian thinking on the subject has been increasingly vigorous and productive in the recent past and promises to continue so, it still generally proceeds on the assumption that Christianity, and the other 'major world religions', form more or less clearly defined belief-systems. The task of theologians of encounter then, it is assumed, is to investigate possible inter-relationships between those systems, and devise theories as to their compatibility or incompatibility.

Even John Hick's 'Copernican revolution' model, effective though it has been in promoting a pluralistic theology of the 'universe of faiths', can still be taken as giving unquestioned priority to the viewpoints of the few major established religions (the 'planets' of the Copernican universe).[8]

But in the cosmos from which Hick's model is drawn, it could be argued, the 'space' between the planets has turned out to be equally rich in informative content: gravitational fields, free-floating dust and gases, cosmic radiation, satellites, comets and asteroids . . . even a growing number of space-travellers. Too much attention to the nature and behaviour of the named planets can lead to our missing a wealth of relevant data which exists elsewhere, and which throws considerable light on the universe's origins and its possible future. The parallel with the religious universe is obvious.

John Hick himself is well aware of the need to include more than simply the familiar, 'domesticated' forms of religious experience in framing a philosophy of religious pluralism. Thus after writing

> a mutual mission of the sharing of experiences and insights can proceed through the growing network of inter-faith dialogue and the interactions of the faith-communities . . .

he admits to having mentioned only 'the great world religions' and asks:

> What about the other smaller ones, including the many new religious movements which are springing up around us today? And what about the great secular faiths of Marxism . . . and humanism?[9]

But even there, the primary reference-points still seem to be positions within some distinguishable tradition or path, some system or other.

A proper appreciation of the theological significance of the experiential 'raw material' in inter-faith encounters will not be well served by that assumption. For it makes it difficult to give adequate weight to the element of inchoate and unselfconscious, pre-theological human experience, in which religious response and spiritual sensitivity are essentially located. There is, after all, no good reason to assume that the work of God in the world, nowadays any more than in the past, will be confined to the articulate representatives of distinguishable belief-systems.

It is commonly maintained, particularly when inter-religious dialogue is being fostered at institutional levels, that the best people to take part are those firmly committed to their own faiths and sure of their convictions, while at the same time willing to hear and appreciate the convictions of others. Thus we are told:

> For Christians commitment to inter-faith dialogue has to go hand in hand with a deeper commitment to the Christian tradition. This comes from living within the worshipping community and engaging with the central truths of Christianity in eucharistic celebration.[10]

Not only is that a counsel of perfection; it also overlooks the fact, already noted, that many nowadays who experience genuine inter-faith encounters may well be at the very outskirts, if not beyond the bounds, of the Christian faith and its traditional institutions.[11]

That such a state of affairs may nonetheless open up fresh theological vistas appears to be supported by the experience of those attending a World Council of Churches sponsored women's inter-faith dialogue held in Toronto in June 1988. There participants apparently found themselves sharing a deep sense of spiritual common ground precisely because, as women, they held only marginal status in their respective religions, at least as traditionally interpreted.[12]

Thus multi-faith dialogue and interaction between the critics of institutions, the disaffected, the extraditionalists and post-religionists, should not be underrated as a source of theological insight. While from the point of view of the religious 'mainstream' it is perhaps inevitable that such people's experience should be discounted, there is much to be lost theologically in doing so. Those at the fringes of religions, and beyond, are every bit as much citizens of the wider world of faith to which, more than ever before, theology must nowadays turn its attention to find its experiential point of reference.[13]

For all its usefulness in mapping possible responses to religious plurality, then, the by-now familiar triad of *exclusivism, inclusivism,* or *pluralism* seems more of a hindrance than a help, when approaching the wider domain of personal and communal experience of inter-faith encounter in modern societies.

That triad itself presupposes an insider's point of view, a position from within a defined belief-system. It asks how, from that point of view, the existence of other such systems may be regarded. While that will, of course, be the point of view of most who write or theorize about the subject, it by no means adequately fits the situation of a great many whose experience is nonetheless vitally relevant to any theological judgement on the matter.

It would be a disaster for Christian theology if 'the challenge of other religions', or 'the debate between exclusivists, inclusivists and pluralists' were to turn into a set-piece academic exercise, the mere re-shuffling of a neat pack of abstractions, bearing little relation to the untidy, complex, and rapidly developing realm of inter-faith encounter in the 1990s.

The theological net must be cast wider still. Christian theologians applying their skills to the subject of religious diversity must be prepared to theologize on behalf of the religiously 'unchurched' as well as their fellow-believers. Such 'free-lance' theologizing is far from being a bad thing. It is likely to have very positive feedback for the more specific theologies demanded by confessional commitments.

For Christian theology, the 'challenge of inter-faith encounter' is neither simply an issue in the field of the Church's mission or social responsibility, nor just an occasion for hermeneutical and doctrinal ingenuity. Participation in inter-religious encounter can put vital, fresh content into conventional talk about faith, spirituality, and salvation. It is an opportunity for growth not only in the Christian idea of God but in the sense of God in general. Only as theologies of religious pluralism are matched with a grasp of just how widely that sense is to be encountered today, will they have the power to lead to greater knowledge and understanding, on the part of Christians and of all others who respond to truth when they meet with it.

But what will be the long-term outcome for Christian faith? Can the uniqueness of Christ be preserved? Where will Revelation, Incarnation or the Church's Great Commission find their place? Will a form of unified religious experience emerge, as John Macquarrie has suggested?[14] Are we moving towards a 'world theology', as proposed by Wilfred Cantwell Smith?[15]

Such questions are being debated and inevitably will continue to be. There is a case to be made, however, for self-restraint by theologians; for not being too eager to formulate answers on those issues until the experience of inter-faith encounter itself has been more widely shared, and the awareness and knowledge of God it brings more generally recognised as an undisputed reality.

References

[1] London: Epworth Press 1968, p. 137.

[2] 'A Decade of Theology', in *Theology*, July 1988, p. 277.

[3] *Towards a Theology for Inter-Faith Dialogue*, Second edition, published for the Anglican Consultative Council, London: Church House Publishing 1986, p. 1.

[4] ibid.

[5] The Inter Faith Network, formed in March 1987, links more than sixty groups and organisations, large and small, throughout Britain, concerned with inter-faith relations. Address: 5–7 Tavistock Place, London, WC1H 9SS.

[6] See chapter by Jean Holm, below.

[7] *Towards a Theology for Inter-Faith Dialogue*, p. 1.

[8] *God and the Universe of Faiths*, London: Macmillan 1973, chapters 9 and 10.

[9] 'A Philosophy of Religious Pluralism', reprinted in *Problems of Religious Pluralism*, London: Macmillan 1985, p. 44.

[10] *Towards a Theology for Inter-Faith Dialogue*, p. 30.

[11] cf. John Bowden, *Jesus: The Unanswered Questions*, London: S.C.M. Press 1988, p. 179.

[12] Reported by Pauline Webb in *One World*, No. 139, October 1988, pp. 6–7.

[13] On the implications of including sects, cults and new religions in the multi-faith dialogue, see Kenneth Cracknell, 'Dialogue with New Religious Movements?', in *New Religious Movements and the Churches*, edited by Allan R. Brockway and J. Paul Rajashekar, Geneva: WCC Publications 1987, pp. 157–67.

[14] 'The Convergence of Religious Traditions upon One Experience', in *The Scottish Journal of Religious Studies*, Volume X, No. 2, Autumn 1989, pp. 75–85.

[15] *Towards a World Theology*, London: Macmillan 1981.

CHINA:
SOME THINGS TO
THINK ABOUT

David Paton

What follows is one man's attempt to suggest what those of us who care about China and the world might be thinking about. It may be desirable to indicate the experiences which led the author to these perspectives.

I arrived in Hong Kong in December 1939, and after a month there and a few days in Shanghai went up to the Language School in Peking for the best part of a year and a half. Then in the summer of 1941 I was made priest in Hong Kong and travelled overland into 'Free China' with two Chinese colleagues, one of whom was, like me, in the Student Division of the Y.M.C.A. and the other in the Student Division of the Y.W.C.A. For three years I was stationed in Y.M./Y.W. Student Centre of the academic community at Shaping Pa a few miles outside the wartime capital Chungking. I was I think the only foreigner in this academic community of about 10,000 which included two universities and other nationally important institutions.

I left for home in the summer of 1944, waiting in India for a free passage on a troopship. When I got home I married an S.C.M. secretary, herself born in China, and at the end of 1946 we came out with the Church Missionary Society to Foochow to the staff of the Fukien Union Theological College. We were liberated by the People's Liberation Army but our work in the College continued to the end of the academic year. After term ended we set about getting ready for the journey home, the family now including three small boys. It was exactly one hundred years since the beginning of Anglican work in Fukien.

This is not a particularly unusual missionary experience but there were unusual features about my own experience. As the son of William Paton Secretary of the International Missionary Council I inherited some of my father's friends, notably Timothy Ting Fang Lew and, still more important, T. C. Chao, a poet as well as a theologian and China's top Christian intellectual.

I also had the luck for nine of the fifteen months in Peking to live not in the Language School but in a cultured Chinese family, much of whose property had been lost because of the Japanese occupation. The family was educated and cultured; some had Christian friends. They let me share their life and with them I joined in the 'ancestor worship' at the New Year.

A third and very important fact derived from the way that decisions were taken in the Student Y.M.C.A. I asked my colleague Lyman Hoover, an American, what were the rules for a foreigner in a staff otherwise Chinese with Kiang Wen-han as Executive Secretary. The reply was 'they want to know what we think so we say our piece. If we think it has not been understood we say it again. On rare occasions we may say it a third time, if we think it is really important and has not got through. After that we shut up. It is their show and they make the decisions.' All this meant that I had a wider acquaintance with Chinese Christian leaders and Chinese ways of doing things. It also meant much wider opportunities of close friendship. Years later, after the Cultural Revolution, I asked someone back from China whether the two with whom I had made the overland journey to Chungking in 1941 were still alive. I was told that they were both dead: and something died in me.

I have never been back to China. In the later 1970s meeting was possible but serious conversation was not. I don't mind talking trivialities with strangers or mere acquaintances but the friends of one's youth are sacred and when conversation with them in China became possible I was not fit enough for the journey. But one can write letters, and surprising numbers of people do that, and even find their way to come and stay with us. So our Chinese friendships have continued to grow, and there are still things like the Edinburgh 1989 Conference (for the time being postponed indefinitely) in which one can get involved.

1. *OUR PLACE IN THE WORLD*

In the ancient world there were a few centres or civilisations or empires, often in a river valley. The Egyptian civilisation of the Nile, successive empires of the Tigris and Euphrates, Rome on the Tiber, and in China of course successive capitals on or near the Yellow River. But it wasn't always a river – it might be landbased or with access to the sea, for example, Athens or Istanbul. Then time marched on. Civilisation spread to the barbarians, ocean-going trading ships were discovered, built and used, and we began to speak of Western Europe, Indian civilisation, and so on. More time passed, technology advanced, and we began to speak of the North Atlantic, the Far East and the Third World. The rich countries spawn companies which they call multinational but this suggests an activity in which several nations join. They are really transnational, for their influence transcends and weakens the separate nations.

People begin to talk of One World. It becomes easier and easier to travel widely and safely in lands where we do not know the language but the locals have enough English to do some business with us. All kinds of cultural phenomena spread, contract, change. The centre of the Christian world moves away from the Mediterranean. All of this has worldwide effects, but nowhere are they precisely the same. Some things remain apparently unaltered, others change radically and without warning. (Who predicted the rise of Mikhail Gorbachev and the fall of the Berlin Wall?) Whoever we are, whether an ancient and massive civilisation or a smallish people who recently attained independence, we have to find our place in this One World which is infinitely varied.

2. THE MIDDLE KINGDOM/THE CENTRAL COUNTRY

Of all the peoples of the world the Chinese have claims to be the most remarkable. They are about one-quarter of the human race, which they contrive to feed on one-seventh of the world's arable land. Dr C. P. Fitzgerald has described the fundamental Chinese style of government as 'a centralised ideological bureaucracy' and with periodic interruptions that has been true since the establishment of the Han empire about 200 B.C. and remains true today. It is not only age and continuity which are remarkable. There is also a fundamental Chineseness which is recognisable, though hard to describe.

There was a time when 'the Middle Kingdom' or 'the Central Country' seemed to be a reasonably accurate description. There was China, large, diverse and yet one. It was surrounded by partially independent client states sharing in some degree the characteristics of Chinese culture – countries such as Japan, Vietnam, Korea, Mongolia and so on. Beyond this great land mass there were oceans to the East and the South which virtually precluded any communication with the rest of the world. There was the Central Country, there were the client states, and there were the outer barbarians. The Chinese vision of the world made sense.

It makes sense no longer. The British ought to be among the first to recognise this because the British Navy, backed by British commerce, had or thought it had a similar uniqueness. 'Britannia Rules the Waves' still resonates in the hearts of many Brits, but the trouble is, she doesn't. In one way or another modern technology, human imagination and many other factors land us all, whether we be an ancient civilisation or a newly established African state, in this One world. This applies to us all, whether we be Chinese, or British or anything else. It applies also, though doubtless in varying measure, to all the peoples of the world whether they be ancient civilisations or some small tribe which only recently had to bother about anyone else. What do we do in this situation? Where do we go to find or create a world which will become a home for both our local peculiarities and our common humanity? What does it mean, to come back to China, to be the 'Central Country' in a world where there is no Central Country? What does it mean to recognise that 'foreign devils' cannot be adequately described as 'hairy ones'? What does it mean to the British to find themselves in a world where pukka sahibs are the subjects of jokes and country gentlemen are giving way to brash young men from merchant banks? The instinct anywhere is to try to seek to recover the past. The Chinese people made a prolonged effort to keep the West at bay and preserve its own cultural integrity, but it failed – just as the British Empire was not restored by the operation in the Falkland Islands. The question of where we stand today and where we will stand tomorrow is not only a Chinese question of course; and many observers of China are perplexed and indeed deeply hurt by the events in the summer of 1989 ('Tien an men') and it is difficult for those in China as well as those outside to know and understand what is going on. Moreover the Chinese have their particular problems. As we have seen there are good reasons for attending to the Chinese experience and among the most important is one upon which I have not yet touched – the most inconsiderable matter of Chinese religion, to which we shall come shortly.

So the question of where we stand today and where we will stand tomorrow is not only a Chinese question. The question for the Chinese, I suppose, is 'What do the words *Chung Kuo* mean in the world today when no country can be central?' But underlying it is the truth that in one way or another this is a question for all of us – where do we find our place in this pluriform world? 'Within the four seas all men are brothers'; but most countries have some Ayatollahs wanting to go it alone and have their own way. Underlying so much in the modern world are questions to which 'the media' devote too little attention. How do we combine the affirmation of our own identity with the full recognition of the different identity of others, all in the one world in which, because of radio and television, we are present to one another more sharply than ever before.

3. WHO IS JESUS CHRIST FOR US TODAY?

This is the famous question of Dietrich Bonhoeffer, brooding towards the end of the Second World War in a prison cell. It is inescapable, if what I have said here so far is anywhere near the truth. The Gospel is universal but also must be local. Too often, especially if consideration of politics and power have come to be part of the picture, we have given people a version of the Gospel too much of which is British or American or German or Spanish, etc. and too little an answer to the local question about who is Jesus Christ presented in a local form. This is partly because too often we have not listened or have not heard the local question, but have too readily undone our own supposedly universal package, without much consideration of the existing local culture. One can indeed argue that far too much theology today is still answering contemporary questions with formulae which are really Greek or Latin or German or British or American answers which belong to the past and do not fulfil Bonhoeffer's demand to know who is Jesus Christ for *us today*.

This of course is a large range of difficult questions. We write theological books from our own standpoint, which is a mixture of our understanding of the Gospel and our understanding of our own cultural tradition. So we find ourselves having to look for new theologies in written form as elsewhere. There is some attempt to find out where we are now that the excitements of the Enlightenment seem somewhat dimmed, and under renewed attack. Elsewhere Latin Americans develop a new theology for the poor. But some others will ask questions about the reality of liberation.

In this situation it seems that we need one another. We have to find ways of listening to the questions, and must ask and answer and try to understand. We need each other. We need not one theology (which we won't get) but an increased capacity to listen to one another and so help one another.

I make two further comments. It was often assumed in the West that the religions that mattered were either the religions of the Book, Judaism, Christianity, Islam, or some form of mystical downgrading of much human religious experience, as in Buddhism and Hinduism. Books on 'comparative religion' didn't bother much with the Chinese, who express themselves not primarily in religion, but in painting and poetry, food and friendship. We also tended to ignore religions which had not got extensive sacred scriptures and relied on an oral tradition. This resulted in the dismissal of most of the African, Amerindian and South Pacific religions simply as 'the heathen'. It is beginning to be evident that this won't do. We assume that because people operate without written literature and without the immense quantity of words to which some of us are accustomed, there is nothing but 'heathen superstition' in their point of view.

We have to take them seriously. This means that we have not only to compare the written religious classics of one area or religion with others; we have also to seek for its deepest meaning on, so to speak, its own terms.

So what is the solution? How should we behave? The answer I think can only be a steady attention to the development of what I will call educated friendship. I put in the first paragraphs of this article because it seems to me, and it seemed to Ronald Hall, Bishop of Hong Kong (who was my mentor) that without understanding and friendship one cannot get very far.

4. *THE TAO*

I have come to feel in these last years, when fresh thinking is emerging from Chinese Christians, and perhaps others of us are beginning to learn to listen as well as preach, that the one point at which everything meets is the assertion in the first chapter of St. John's Gospel that the Word was in the beginning with God and that the Word was made flesh. In the early centuries the Church's theologians, moving from their familiar Jewish world into the Greek world, used the word *logos* to translate its Jewish original into Greek. Centuries later when the New Testament was translated into Chinese *logos* was replaced by *tao*, the Way – or if you prefer as I do the title of Waley's translation of the *Tao Te China* 'The Way and its Power'.

It has been customary to treat the Chinese translations simply as translations: but I become increasingly uneasy about this procedure because it unconsciously assumes that everybody thinks like 4th and 5th century Greek theologians. What does 'the Tao was made flesh in our Lord Jesus Christ' mean? Is there some truth to be unpacked from this ancient formula in response to Chinese and other questioning? Does the process of theology in one new culture after another mean that there is more to be learnt? Does it mean that the Chinese ways of understanding the Christian faith which are beginning to appear (I am thinking, for example, of that profound little book of Wang Weifan *Lilies of the Field*) are going to alter and enrich our understanding of the faith? Does it mean (which some people will think more dangerous) that we no longer need to teach our theological students or our congregations Greek Christian answers to questions asked by Greeks fifteen hundred years ago in another country? Or does it rather mean that there are signs that there are lessons to be learned from all the human wrestlings for gospel truth and this we in the older theological conditions need to wait expectantly for new light? Does it mean that we cannot answer Bonhoeffer's enquiry about the meaning of Jesus Christ today without taking seriously what is being heard by our fellow Christians (and perhaps not only our fellow Christians) in other cultures? What I am sensing, hardly understand, and cannot properly express is that the consequence of being placed by God in a world which is both one and exceedingly diverse is that we cannot avoid the others. Members of the human race sometimes feel that all men are brothers, and sometimes that all men other than believers in their own brand of Christianity are emissaries of Satan. The plain truth is that we have to cultivate the pursuit of truth with people who are friends. Indeed, if we avoid the issue of friendship we are beaten before we start.

The other thing I would like to insist upon, even though I am not sure of the implications, is that for Western Christians and their fellows in other parts of the world who have been unduly Westernised it is important that they pay much greater attention to the Eastern Orthodox tradition.

In the course of the twentieth century the understanding of the mystical tradition has altered dramatically but very quietly. I remember the alarm at a study conference in the 1930s occasioned by the disappearance of *The Cloud of Unknowing* which was in those days held to be quite unsuitable reading for anyone inexperienced in these matters. Now Julian Meetings, parish retreats, and many other things are growing rapidly and widely welcomed. This not inconsiderable shift in understanding has spread widely and quietly and apparently occasioned no alarm. Moreover there are interconnections between East and West which are mostly new. I once asked Bishop Michael Ramsey where he would advise a young American Presbyterian missionary to start in pursuing an understanding of Orthodoxy which was so far strange to him. The answer I got from Michael Ramsey was 'Let him start on the 14th century English mystics'. From my friend's later writings it is obvious that he has greatly profited. The Desert Fathers are also beginning to come into their own.

5. *TODAY*

What all this means is, for example, that we have to learn to look at other people, especially those about whom we know little or nothing, in a spirit of hopefulness. It means, secondly, that the primary task is exploration of other people's strange ideas rather than hitting them on the head with our traditions. Be it noted, however, that in our traditions other people may see in among the dross, nuggets of truth which we have not noticed until they point them out to us! Thirdly it means that we proceed with these tasks in expectant joy, rejoicing that we are entering a strange new world in which we are enriched if we persevere expectantly. In fact, we must give ourselves, in the best Chinese tradition, to happy feasting with poets and sages.

EPILOGUE:
THE STRATEGY OF LIBERALISM

Daniel W. Hardy

Drawn together in this book are essays by a wide variety of people who number themselves amongst Peter Baelz's friends. They are joined together as tributes intended to honour him and the contribution he has made; they are from those who also respect the position which he holds, even if not necessarily agreeing with it. Overall, they are intended to show the liberal position, the variety of views to be found in it and the views of those who are sympathetic but differ.

Such a polychromatic presentation accords very well with the liberal position, which has no sharp boundaries; it is as broad in its interests as in the means by which it pursues them. Diversity is its identifying feature, and one of the ways by which it responds to the diversity of the age in which it finds itself. If positions have to be constituted by a simple unity, it is doubtful, as John Habgood says at the outset, whether the liberal position exists as such, whether those who value the word 'liberal' would agree on any one set of ideas or attitudes or whether there can be a 'cohort of liberals' who set out to foster a liberal ascendancy.

But there can still be a unity achieved in their diversity by people with similar interests. And the tendencies which bring liberals to converge can be singled out. They may be respected, even if the conclusions which they bring are not agreed, either by those who count themselves liberals or by those normally opposed. For the intellectual and practical situation which confronts Christians in modern times may bring both liberals and their opponents to share certain concerns which are quite different from those of previous times. All, for example, may be concerned with modern life, which appears in so many ways to have set aside the need for religious belief, and with the variety of forces – philosophical, scientific, cultural, social – which support such secularism. The difference between liberals and others may be more in how they follow these concerns than in the concerns as such, for example, in how readily – or how deeply – they embrace the challenges of 'modernity'.

299

There is little question that one identifying feature of liberalism is its willingness to face and interact with the changes brought about by modern understanding, and in that to defend Christian faith. But what such changes are is by nor means as clear as might be wished. Some of these causes can sometimes be stated in general terms – the impact of science, the influence of positivism, the importance of historical contingency – but the nature and effect of the changes are no so clear. In any case, if one can speak in these terms, the changes themselves are changing. Any Christian who wishes to interact with modern understanding must stand with those who are pressing forward with it, hoping to avoid what is of only transient importance and to find what is more enduringly important. Anyone who attempts this may be too naive in his appreciation of the implications of modernity, and certainly no one can hope to be successful in responding to the whole range of the movement of modern thought and life. The essays here come from people who have been deeply immersed in special and different aspects of modern thought and life as they probe their implications for Christian faith.

Unless Christian faith consists in simple assent to fixed tenets of belief, or some other equally time-bound position, engagement with the changes of modernity is not necessarily a departure from the ways of Christian faith. It is instead a looking for the possibility of a deeper Christian faith through modern understanding, in which the possibilities of faith are actually enriched through modern ways. But this exploration is likely to develop faith in ways not easily – or well-understood by those who have stood apart from the challenges of modernity. They may find it difficult to understand what is happening, and may even impute faithlessness to those whom they simply fail to understand.

Even if liberals – much as they may try to make their views accessible – cannot always be expected to make themselves understood, they can be held responsible for what they say. The results of the deeper engagement of Christian faith with modernity may – remembering Hans Christian Andersen's story of 'The Emperor's New Clothes' – be a set of imaginary new clothes to delude the emperor about his elegance while satisfying no one else. In other words, it is at least possible that deeper engagement with aspects of modernity (those which are incompatible with Christian faith) may produce a lesser form of Christian faith which at the same time inflates Christians with their own importance while not enhancing the credibility of Christian faith. The history of theology in the modern period abounds with examples of 'deeper' forms of faith which are also more vapid. That is certainly not what the liberals themselves intend. In this respect, there is a genuine difference between serious liberal thought of the sort found in this book and other forms which glide over the difficulties. The purpose of liberal thought is not to compromise Christian faith, but to rediscover the means of maintaining it in the modern world.

That is a bewilderingly large task, leading in all the directions of modern life, as can be seen from the wide range of issues discussed in this book. It is almost inconceivable that any group of people should be able to succeed. And failure, whether measured by the old tradition of Christian faith which people remember and suppose still to be possible, or by a present wish for a credibility which will convince everyone, is what the opponents of liberalism often remember. That sort of failure can, perhaps too easily, become their reason for rejecting liberalism and all its stands for. But they, in their turn, need to remember the image once used to describe Karl Barth's theology; it was likened to a marvellous castle built on a high hill, with no access roads. If the principal danger for the liberal theologian is vapidity or banality, theirs is irrelevance and unintelligibility for modern life.

Most of the contributors to this book, as well as Peter Baelz, are what might be called 'qualified liberals', their liberalism qualified by some other concern or starting-point – liberals 'but also . . .' That is a more important characteristic than may first appear. If one likens the Christian Church to a well-developed company, the social psychology of management suggests that the ongoing work of the company requires those who are simply expert in its familiar operations, whereas executive officers are expected to be much more creative and adaptive in their operation of the company, to develop it for its future; and there needs also to be an intermediate level capable of holding the two together as business proceeds while adapting to new possibilities. So far as this analogy holds, liberals often follow the style of executive officers, not because they are more in command, but because they are preoccupied with vision and creative adaptation.

The differences between them can still be considerable. One way in which they often differ is in how creative or adaptive they are prepared to be. The liberalism most frequently found here is 'qualified' by allegiance to what Christian faith has meant in the past. The allegiance is not to the 'givenness' of certain statements of faith, however, but to a tradition which revivifies itself in creative reappropriation. While they would probably accept definition as 'critical theological realists', it is their insistence on creative reappropriation of the tradition which differentiates them from the more stern forms of theological realism which mark those of more conservative disposition. Unless it is used as a way of bringing the two – liberals and conservatives – into contact with each other, to lump the two together as varieties of conservatism serves the purpose only of those who argue that a still more radical alternative is necessary for the 'post modern' situation, a completely unqualified or 'ecstatic' liberalism – in which 'nothing is sacrosanct, everything is revisable'. Whatever value it may have, that is not liberalism in the sense discussed by most of the essayists here. They believe in a God who is eminently gracious, whose grace may be freshly discovered in the modern situation insofar as people allow themselves to be enlarged by it.

The 'I am a liberal but also' stance suggests that the analogy with company officers is apt, at least to a degree; it shows the liberal as one engaged in the visionary, creative and adaptive aspect of Christianity, trying to fit it for its future, but doing so with a conscious loyalty to the ongoing culture of 'the company'. Neither the creative adaptation nor the loyalty to the culture are simple, as may be seen from Peter Baelz's description of a 'dialectical relation between a contemplative catholicism and a critical liberalism, . . . [between] the givenness of Christian faith [and] a corresponding emphasis on its questing and questioning'. And there are no sharp lines between those considered fit to carry on this dialectic and those who are not. The 'company' is not simply its members, but all – whether believer, half-believer or agnostic – who in any degree, and by whatever means, are prepared to engage in the struggle for faith, and to engage in a constant dialogue of affirmation with the critical and questioning spirit. From this combination of contemplation and questing, it is suggested, emerges the possibility for Christians to talk creatively about the central questions of faith in a believable manner, unhindered by narrow or 'reductive' theological habits.

Whether such a subtle set of loyalties satisfies the other 'workers' is another matter. For such a creative use of the tradition implies that Christian belief and practice for the present day cannot be read off, directly or indirectly, from what the Church has taught in previous times. What seems most frequently to bother liberals about the sterner forms of Christian position are two things, their tendency toward dogmatism (whether of content or method) in belief and moral absolutism on the one hand, and their tendency to a cumulative overspecification in matters of belief and practice. The one, dogmatism and absolutism, manifests a refusal to recognise the most important lessons of post-Renaissance understanding, that all belief and life are conditioned by history and political interest. The other, the cumulative over-specification of belief and practice, is problematic, even apart from other difficulties which it may introduce, because it ties theology to an increasingly heavy weight of tradition, thereby blocking out the new and often secular situations and interpretations with which theology should be concerned.

The alternative which liberalism provides is that of a dialectical relation between a contemplative traditionality and a liberal and critical modernity. But in this dialectical relation, there are varieties of balance; and differences of balance are much in evidence amongst the authors of the essays included here. The issue between them is a simple but intractably difficult one. If one accepts that the tradition, the 'givenness', continually renews itself through creative interpretation, how is this tradition-recreating interpretation to be carried on? There is no wish amongst liberals to avoid the responsibility – to the tradition as well as to the present and the future – conferred upon them by creativity. But what it is to be responsible in creative adaptation is very much more difficult to specify, not least because there are so many judges. Here again, it is easier to speak in general programmatic terms than to provide more detailed help. Perhaps all that can be expected is case-studies in practice. If so, this book provides many fascinating examples.

Within them all, however, is the search for the right kind of liberality, the possibility of responding to, and being shaped by, 'the gracious liberality of God ... [in order to] display its marks in ... liberality towards all that God has made' (Habgood). What is more surprising is the relatively scant attention given to the character of the 'graciously liberal God'; most attention is paid to the marks of liberality in God's creation and redemption. Perhaps in itself this is an indication of the norms within which this liberalism operates. They are those of the 'turn to the subject' characteristic of post-Kantian thought, with all the possibilities for mystery-centred theology which that promotes.

Even so, the learning of such liberality embraces a vast variety of kinds and levels. It is aesthetic, concerned with the 'sheer numinousness' which Peter Baelz found and fostered in buildings, art and words as preparation for faith. It is imaginative, concerned with fundamental forms of enlargement and disciplining for the human heart and mind in the perception of God, those which will produce a sharpened awareness and tenderness amidst the fragility of the world. It is one of worship, through which perception and response are 'ex-centered'. It is cognitive, concerned not only with the understanding of God but with the rebirthing of the traditional images of theology in the light of the best philosophical and scientific thought. But all these are inextricably connected – 'integrating' was Peter Baelz's word – with issues, both theoretical and practical, in the wider life of society and in the life of the Church, particularly those by which Christians may learn new, more natural and less narrow forms of spirituality and society, and may respond to the growing flood of issues about the Western Christian tradition itself.

As this Epilogue has sketched some of the main issues at stake in the liberalism presented or discussed in these essays, so the essays themselves are sketches of some of the implications of liberalism. By the very nature of liberalism, their success in promoting a deepended appropriation of the Christian tradition through the use of critical modernity must be left to readers. 'Try it and see.' At the least, it may be hoped that they will bring a greater awareness of the character of liberalism and its particular practice and conviction of the gracious liberality of God.

BIBLIOGRAPHY

BOOKS

Christian Theology and Metaphysics. Epworth Press, London 1968.
Prayer and Providence. The Hulsean Lectures for 1966. S.C.M. Press, London 1968.
The Forgotten Dream. The Bampton Lectures for 1974. Mowbrays, London & Oxford 1975.
Ethics and Belief. Sheldon Press, London 1977.
Does God Answer Prayer? Darton, Longman & Todd, London 1982.

LECTURES AND ARTICLES

Obedience. In *Theology*, Vol. LXVI, No. 515 (May 1963). Reprinted in 'Traditional Virtues Reassessed', ed. A. R. Vidler, S.P.C.K., London 1964.
Is God Real? In 'Faith, Fact & Fantasy', Collins Fontana 1964.
A Deliberate Mistake? In 'Christ, Faith & History: Cambridge Studies in Christology', ed. S. W. Sykes and J. P. Clayton, Cambridge University Press 1972.
Voluntary Euthanasia. In *Theology*, Vol. LXXV, No. 623 (May 1972). Reprinted in 'Suicide: The Philosophical Issues', ed. M. Pabst Battin and David J. Mayo, St. Martin's Press, New York 1980.
Old Wine in New Bottles. In *Theology*, Vol. LXXVI, No. 623 (May 1972).
Christian Obedience in a Permissive Context. The John Coffin Memorial Lecture for 1973. Athlone Press, London 1973.
Abortion: Anglican Attitudes Reconsidered. Crucible July–December 1974.
The Ethics of Strikes in the Caring-Professions. October–December 1975.
Is Christianity Credible? In *Epworth Review*, Vol. 4, No. 3 (September 1977). Reprinted in 'Is Christianity Credible?', Epworth Press, London 1981.

305

Philosophy of Health Education. In 'Health Education: Perspectives and Choices', ed. Ian Sutherland, George Allen & Unwin, London 1979.

A Sermon for Christmas Day 1980. In 'God Incarnate: Story and Belief', ed. A. E. Harvey, S.P.C.K., London 1981.

Give Us A Blessing, Crucible January–March 1981.

An Integrating Theology. A.C.C.M. Occasional Paper, No. 15. C.I.O., London 1983.

A Christian Perspective on the Biological Scene. In *Zygon,* Vol. 19, No. 2 (June 1984).

Ministers of the Kingdom. In 'Ministers of the Kingdom', ed. Peter Baelz and Michael Jacob, C.I.O., London 1985.

What is Faith? In *Epworth Review,* Vol. 14, No. 1 (January 1987).

The Authority of Reason and Conscience. In 'By What Authority?', ed. Robert Jeffery. Mowbrays, London 1987.

What Sort of World? What Sort of God? In 'Embracing the Chaos: Theological Responses to AIDS', ed. James Woodward, S.P.C.K., London 1990.

CONTRIBUTIONS TO CHURCH WORKING PARTY REPORTS

On Dying Well. C.I.O., London 1975.

Marriage and the Church's Task. C.I.O., London 1978.

Homosexual Relationships. C.I.O., London 1979.

Choices in Childlessness.* Free Church Federal Council and British Council of Churches 1982.

Perspectives on Economics.* C.I.O., London 1984.

Call to Order.* A.C.C.M., London 1989.

* Signifies that the contribution included chairing the working party.

INDEX OF NAMES

307

INDEX OF TOPICS